# For The Love Of Money

*Colin —*
*Thanks so much for your support! I hope this is helpful.*
*Enjoy*
*Shannon 06'*
*(*I'm really 25!)*

2006 EDITION (FOR 2005 TAX RETURNS)

# For The Love Of Money

"The 411 To Taking Control Of Your Taxes and Building Your Net Worth"

Shannon K. Nash, Esq., CPA

iUniverse, Inc.
New York  Lincoln  Shanghai

For The Love Of Money
"The 411 To Taking Control Of Your Taxes and Building Your Net Worth"

Copyright © 2005 by Shannon King Nash

All rights reserved. No part of this book may be used or reproduced by any means, graphic, electronic, or mechanical, including photocopying, recording, taping or by any information storage retrieval system without the written permission of the publisher except in the case of brief quotations embodied in critical articles and reviews.

iUniverse books may be ordered through booksellers or by contacting:

iUniverse
2021 Pine Lake Road, Suite 100
Lincoln, NE 68512
www.iuniverse.com
1-800-Authors (1-800-288-4677)

ISBN-13: 978-0-595-34895-4 (pbk)
ISBN-13: 978-0-595-79613-7 (ebk)
ISBN-10: 0-595-34895-5 (pbk)
ISBN-10: 0-595-79613-3 (ebk)

Printed in the United States of America

# SHOUT-OUTS

Most books call this the Acknowledgement Section, but I'm calling it exactly what it is—Shout-Outs. First, I would like to thank God for all the many blessings he has bestowed upon me. To Bill, Kyle, Jason and Charlie—thanks for being the light at the end of my tunnel. I love all my "guys." Thanks so much for believing in me and helping me to find the "time" for this book.

To my parents Billy and Gwen King—thanks for putting a law book in my hand at the very early age of six! To my sister Nikki—thanks lil' sis for being there. To my very large extended family—thanks for always believing in me and supporting me, including: my grandparents, Carolyn and Milton Nickerson and Nona and Alvin King, Sr.; my aunts, Linda Nickerson Drane, Cynthia Nickerson, Glenda Faye Richardson, Denise Welch, Sandra Montague, Samantha King, Jaqui King; my uncles, Broderick King, Keith King, Alvin King Jr., Bob Montague; and my many cousins, in-laws, and everyone else who is somehow related to me.

To the three contributors to this book, who gave me many comments, suggestions, and more comments—We finally finished! Thanks to O'Sumby Kuti, Wayne Hamilton and Don Moragne. Keep, keepin' on, you got to keep keepin' on!

To Petrice Young—you are the best friend a girl could have. To Dee Baker Amos, my other best sister, and marketer extraordinaire—many thanks. To Deshong Perry, thanks for your marketing expertise and for always looking out. To Stacey Montgomery, thank you for continually reminding me why I should write this book, even when it looked like it would never happen. Thanks for your constant, unwavering encouragement. Skeewee love to all of you!!!!!

To my LA girls: Kathy Shirley, Tanya Greig, Shelia Ducksworth, Deanna Thomas, Barbara Bronson Gray, and Cheryl Argrett—thanks for believing in me, no matter what! To my Chi-town buddies N'gai Merrill and Steve Thomas—keep living the entrepreneur's dream! To my Orlando angel Mayra Sutton—thank you so much for your support! And I can't forget about my DC/Virginia/Maryland Crew—Sid Smith, Jackie Wilson Cranston, Judith Dozier, Carla Partlow, Juanita Woods, Sean White, Anne Kim, Maxine McBean, John Jones, Nicole Livas Webster, Rich and Stephanie Bryant, and the partners and associates at Dorn & Klamp (particularly Susan Dorn & Carolyn Klamp)—you've always got my back!

Nor can I forget about the UVA Crew—Danyale Price Dumas, Ackneil Muldrow, III, Brian Booker, Janice Johnston, Wilfredo Pesante, Jr., Ramona Prioleau, Kim Clark, Shanna Batten Aguirre and Bianca Bennett Alexander—some of us are still practicing and others are doing completely different things. I'm so proud of what we have all accomplished post-Mr. Jefferson's University!

To my writing buddies—Angela Scott, Shelia Harvey and Darryl Amos—thanks for being that voice of reason when no one understands why we even "write" in the first place.

To my assistant, Sabrina Morales for her patience, excellent proof reading, formatting, and all-around listening skills. Thanks for all of your hard work and encouragement. To Ben Young—thanks for your patience and excellent brand marketing skills.

To the Debbie Allen Dance Academy, in particular the founders, Debbie Allen and Norman Nixon, and the staff, including: Adrienne Dellas Thornton, Steve Brown, Denise Harris, Juan Session, Bill Bowles, Steven Smith, Karen McDonald, Bronwyn Thomas-Hodgson, Chloe Arnold, and Dianne Guess—your dedication and pursuit of the arts and children is impressive and inspiring. Thank you for allowing me to share in helping your dreams to become realities.

Also, to Veronica Coffield and Tammy McCrary at the Chaka Khan Foundation for your inspiring dedication to helping children; particularly those suffering from autism. To Rodney Jackson and the folks over at the National Center for Black Philanthropy for their tireless dedication to Black philanthropy.

To my tax buddies, who were there from the start of this tax "thang" and who continue to blaze the trail: Randle Pollard, Richard Larkins, Jo-Renee Hunter, Kari Gibbs, Lilo Hester, Dwight Jones, Wayne Monfries, Lisa Tavares, Mildeen Worrell, Linda Holoman, Jack Harper, Veronica Rouse, Craig Boise, Walter Burford, and Gilbert Boyce. To Tony Santiago at Tax Search, and John O'Neill and the rest of the folks at Taxtalent.com for caring to even have a Diversity forum and a Diversity Advisory Board, in the hopes of bettering the tax profession.

Finally, to all the many friends and colleagues over the years who have supported me on this project, and every other "next thing"—thanks so much for being a stable force in my life. Much Love!!

Shan

\*\*\*

I dedicate this book to the few tax folks who paved the way, in particular: Loretta Argrett, Larry Bailey, Samuel Thompson, Jr., Glenn Carrington, and The Honorable Maurice Foley. Also, I dedicate this book to my friends, families, colleagues, clients and to everyone who asked that one tax question—which inevitably led to three, then four, then five questions—and in many cases, doing the actual tax return.

# CONTENTS

| | | |
|---|---|---|
| Introduction | | xi |
| CHAPTER 1 | Tax Basics | 1 |
| CHAPTER 2 | Side Business | 53 |
| CHAPTER 3 | Side Business Part II | 85 |
| CHAPTER 4 | Capital Gains | 131 |
| CHAPTER 5 | Itemized Deductions | 157 |
| CHAPTER 6 | Itemized Deduction Part II | 187 |
| CHAPTER 7 | Alternative Minimum Tax | 221 |
| CHAPTER 8 | Investment, Education & Estate | 237 |
| CHAPTER 9 | IRS Audits | 275 |
| CHAPTER 10 | Frequently Asked Questions | 297 |
| The Next Track | | 329 |
| Appendix | | 333 |
| About the Author | | 385 |
| Contributions | | 387 |
| The Ultimate Resource Guide | | 391 |
| Index | | 399 |

# INTRODUCTION

First, thank you for purchasing this book. I hope you will find it educational, empowering, entertaining, and overall, the best tax book you've ever read (assuming you've ever read a tax book from cover to cover before).

## WHAT'S FOR THE LOVE OF MONEY?

*For The Love Of Money* is not your typical 1,000-page tax or business book. You will not find a lot of tax forms, line-by-line instructions, math, accounting or legal cases. *For The Love Of Money* takes common tax problems and issues, and gives real life explanations. There are no Jane and John Doe examples in this book. You'll find everyday examples, using some of your favorite popular songs.

*For The Love Of Money* is "tax explained through music." Each chapter starts with a popular song that inspires the focus of that chapter, and will take you back down "Memory Lane," (Minnie Riperton, 1973), while learning how to save money on taxes. *For The Love Of Money* devotes 10 Chapters on tax and finance issues to help you save your, "Money, Money, Money, Money—Money" (O'Jays, 1973).

- 🔊 The nuts and bolts of Form 1040
- 🔊 Organizing and operating your side business
- 🔊 Capital gains strategies to help you build wealth
- 🔊 Making the most of your itemized deductions
- 🔊 Alternative minimum taxes that can creep up
- 🔊 Saving for education and retirement
- 🔊 Relaxation techniques for an IRS audit
- 🔊 The all-star frequently asked tax questions

Each chapter ends with a short list called the Remix, reflecting the lessons learned in that chapter. As an added bonus, check out the *For The Love Of Money* lists on subjects that matter to you the most like:

- For Landlords
- For Single Parents
- For New Parents
- For Newlyweds
- For Lawyers
- For Freelancers
- For The College Grad
- For Doctors
- For New Homeowners
- For Stylists
- For Charities
- For The Self-Employed
- For Entertainers And Athletes
- For Good Stewards Of Blessings
- For New Money
- Reasons To Pay Your Taxes
- Check-Up List for Individuals
- Check-Up List for Side Businesses
- Ways To Avoid A Tax Audit
- Signs You Need Tax Help

**INSPIRATION**

I wrote this book to specifically address people like me—professional, hard-working, hard-playing, fun-loving, prayerful and proud folks. I'm targeting financially-savvy, money-smart, savings-mentality, sacrificing-for-that-first-home, credit card management, full of self-esteem (not into material trappings, but into wealth accumulation) folks. Can people do it all at the same time? Certainly—with education and guidance.

I hope to convey what we all need to know to benefit from the tax laws, for people who are interested in paying their fair share of taxes—nothing more, nothing less. Whether you do your own taxes or have them done, I focus on what you need to know to make you more financially and tax intelligent so you can save money and start building your net worth. Everyone, whether rich, middle class, or poor can benefit from some basic tax knowledge. People come to me all the time with tax questions; from the easy to the absolutely hilarious with questions like:

*Question*: If I hit the lottery, do I need to pay taxes on my winnings?

*Answer:* Yes. Just because you hit the jackpot, doesn't mean you don't have to pay taxes. You aren't that lucky. The IRS wants its cut, too. If your gambling winnings for the year are greater than your gambling losses, you will have to pay taxes on the difference.

*Question:* Do I need a social security number for my child to claim him on my tax return?

*Answer:* Yes. This is how the IRS can verify that your Lil' (you insert the name) is really a living, breathing person.

*Question:* How can I deduct my share of the reparations (government payments to descendants of slaves)?

*Answer:* You can't. Let's get this clear once and for all: There are no reparation payments; not yesterday, not today, probably not ever. This is an unfortunate rumor that some folks have been spreading in the African-American community and they need to stop it. The IRS has made efforts to alert folks of these fraud schemes. For more information about this, see *IRS Fact Sheet 2002-08, "Reparation Scams Carry a Price."* If you hear of any tax credit or scheme that seems just too good to be true and it doesn't cost you more than something ending with 99 cents on the end, be wary. Always test the validity of these credits or schemes with your tax advisor.

This list of questions can go on and on for pages (check-out Chapter 10: FAQ for questions that did make the book). The point is, I was inspired by everyday questions, problems and dilemmas like these. But what really served as the final straw, were the horror stories of famous folks falling prey to ordinary tax problems. These are people who can clearly afford competent tax and finance help. The real problem is that they, more than likely, didn't have a basic understanding of the tax issues.

Perhaps the most publicized case of an entertainer in trouble with the taxman is country singer Willie Nelson, who in the 1980s supposedly owed the IRS over $16.7 million in back taxes. The IRS took his houses, farms and most of his belongings to satisfy his debts. Luckily, Willie's friends and fans bought most of his belongings back from the IRS. He also made an album to help pay off this debt—"The IRS Tapes: Who'll Buy My Memories?" He even had the profits from the album sent directly to the IRS. By the mid 1990s he was able to put his financial life back on track.

Willie's far from being the only entertainer to have these problems. Take the case of Peabo Bryson. It is reported that Peabo owed over $1.2 million in taxes, spanning over two decades. Comedian, Richard Pryor was arrested for tax evasion back in 1974. Singer Chuck Berry, of "Johnny B. Goode" and "My Ding-a-Ling" fame, plead guilty to tax evasion back in 1979. Soon after his famous sitcom, "The Jeffersons" was canceled, Sherman Hemsley found himself with tax problems; owing thousands of dollars and eventually filing for bankruptcy in 1999.

Sadly, before their deaths, Sammy Davis Jr., Phyllis Hyman and Marvin Gaye all had significant tax deficiencies. In 1997, Altovise Davis, Sammy's wife, was finally able to reach a settlement with the IRS (some seven years after his death) to take care of almost $7.5 million in back taxes. Before her tragic suicide in 1995, Phyllis Hyman reportedly owed the IRS millions of dollars, and even referred to her financial wows in her suicide letter. Even as he was making some of his best music in the 70s with hits like "What's Going On," Marvin Gaye owed a reported $4 million to the IRS and wound up filing for bankruptcy, selling homes and taking his friends and family off the payroll.

Artists today are still falling prey to the tax man. In 2002, hit maker and rapper, Jermaine Dupri, was served with a whopping $2.5 million tax bill for failing to report his taxes. Master P. (aka, Percy Miller) apparently didn't file a corporate tax return for his business for over seven years. In October 2004, Mr. Big, aka, Ronald Isley of the famous Isley Brothers, was indicted on tax evasion charges. He was accused of not filing tax returns for over five years and not claiming all of his income. In January 2005, the IRS foreclosed on Death Row Record's headquarters in Beverly Hills, California to pay a reported $6.5 million back tax bill.

There are so many more examples of this every day. I'm simply tired of seeing these headlines and want to make a difference. I wrote this book with the hope that I can help folks become more savvy about taxes and finances; so that they can ask their advisors the right questions, before the headlines and before it's too late.

## THE THREE E'S

*For the Love of Money* follows the Three E's: Educate, Empower, and Entertain.

**Educate**—First and foremost *For The Love Of Money* seeks to help you become *Educated* on taxes so that you can take control of your financial life and save money.

**Empower**—As an "educated person," you can realize *Empowerment* to take your dreams to the next level; whether it's starting a side business, sending a child to the best college, or saving for a retirement home in the Bahamas. You need to be empowered to build your net worth.

**Entertain**—Of course, I realize that thinking about taxes is almost as exciting as reading a book on nuclear physics. In an effort to capture your attention, I'm working hard to *Entertain* you through humor and analogies using your favorite songs.

I hope the Three E's will help give you a better understanding of the tax and finance game. I also want to inspire more women and minorities to enter the tax field—it gets kind of lonely!

\*\*\*

Now that you're finished with the Intro, it's time to "Keep On Moving," (Soul II Soul, 1989). Get ready for 10 chapters jammed pack full of tax details, wisdom and even games in *For The Love Of Money*.

**Note to Readers:** *For The Love Of Money* focuses on individual federal income taxes and related issues. It does not generally cover state and local taxes. When the term "tax return" is used, it generally means Form 1040. The examples used in *For The Love Of Money* (including the names of the individuals, situations and events) are purely fictional and are not in any way meant to be real persons, situations or events. *For The Love Of Money* is by no means meant to be tax, accounting or legal advice. *For The Love Of Money* seeks to give you general information to help you ask the right questions and plan your own financial lives. Readers should always consult with their individual tax and legal advisors on how to handle any personal tax and legal issues.

# Chapter 1

# Tax Basics

*Understanding the Tax Basics*

> *Everybody, everybody, let's get into it.*
> *Get stupid*
> *Get it started, get it started, get it started.*
> *Let's get its started (ha), let's get it started in here.*

**"Let's Get It Started," Black Eyed Peas (2003)**

---

It all starts with taxes. If you want to keep your money and make it grow, you must understand tax basics. *For The Love Of Money* is bringing you the 411 on America's favorite tax return—the Form 1040. There are many songs that can get you in the mood for getting this tax party started; from "Let's Get It On," by Marvin Gaye (1973), to "Set It Off," by Strafe (originally mixed by Walter Gibbons, 1984). The Tax Basics may not be as fun as the "Fantastic Voyage" envisioned by Lakeside circa 1981, but I promise to give you chapter jammed pack with practical tips and a little entertainment to help you get through it all.

In this Chapter, get the lowdown on the following major parts of Form 1040:

- Filing Status
- Exemptions
- Income
- Adjusted Gross Income
- Taxes and Credits
- Other Taxes
- Payments
- Refunds
- Amount You Owe

## Filing Status

There are five filing status categories to choose from:

➢ Single
➢ Married Filing Jointly
➢ Married Filing Separately
➢ Head of Household
➢ Qualifying Widow(er) with Dependents

Your filing status can have a big impact on the amount of taxes you actually have to pay. Why? Because some of your tax deductions and credits are based on your filing status. Generally speaking, if you file as head of household, your taxes will be lower and your standard deduction will be higher than single status or married/filing separately. For example, the amount of the standard deduction depends heavily on your filing status, which is provided below for 2005:

| | |
|---|---|
| Single | $ 5,000 |
| Head of Household | $ 7,300 |
| Married, filing a joint return | $10,000 |
| Married, filing a separate return | $ 5,000 |
| Qualifying Widow(er) | $10,000 |

Your filing status is always determined as of the last day of a given year. For example, if you become legally divorced by December 31$^{st}$, you cannot file as married/filing jointly or married/filing separately since you are no longer married. You will be treated as single or head of household, assuming you can qualify for the latter. Note: There is an exception for the first year your spouse dies. See pointer Number 5 for more details.

Finally, if you qualify for more than one filing status, choose the one that will give you the lowest tax. For example, people who qualify for head of household filing status may also qualify for single filing status. In most cases, a lower tax will result from the head of household filing status.

Here are seven pointers to keep in mind when choosing the right filing status:

### Pointer 1: Shackin' Up

Just because you've decided that you and your "boo" are together and you share everything, including all of your expenses, the IRS may not see it that way. Generally, you can't use the married/filing jointly category unless you are legally married. Moreover, calling someone your "Wifey," (Next, 2000) is not going to change this. Yes, the term is supposed to be a compliment-meaning the woman has moved up in status from just a girlfriend to the number one girl, or in football jargon, the first string starting quarterback. But in the tax world, Wifey's status is somewhere below the legal status of "wife." So a "Wifey" generally can't use any of the filing statuses that start with "married." Look to the single filing status or head of household if you have a dependent child. However, certain states have an exception that recognizes common law marriages. So even if you never meet at the altar with your white dress, (aka, Jagged Edge style, "Let's Get Married," 2000), you may be treated as married because you've been living together for many years and act like you're married (i.e., you tell everyone this, call each other "husband" and "wife," etc.).

**Pointer 2: Qualifying Child**

Many tax benefits will depend on whether or not your child can be seen as a dependent (known as a "qualifying child"). The qualifying child rules apply to the head of household filing status, the personal exemption for a dependent, the child tax credit, the child and dependent care credit and the earned income tax credit. Under these rules a "qualifying child" must satisfy <u>all</u> of the following four tests:

- ✓ **Relationship**—It must be your child, stepchild, grandchild (whether by blood or adoption), foster child. Also, your sibling or stepsibling can count. Finally, even your niece and nephew may count as a qualifying child.
- ✓ **Residence**—The person must live with you for more than half the tax year. But there are exceptions for example, for cases like children of divorced or separated parents.
- ✓ **Age**—The person must be under the age of 19 at the end of the tax year, or under the age of 24 if a full-time student for at least five months of the year. Note: There is no age limit for special needs children (i.e., those who are permanently and totally disabled).
- ✓ **Support**—You must provide more than half of the financial support for child for the year.

For more on the qualifying child rules, see the IRS website at http://www.irs.gov and see FS-2005-7, January 2005.

**Pointer 3: The Real Head of Household**

This may be the most confusing filing status. Many people consider themselves "head of household" when they don't qualify. First, you must be unmarried to claim this status. But if you are legally married and your spouse has not lived with you in your home for at least 6 months, you may be able to qualify as head of household.

Second, you must provide more than half the costs for keeping up a home for your dependent. For most people, this dependent will be their child (i.e., a qualifying child, as under Pointer 2 above).

But the dependent can be a relative who does not live with you (i.e., they live in their own home or a retirement home), but for whom you pay more than half the cost of keeping up a home. They key is that you must be able to claim a personal exemption for this relative (described below in the next section) before they will count as a dependent under the head of household rules. Finally, you may be able to claim head of household status for people who aren't true relatives (i.e., play cousins) if you can claim a personal exemption for them (i.e., they live with you all year and you provide over half of their support). For more on this see the personal exemption rules in the next section.

Note: In the case of divorce, you can't generally negotiate or trade which parent will get head of household status. This means, the parent who has physical custody of the child (i.e., the child lives with them for the majority of the year), typically can claim head of household status. But if you have more than one child, you can agree to have one parent claim head of household status for one child and the other parent claim it for the second child. But these rules are different than those for claiming personal exemptions for children in the next section; where you can barter, trade and negotiate who gets to take the deductions. So it's possible for a child to qualify as a dependent under these rules and not under the personal exemption rules (described below in the next section). This means that you could claim the head of household filing status, even though you can't also take a personal exemption for that child. Please see the discussion below in this Chapter for more on personal exemptions.

**Pointer 4: Baby's Momma & Baby's Daddy**
Remember when you first heard the lyrics "Who that is, that's just my baby's daddy?" (B Rock and the Bizz, "My Baby Daddy," 1997)? Now fast forward to 2004; a time when Hollywood even made a movie called "My

Baby Daddy." We live in a world where Baby's Momma and Baby's Daddy may next become official terms in Webster's dictionary. In the tax world, if you are a Baby's Momma or Baby's Daddy, this typically means you aren't married. So the married/filing separately, married/filing jointly, or qualifying widow(er) statuses are probably not available to you. This leaves the single and head of household filing statuses. If you can prove that you provide more than half the costs of keeping a home for you and your child(ren), you may qualify as head of household. Otherwise use the single filing status.

**Pointer 5: Living All Alone**

The next filing status may best be summarized by the lyrics from Phyllis Hyman's "Living All Alone," (1987). The qualifying widow(er) filing status can be used by unmarried widows, with at least one dependent child, for up to 2 years after their spouse's death. With this status, you still get the same tax rate and the higher standard deduction as the married/filing jointly status. Here's how it works: The year in which your spouse dies, you can still file as married/filing jointly. For the next two years after your spouse's death, you can file as qualifying widow(er) status, but you must have a dependent child for whom you pay more than half the costs of keeping a home to claim this status. Once two years have passed since your spouse's death, you may be able to qualify as head of household if your child is still a dependent.

**Pointer 6: Same Sex Marriages**

Currently, only the state of Massachusetts recognizes same sex marriages. The IRS does not see it this way. If you are in a same sex marriage, even one that is legal in your state, you cannot use any of the married filing statuses (i.e., married/filing jointly, married/filing separately, or qualifying widow(er) with a dependent child). You must file as single or head or household (if you can qualify). Note: Massachusetts has indicated that it will allow a same sex couple, who was married in the state and are residents of the state, to file a joint tax return for their state taxes.

**Pointer 7: No Romance without Finance**
Like Gwen Guthrie said, "No romance without finance" ("Ain't Nothing Going On But The Rent," 1986). There are many legally married couples who choose not to treat common expenses as one joint expense. For example, they have separate bank accounts and split paying joint expenses based on some formula like their relative earnings (i.e., she pays 40% of the mortgage and he pays 60%) or the type of bill (i.e., she pays the mortgage and he pays the car notes). These couples may also consider filing their tax returns separately, but in most cases, using the married/filing separately status will cause you to pay more taxes than filing as married/filing jointly.

However, there are numerous non-financial reasons for couples to want to file separately. One common reason arises in the case of a legally married couple that is separating, or no longer lives together. Emotions, in such cases, are so high that the individuals don't want to have anything to do with each other—which include having as few financial ties as possible. They simply don't care that filing separately will cost them more money.

Also, some people use this filing status where they believe that their spouse is not accurately reporting tax information. Keep in mind, with a joint return you are both stating that all the information provided to the IRS is accurate and correct. If you know your spouse is not reporting all of his or her income, it will be no defense if he or she is caught that you didn't personally lie. To protect yourself in this case, you may want to consider filing a separate tax return. Note: There is an innocent spouse exception that may help you in this situation. Under the innocent spouse rules, the IRS may agree to only go after the spouse who lied or misrepresented the tax information. Please see Chapter 10, FAQ #20, for more on the Innocent Spouse Relief. Also, for more on this see *IRS Publication 971, Innocent Spouse Relief*, and *Form 8857, Request for Innocent Spouse Relief*.

# Exemptions

Exemptions are deductions that you can take for yourself, your spouse and your dependents. For 2005, you can take $3,200 for each person who qualifies. To figure out your total exemptions, you will need to make sure that your dependents qualify. In addition to the dependency test below, get the lowdown on how these rules work when you have the following situations: college-aged children, divorces, and elderly parents whom you support. Also, keep reading to see how your total exemptions may need to be decreased (i.e., phased-out) if your income is too high.

### DEPENDENTS

You can take a personal exemption for anyone who qualifies as your dependent. Individuals who meet the qualifying child rules under pointer 2, will be treated as your dependent. For everybody else they must meet the following 5 tests to qualify as your dependent:

① **Member of Household or Relationship Test**—Under this test, the person must either live with you for the entire year or be related to you. Relatives include folks like: your siblings, parents, grandparents, aunts, uncles, niece, nephew, and in-laws. Everyone else must live in your house for the entire year in order for you to claim a personal exemption for them. This includes your: boyfriends, girlfriends, "play" cousins, aunts and uncles, godparents or anyone else who lives with you all year, even if they are not legally related to you.

### EXAMPLE 1.1

Just off of their hot single "Yells of Passion," The Peeps was a music group of extended family and friends. The vision for the band was all owed to King. In addition to writing the song, King provided almost all of the financial support for the band members. In fact, three of the members (there were five in total) lived in

King's house all year. Of the remaining two, St. James was King's nephew and he lived in a condo, but King owned the condo and paid for most of St. James' expenses. The other member, Susana M., lived in her own house with her twin sister, Wendi M, who was a superstar in one of King's other singing groups; Wendi and Liza. Although King considered Wendi and Susana to be his "play" sisters, there was no blood relation.

Assuming all of the other personal exemption tests are met, King should be able to claim personal exemptions for the three band members who lived in his home all year. He also should be able to claim a personal exemption for his nephew, St. James. Even though St. James did not live with King, he is one of the "qualified" relatives under the personal exemption rules. Finally, King will not be able to claim an exemption for Susana M., since she did not live with King and she is not a relative; she's just a play thing.

Note: Paying for the support of your relative may also allow single taxpayers to qualify for head of household filing status (see the discussion above in this Chapter). You may also be able to claim some of the medical expenses that your pay for your relatives. For more on medical expenses, see Chapter 5: Itemized Deductions Part I.

② **Citizen or Resident Test**—The person must be a U.S. citizen and resident or a resident of Canada or Mexico.

③ **Joint Return Test**—This test typically becomes an issue where you are providing support for your adult who happens to be married. The test typically prevents this person from filing a joint tax return with their own spouse, unless they only file a tax return to get a tax refund; in which case you can still claim them as your dependent.

④ **Gross Income Test**—You generally cannot claim someone as a dependent if they have more than $3,200 in gross income. But there is an exception for children who are either under the age of 19 or who are college students under the age of 24. For more on college aged children see the discussion below in this Chapter.

⑤ **Support Test**—Under the final test, you must "support" the person. Support can be defined many ways; there's emotional support, seasonal support, or plain old physical support (i.e., "Booty Call," style, Blackstreet, 1994). But the IRS is talking about providing at least over half of the person's financial support.

To calculate the costs for supporting your dependents, add up all the following:

- Clothing expenses
- Education expenses
- Medical expenses
- Household expenses (such as rent, utility charges, food, upkeep and repairs or fair rental value of a house that you own).
- Transportation
- Travel and vacation

Out of this total, figure out how much you pay personally for these expenses and how much someone else pays. If your amount is more than 50% of the total, you meet the test.

**Pointer 8: Social Security Number**
You must provide a social security number for your dependent on your tax return. If your dependent does not have a social security number, file *Form SS-5, Application for a Social Security Card* with the Social Security Administration.

## COLLEGE-AGED CHILDREN

You can still claim personal exemptions for your college-aged children who are under the age of 24; even if they earn more than $3,200 for 2005. Your child must be a full-time student at a school for at least 5 months in the year. Also, the term "school" includes programs, like: colleges, universities, technical and trade schools. It does not include on-the-job training courses, correspondence schools and night schools. So if your college bound child has a job but you still provide over half of her support, you should claim that child's personal exemption. Make sure, however, that you discuss all of this with your child. Why? Because once you claim your child on your tax return, they can no longer claim themselves on their own tax return.

## DIVORCE

For some, there comes a point when "Love Don't Live Here Anymore," (aka, Rose Royce in 1978, or the Faith Evans and Mary J. Blige version in 1995). Couples find themselves asking "Is This The End," (New Edition, 1983)? Divorce can be a way to cut your losses or it may be a sad ending and the break—up of a "happy home," ("If You Don't Know Me By Now," Harold Melvin & the Blue Notes, 1972, or the Simply Red version, 1989). Before you sign the paper and start singing "It's Over Now," (Luther Vandross, 1985) or "Me Myself And I" (Beyonce, 2003 or De La Soul version, 1989), make sure you have formally figured out how some of the many tax benefits will be shared.

One of the most common tax issues that divorced parents must resolve is who gets the personal exemptions for the children. If you say nothing, zilch, nada on the issue, then the parent who the child lives with will get the personal exemptions (called the custodial parent, in tax talk). This is the case even if that parent (i.e., the non-custodial parent) does not provide more than fifty percent of the child's support. Divorced parents can agree to share the exemption over various years (such as one parent gets it for the first three years then the other parent gets it for three years, etc.).

**Pointer 9: Form 8332**

Use *Form 8332, Release of Claim to Exemption for Child of Divorced or Separated*, to show that you are giving the personal exemption to your ex-spouse. This form must be attached to the non-custodial parent's tax return. The original Form 8332 is attached in the first year that the exemption is released, and then a photocopy is attached in all subsequent years that the non-custodial parent claims the personal exemptions.

## ELDERLY RELATIVES

If you provide support for your elderly relatives, even if they live in a nursing home or their own home, you may be able to claim a personal exemption for them. Keep in mind, your elderly relative cannot have more than $3,200 in income for 2005. This could potentially disqualify your parent as a dependent where they have more than $3,200 in income from sources like investment income or pension income. Note: Some of your parent's social security payments may be ignored when calculating their income under these rules.

In some cases, you may be able to claim a personal exemption for your elderly relative, even if you don't provide over half their support, but you must provide at least 10%. For example, if you and your siblings all chip in to help pay the majority of the support for your parent, but no one person provides over 50% individually, you may file a multiple support agreement (*Form 2120 Multiple Support Declaration*); so at least someone gets the benefit of the tax deduction. With this agreement, you sign a contract with your siblings allowing for one of you to claim the personal exemption for your parent.

**Pointer 10: Multiple Agreement**

If you and your siblings share the expenses of providing most of your parent's support, consider filing a multiple support agreement with siblings, then agree to rotate the tax benefits each year so that each sibling can get the benefit. Otherwise, without an agreement no one will be able to claim the tax benefits (i.e., personal exemptions and other deductions like medical expenses). The person claiming the personal exemption should attach a copy of *Form 2120, Multiple Support Declaration*, to his tax return.

### PHASE-OUT

What the tax man "giveth," he can surely "taketh" away. This is the basic concept behind phase-outs. As mentioned above, everyone can deduct personal exemptions. How much you can deduct depends on your filing status and your number of dependents. If you make too much money, you will start to lose this deduction, to the point where you can't take it at all. The following chart shows when your income level causes you to start losing your exemption up to the point that you lose it completely:

For 2005:

| | Phase-out Begins | Completely Phased-out |
|---|---|---|
| Married Filing Separate | $109,475 | $170,725 |
| Single | $145,950 | $268,450 |
| Head of Household | $182,450 | $304,950 |
| Married Filing Jointly or Qualifying Widow(er) | $218,950 | $341,450 |

## Income

What is income? We all know what cold hard cash is—just like the title of this book—"For The Love Of Money," (O'Jays, 1973 or New Jack City Style, by Troop, Levert and Queen Latifah, 1991) and songs like "It's All About The Benjamins," (Puff Daddy and the Family, 1998), and "C.R.E.A.M.," (Wu-Tang Clan, 1994). But, what does the IRS consider as income? If you started out thinking that almost anything you earn of value could potentially be income, you're pretty close. Below, get the 411 on some of the common types of income:

- Wages
- Dividends and Interest
- Tax Refunds
- Alimony
- Side Business Income
- Rental Real Estate
- Gambling Income
- Prizes

Also, there are certain types of income that the IRS won't tax you on. Keep reading this Chapter for the 411 on two of these lucky exclusions:

- Employer provided educational assistance
- Gifts and inheritances

Note: There are many other items that may be taxable income or excluded from taxes. For example, if you make a living dancing to "Lights, Camera, Action," (Mr. Cheeks, 2001), you will probably have some tip income that needs reporting. For more details on other types of income, please see *IRS Publication 535, Taxable and Nontaxable Income*. For more on capital gains or losses, see Chapter 4: Capital Gains.

### WAGES

Some of the best moments in your life come on Friday night when you "Just Got Paid," (Johnny Kemp, 1988) and you "hop in the Escalade," ("Whatever," by Ideal, featuring Lil' Mo, 2000). For many people, the money they get from their "J-O-B" will be the biggest amount of their income. In January of each year, you should receive a *Form W-2, Wage and Tax Statement* from your employer which lists your income for the year. Include this amount on your tax return and attach a copy of the Form W-2. If you don't get your Form W-2 by the middle of February, contact your employer; maybe it really did get lost in the mail, or your dog ate it, or whatever other crazy excuse you can think of. Keep in mind that you still have to report your salary income even if you don't have a Form W-2.

 **Pointer 11: Form W-2**
You should keep a copy of your *Form W-2, Wage and Tax Statement,* for at least 3 years. You will find your federal taxable income in Box 1. Keep in mind, pre-tax dollars, like amounts contributed to your 401(k), are not included in this box, because you aren't paying taxes on them.

### DIVIDENDS AND INTEREST

If you own investments in stock, bonds, mutual funds, other investments and savings accounts, you will probably have interest and dividend income. Report your interest and dividend income on *Schedule B, Interest and Dividend Income (1040).*

Interest income is your earnings on investments. It typically includes interest that you receive from bank accounts, loans you made to others, and amounts called "dividends" (even though they are really interest) when paid by cooperative banks, credit unions, savings and loan associations, and mutual savings banks. You should receive a *Form 1099-INT, Interest Income* from a bank or other financial institution reflecting your interest income. You may not have to pay taxes on interest income from certain types of investments, like US Savings Bonds, until the bonds are redeemed (i.e., cashed in) and you may be able to avoid state and local taxes.

Dividend income is money you receive as a stockholder, out of a company's earnings and profits for the year. You will generally receive a *Form 1099-DIV, Dividend Income* from a company or financial institution. On this form, your dividends will be broken out into three types. First, ordinary, dividends (Box 1 of Form 1099-Div) are those monies paid to you from a company in which you own stock. These dividends are fully taxable and you must include them in your income. You may also have dividends, called capital gains distributions (Box 2 of Form 1099-Div). These typically come from owning mutual funds or REITS (Real Estate Investment Trusts). They are also fully taxable and must be included in your income. Finally, you can receive dividends that are a return of your capital (Box 3 of

Form 1099-Div). You don't pay taxes on these amounts as they are simply returning your initial investment (i.e., the money does not come out of the company's earnings and profits).

Note: Any expenses related to earning your interest income may be deductible as miscellaneous itemized deductions. For more on this, see Chapter 5, Itemized Deductions Part I. Also, for more on interest and dividend income, see *IRS Publication 550, Investment Income and Expenses.*

**Pointer 12: Schedule B**

Fill in Part I to *Schedule B, Interest and Dividend Income (1040)* with all of your interest income, and Part II with all of your dividend income. You must attach *Schedule B* to your tax return if your dividend or interest income totals more than $1,500. If your interest or dividend income is $1,500 or less, enter your income on line 8a and 9a of Form 1040. Also, you do not need to attach Form 1099-INT or Form 1099-DIV to your tax return, but you should keep these records in your tax files for at least 3 years.

## TAX REFUNDS

It's great news when you find out you are getting a tax refund. But did you know that one year later, you might have income? If you deduct your state income taxes as itemized deductions on your federal tax return and then later you get a refund check for those taxes, you have to report that refund in your income the following year. Why? Because you took a deduction for a certain amount, when in fact the amount you paid in state taxes was less, thanks to the refund. Note: This only applies to people who itemize and take a deduction for state income taxes. If you use the standard deduction, you don't have to report your state tax refund as income and you can skip this section (unless you like reading my examples).

## EXAMPLE 1.2

Maria Scary was so happy when she got her $2,000 refund check for her 2003 state income taxes in May 2004. She already knew what she was going to spend the money on—a new diamond tennis bracelet. Her man, Jason, a self proclaimed "Ruffneck" (MC Lyte, 1993) really needed the money to "get right" with his creditors. Being a girl who was "down with the team" (i.e., like the "Bonnie and Clyde" theme, by Yo-Yo and Ice Cube, 1993, or the Jay Z and Beyonce version, 2003), she decided to give her man the refund check. Jason thanked Maria by giving her a K-I-S-S (i.e., "U Make Me Wanna," Jadakiss, featuring Mariah Carey, 2004).

But by January 2005, Maria and Jason had broken up. Although Jason still hadn't paid the $2,000 back, Maria had moved on and couldn't stop saying "U Don't Have To Call," (Usher, 2001). She was "Looking for A New Love," (Jody Watley, 1987) and had found someone who made her "wanna" leave the one she was with (aka, "You Make Me Wanna," Usher, 1997).

As she was going through her tax files for 2003, she noticed that she got a Form 1099-G from her state stating that she had gotten a $2,000 state tax refund. Maria had ignored this form since she was busy kissing her man, but when she went to see her tax advisor, she was shocked to learn that she would have to pay income taxes on this refund. Why? Because Maria took itemized deductions on her previous tax return which included deducting these state income taxes.

### Pointer 13: Form 1099-G
Your state tax refund is reported on *Form 1099-G, Certain Government Payments.* You don't have to attach this form to your tax return.

## ALIMONY

You must include all alimony payments in your income. What is alimony? For IRS purposes, alimony is more than the cash payments you make to your ex-spouse under a divorce or separation agreement. It may also include payments made by one spouse on behalf of the other such as: rent, utilities, health or life insurance premiums, medical expenses, car notes, tuition, or taxes; so long as the payment is required under the divorce or separation agreement. Payments for a mortgage (including property taxes) on a jointly owned house, but in which only one spouse lives, may not completely count as alimony. In many cases, only half of the mortgage and interest payments count as alimony.

What about other payments you make outside of those required under the divorce or separation agreement? If you give your ex-spouse money, out of the goodness of your heart, this does not count as alimony. However, you may have a gift tax if you give your ex-spouse more than $11,000 in a single year. For more on gift taxes, see Chapter 8: Investments, Education and Estate. Finally, alimony payments should not be confused with child support payments. Child support payments are made by you to take care of your child; they are not income.

This is intended to be a brief overview on some of the extremely complicated rules around alimony and tax issues that arise in a divorce. For more information, see IRS *Publication 504, Divorced and Separated Individuals*. If you are going through a divorce, you should contact a tax advisor for specialized assistance. Note: The person paying the alimony gets a tax deduction for the payments. For more on this, see the discussion below under Adjusted Gross Income.

### Pointer 14: Line 11 (Form 1040)
Report your alimony that you receive on line 11 of Form 1040. Keep in mind; you must also include your ex-spouse's social security number. If you don't include this you may have to pay a $50 penalty tax.

## SIDE BUSINESS INCOME

You must report income from your side business. What is a side business? Anything that you do with a profit motive, from braiding hair to running your own bed and breakfast, will qualify. Even if you don't have income, you can report your business losses and use them as a deduction against your other income (i.e., from your "9 to 5" job).

If you are doing this activity, just for the fun of it with no profit motive whatsoever, you may be engaging in a hobby. You must still report all of the income from your hobby, but you may not be able to take all of your hobby related deductions. These deductions are treated as miscellaneous itemized deductions (i.e., which must be greater than 2% of your adjusted gross income before they are deductible). Also, hobby losses can only be deducted up to the amount of hobby income. If your losses are greater than your income, you cannot take the extra deduction. Finally these hobby losses do not reduce the amount of your hobby gains. You must still report all of your hobby gains on your tax return.

For more help on organizing and operating your side business, see Chapter 2: Side Business Part I and Chapter 3: Side Business Part II. For more on miscellaneous itemized deductions, see Chapter 6, Itemized Deductions Part II. Note: For most people, any income from a rental real estate side business should be included on *Schedule E, Supplemental Income and Loss (Form 1040)*. For more on this, see the discussion below in this Chapter under rental real estate.

**Pointer 15: Reporting Side Business Income**
If you have a sole proprietorship, report this income on *Schedule C, Profit or Loss from Business (Sole Proprietorship) (Form 1040)*, then include it on line 12 of Form 1040. Make sure to attach Schedule C to your tax return. If your side business is a partnership or a limited liability company, your share of the organization's income will be reported on *Schedule K-1, US Return of Partnership Income (Form 1065)*. If your side business is an S

Corporation, your share of the organization's income will be reported on *Schedule K-1, US Income Tax Return for an S Corporation (Form 1120S)*. Take the amount listed as income or losses on these forms and report them on line 21 of Form 1040. Note: You do not need to attach Schedule K-1s to your tax return, but you should generally keep it in your tax records for at least 3 years.

## RENTAL REAL ESTATE

Many people are gaining their way to riches by becoming landlords; thanks in part to books like *"The Rich Dad Poor Dad"* series of books by Robert T. Kiyosaki, and Sharon L. Lechter, and articles in magazines like *Black Enterprise, Business 2.0, Fortune, Money, Inc., Entrepreneur* and *Minority Business Entrepreneur*. Here's the 411 on what you need to know.

First, you must include your income and losses from rental real estate. What counts as rental real estate? Any real estate property that you own and rent out to others, even if you also live in the home or if the person renting it is a relative. You must include all rental payments that you receive as income. This includes the first and last month rental payments that you receive in advance. It also includes that value of any services that your tenant provides for you in exchange for reduced or free rent (i.e., a handyman's services). But it does not include the security deposit, if you plan to give that money back to the tenant at the end of the lease. Note: If you use the security deposit to cover the last month's rent, you should treat this as income at that time.

Besides giving you another form of revenue and building a nest egg for your retirement, there are tax benefits, too from being a landlord. Because you are able to deduct your rental real estate expenses, for many folks, this will result in a taxable loss; a loss that can be used to offset your other income (i.e., from your full-time "J-O-B"). This loss often comes from the fact that you can take depreciation deductions for your rental property.

## EXAMPLE 1.3

Kwame purchased a single-family home in 1994 for $155,000. One night while listening to the radio he heard a song called, "Only Ewe," by Kwame (no relation). Sensing that this was an omen, he asked his longtime girlfriend, Eve (he got the "w" and "v" confused), to marry him. She said yes, but she did not want to live in his house, which was known by all of his friends as the "Booty Bachelor Pad." So the couple brought a new house on the other side of town. Being the ever-smart entrepreneur, Kwame decided to keep his house and turn it into a rental property.

He charged the tenant $1,500 a month for rent and received $18,000 for the entire year. Assume he spent $14,500 for repairs, advertising, insurance, taxes, mortgage interest, utilities, and legal fees. From a cash flow perspective, Kwame has an extra $3,500 from renting his home (i.e., he paid out $14,500 but got $18,000 in cash). Assuming his tax rate is 20%, this could add an extra $700 in federal taxes.

But Kwame will probably not have to pay taxes on this income. Why? Because he also gets to deduct depreciation. Assume his depreciation for the year equals $5,818. After depreciation is deducted from his rental income, Kwame actually has a $2,318 loss ($18,000 - $14,500 - $5,818). He can also use this loss as a tax deduction against his other income; from things like his salary, interest dividends, side businesses, etc. Thus, he has $3,500 in extra cash and a $2,318 tax deduction.

---

Depreciation is based on your basis or the cost of the property plus any additions or improvements you make. It is an attempt to allow you to deduct the costs due to wear and tear of your property. You can't depreciate the value of the land, since land is not thought to wear out; it's always valuable. So since residential real estate is made up of a building and land, to calculate your depreciation, you must deduct the cost of the land from your basis. Next, you take this amount and divide it by the property's useful life (which can be found in *IRS Publication 946, How to Depreciate Property*). For most residential real estate the use life will be 27.5 years. Note: repairs can be deducted in full when you pay them and are not added to your basis.

### EXAMPLE 1.4

Using Kwame from example 1.3 above, in addition to the $155,000 he paid for his Booty Bachelor Pad in 1994, he also made $55,000 in improvements and additions over the years. He began renting the house on January 1, 2004. Kwame checked with his tax advisor and found out that $50,000 of his purchase price for the house was attributable to the land. So, his actual basis in the house, for purposes of calculating depreciation, was $160,000 ($155,000 + $55,000 - $50,000). For 2004, Kwame can take a depreciation deduction for his rental real estate equal to $5,818 ($160,000/27.5). He can take this same depreciation deduction for this rental property for the next 26.5 years.

As seen in the above example, since depreciation is a tax deduction and not an actual dollar expenditure, it can result in lowering the taxable amount on a rental property to the point where you may actually have a rental loss. How much of a loss? Most folks can take up $25,000 in losses from rental real estate. But, typically the $25,000 limit must be reduced when your adjusted gross income is more than $100,000, and eventually completely eliminated as your adjusted gross income is more than $150,000. See more on adjusted gross income later in this Chapter. But if you're a full time "playa" in the rental real estate business (i.e., you spend more than 750 hours a year on buying, selling, renting and managing rental real estate property) you may be able to take unlimited losses.

For more on rental real estate, see *Publication 527, Residential Rental Property*. Also, see the discussion regarding rental real estate in Chapter 3:

Side Business Part II, selling your rental real estate in Chapter 4: Capital Gains, and dividing the personal amount of interest and property tax expenses in Chapter 5: Itemized Deductions, Part I.

### Pointer 16: Schedule E and Form 4562

Are you ready to play the tax forms game? Calculate the amount of your depreciation deduction, and any mileage or other car related expenses you have from using your auto in connection with your rental real estate on *Form 4562, Depreciation and Amortization* and then transfer this to *Schedule E, Supplemental Income and Loss*. Use Schedule E to list all of your rental income and rental expenses, and calculate your ultimate rental income or loss. Take the final amount from Schedule E and report your income or losses from rental real estate activities on line 17 on Form 1040. Note: You must attach both Form 4562 and Schedule E to your tax return.

### Pointer 17: Rental Real Estate Expenses

In addition to depreciation, other expenses you might be able to deduct in connection with your rental property include advertising, cleaning, mortgage interest, property taxes, insurance, repairs, supplies, maintenance, utilities, landscaping and yard maintenance, pest control, travel, and professional and management fees. Take all of these expenses against the rental income that you charge to determine if you have income or losses from your rental real estate. Note: Thanks to a concept called amortization, you may only be able to deduct a portion of your mortgage points paid for rental real estate.

## GAMBLING INCOME

Do you have the "Midas Touch" (…everything you touch turns to gold? Midnight Star, 1986). If so, I would like to congratulate you. I hate to rain on your parade, but the Tax Man may be knocking at your door if you don't include these winnings in your taxable income.

You have to include all of your gambling winning in income. Gambling income includes all your winnings from virtually anything that you put a wager on; such as, Keno, slot machines, table games (i.e., twenty-one, black jack, craps, poker, baccarat, roulette, and wheel of fortune), bingo, racing and lotteries. It may also include raffles.

What about gambling losses? They can be deducted as miscellaneous itemized expenses, but in many cases, you probably won't be able to deduct the full value of these gambling losses. For more on gambling losses, see the discussion under miscellaneous itemized deductions under Chapter 6: Itemized Deductions.

To make matters even worse, not all expenses that you pay are gambling losses and in fact, they may not even be deductible. Take the case of a raffle. Assume that you just won the grand prize at your annual sorority fundraiser; a 7 day, 6 night vacation for two worth $6,000 at an all-inclusive resort in San Tropez to "watch a brotha play a mandalay" ("I Need A Girl (Part Two)," P. Diddy, featuring Loon, Ginuwine & Mario Winans, 2002). You paid $100 for the raffle ticket. What's the catch? With most of these prizes, your airfare, hotel and food costs are covered, but you still have to pay the sales taxes and transportation-related fees; in this case, assume you have to come out of pocket on this, to the tune of $750.

And that's not all. Don't forget you will have to report your free vacation on your tax return. How much do you need to report in income? If you guessed $5,150 ($6,000 - $100 - $750) you're wrong. The entire cost of the prize, $6,000 must be included in your income. Assuming a 20% effective tax rate, this could be an additional $1,200 in taxes.

Moreover, your gambling expenses only include the cost of the raffle ticket, or $100. The $750 that you paid in state sales taxes and transportation related fees does not count as gambling expenses. But a portion may be deductible as state sales taxes. For more on state sales taxes, see Chapter 5: Itemized Deductions, Part I. Otherwise chalk it up to getting property worth $6,000 and only paying about $2,000 for it ($100 ticket + $750 in taxes and fees + $1,200 in extra taxes).

**Pointer 18: Form W2-G**

Gambling establishments are required to report your gambling winnings over $600 to the IRS ($1,200 for winnings from bingo or slot machines and $1,500 for winning from Keno) on *Form W2-G, Certain Gambling Winnings*. Also, if you win more than $5,000, they must withhold taxes from your winning (i.e., to the tune of 25% to 28%).

### PRIZES

The tax shock for the raffle winner is not much different from the surprise that comes to many game show winners. Game shows—and every other large gift giver and casino—must report these winners to the IRS. It's often then the responsibility of the winner to fess up on their tax return. Let's take some real life recent examples here.

### EXAMPLE 1.5

Oprah Winfrey started her 19th season in 2004 by giving away Pontiac G6's to everyone that was in her audience that day (a reported 276 cars). Everyone was so happy; after all, who wouldn't like to win a new car. But, because you are reading *For The Love Of Money*, you know most of the audience members forgot about taxes. Although Pontiac paid for all of the local sales taxes and licensing fees, they didn't cover the income taxes that each person would have due to including the prize in their income.

This came as quite a shock to many folks, because these cars were valued at over $28,000. This extra income could cause some of the guests to be in higher tax bracket. Also, they could have additional state income taxes. Can't Oprah solve this problem by just paying the taxes for them? Probably not, because any payments she makes on their behalf would be additional income to them and could also be subject to gift taxes if she pays each person more than $11,000. But, by using a mathematical calculation called a "gross-up" she could figure out how much she would have to pay them so that they wound up in a neutral tax situation (i.e., the same place had they not gotten the cars in the first place). This is unlikely to happen though.

In the end, most people in this situation either pay the additional tax (after all they did get a car worth over $28,000), or they sell the car and use some of the money from the sale to pay off their taxes. Either way they have more money or assets, than before they visited the Oprah show.

## EXAMPLE 1.6

Richard Hatch, the first winner of the TV show, *Survivor*, may be facing IRS trouble for failing to pay taxes on his $1 million in prize winnings from the show. He apparently filed a tax return, but somehow forgot to include his prize money as income. In addition to owing the IRS hundreds of thousand, he could face jail time too! Note: Mr. Hatch is reportedly fighting this matter with the IRS under the theory that he was an employee of CBS and it was their responsibility to withhold any taxes and pay them over to the IRS. Whatever the case may be, someone is going to have to pay taxes off of this prize money.

### EMPLOYER-PROVIDED EDUCATIONAL ASSISTANCE

Employer-provided educational assistance programs come in as many flavors as artists who rapped on Craig Mack's "Flava in Ya Ear," (remix version, with artists like LL Cool J, Notorious BIG, Rampage, and Busta Rhymes, 1994).

Some employers will pay up to a certain dollar amount for any type of class (whether it's at a four-year college, graduate level, community college, or "Basket Weaving 101"). Others will pay for all educational expenses if directly related to your current job. For purposes of the IRS, it does not have to include courses related to your job. So, if you are a secretary and your employer will pay for you to take a $1,000 photography class at your local community college, you won't have to worry about reporting this as income on your tax return. Keep in mind that even though this assistance is income, the IRS allows you to exclude up to $5,250. Since most large corporations and a number of smaller ones offer some form of educational assistance, you should check with your employer to see what type of educational expenses are eligible.

For more on employer provided education assistance, see *IRS Publication 970, Tax Benefits for Education*. Note: If you personally pay expenses for education that your employer requires for your job, you may be able to take a deduction for these costs. For more on unreimbursed employee expenses, see the discussion under miscellaneous itemized deductions in Chapter 6: Itemized Deductions, Part II.

### GIFTS AND INHERITANCES

You generally don't have to include property or money you receive as a gift or from an inheritance in your income. For example, it's reported that before his death, Ray Charles gave each of his twelve children, $1 million each. His children will not have to include this $1 million in their income. But the person giving the property (in this case, Ray Charles) may have gift or estate taxes. For more on this area, see Chapter 8: Investments, Education, Estate.

## Adjusted Gross Income

Adjusted gross income (nicknamed AGI for short) is one of the most important numbers that you need to know. Many of your tax breaks and benefits are dependent on how high or low your AGI is. Calculate your AGI by taking your income and subtracting your "above the line" deductions. The "line" is your AGI, in tax talk and any deductions taken before you reach your AGI are called "above the line." I call these "Above the Rim Deductions."

> **Income − Above the Rim Deductions = AGI**

These "Above the Rim Deductions" are important, because you can take them even if you can't take itemized deductions. That's right. You can take them even if you don't own a home, make charitable contributions or have high medical expenses. Itemized deductions are deducted after you compute AGI and can only be taken if they are greater than your standard deduction. Also, they are subject to various rules, exceptions and phase-outs. In fact, they are significantly decreased (i.e., up to 80%) once your AGI reaches over who make more than $72,975, if single or $145,950 for married folks.

Although you'll take a deduction wherever you can get it, in most cases you come out better if it's an Above the Rim Deduction. For more on itemized deductions see the next section in this Chapter. Get the 411 on the following Above the Rim Deductions:

- IRA Deduction
- Student Loan Interest Deduction
- Tuition and Fees Deduction
- Educator Expenses
- Health Saving Accounts
- Moving Expenses
- Self Employment Tax & Deductions
- Alimony

In addition to these deductions, you may be eligible for certain other Above the Rim Deductions, such as business expenses of reservists, performing artists and fee-basis government officials, or penalties on early withdrawal of savings. Please see, *IRS Publication 17, Your Federal Income Tax (Individuals)* for more on these deductions. Note: In some cases, your tax benefits and deductions are based on a modified AGI. This means you take your AGI and add back certain tax benefits, like: student loan interest deduction. For many people modified AGI and AGI will be the same number, and thus the terms are used interchangeably in this book. See *IRS Publication 970, Tax Benefits for Education* for more on modified AGI.

## IRA DEDUCTION

You may be able to deduct up to $4,000 for your IRA contributions. Also, you have up until the date your tax return is due (i.e., April 15$^{th}$, unless you file for an extension) to make contributions to an IRA and have it count on your tax return. So if it looks like you owe taxes, it might make sense to set up an IRA and take a tax deduction to limit or completely get rid of your taxes.

Keep in mind, this deduction is only for contributions that you make to a Traditional IRA. It does not include contributions that you make to other retirement plans such as: 401(k), Roth IRA, SEP IRAs, SIMPLE IRAs, etc. Of course there are a couple of rules to determine if you get the full $4,000 deduction. The actual amount that you can deduct will primarily depend on your income and if you or your spouse are covered under a retirement plan at work (i.e., a 401(k) plan).

Here is how it works: If you (and if married, your spouse, too) are not covered under any other retirement plan you can take the full IRA deduction, regardless of your income level. But, if you are covered by another retirement plan, the amount of your IRA deduction will depend on your AGI. If your AGI is greater than $50,000 for single folks and $70,000 for married filing jointly, your deduction will start to decrease and will be completely gone by the time your AGI exceeds $60,000 for single folks and $80,000 for married filing jointly taxpayers. See the Instructions to Form 1040 for more on calculating the IRA deduction.

Moreover, if your spouse is covered under a retirement plan, but you aren't, the amount of your AGI limits increase. Your IRA deduction begins to phase-out when your AGI reaches above $150,000 and completely phase out after $160,000. For more on IRAs and other retirement plans, see Chapter 8: Investments, Education and Estate. See also, *IRS Publication 590, Individual Retirement Arrangements*.

**Pointer 19: Line 25 (Form 1040)**
Reporting this deduction is as easy as "ABC," (The Jackson Five, 1970). Put the amount of your IRA deduction on line 25 of Form 1040. There are no additional forms or schedules that you need to attach to take this deduction.

### STUDENT LOAN INTEREST DEDUCTION

Kanye West's "School Spirit Skit 2," talks about a man who has nothing going for him but his degrees. The man is 52 years old and has never made a dime, because he's been in school getting his "masters," "master's masters" and "doctorate." In fact, when he dies he wants to be buried along with his degrees. Although this is an interesting commentary on education and the value of a degree, the bottom line is that even Kanye West, a self-proclaimed "College Dropout," would probably agree that getting a college education is becoming necessary if you want to compete for the best jobs and opportunities.

But, the costs of education can be staggering. Most people must borrow and take out loans to finance at least a part of their education. The good news is that you can take a partial deduction for the interest you pay on student loans. These include student loans (for you, your spouse of your children) to attend an eligible educational institution and where the money is used for thing like: tuition, fees, room and board, books, equipment, transportation and supplies. The school must be a college, university, post-secondary educational institution, certain vocational schools, or other institutions eligible to participate in Department of Education student aid programs. Also, the student must carry at least half of the normal full time student workload.

The maximum deduction is $2,500. However, the deduction begins to phase-out for taxpayers who are married filing jointly with AGI over $105,000 and $50,000 for single folks. It's completely gone when your AGI reaches over $135,000 for married folks filing jointly and $65,000 for singe taxpayers.

Finally, if you are claiming student loan interest for your child's education, you must be able to claim the child as a dependent when the loan is made. So you can still take the deduction even if, by the time you actually pay it back, your child is no longer your dependent. For example, say that you took out a loan to pay your daughter's, Monica, education. Monica was your dependent when you took out the loan, but like Janet Jackson, she's now in "Control," (1986). She has graduated, is working, and is no longer calling home for money (at least not that much). You can still deduct the student loan interest that you pay, because Monica was your dependent when you took out the loan. Note: On the flip side, you cannot claim the student loan interest deduction on your tax return if you are claimed as a dependent on your parent's tax return. For more on this deduction see *IRS Publication 970, Tax Benefits for Education.*

### Pointer 20: Form 1098-E

You can find your student loan interest amount on *Form 1098-E, Student Loan Interest Statement*, check Box 1. You don't have to include this with your tax return, but you should keep a copy in your tax files. It should be mailed to you on or before Jan. 31st of each year by your lending institution.

## TUITION AND FEES DEDUCTION

In addition to student loan interest, there's another education related deduction called the tuition and fees deduction. You can take a deduction up to $4,000 in tuition and related expenses for you, you spouse or your dependents. Tuition and related expenses (like books and supplies) include those spent pursuing a degree at a college, university, vocational school or postsecondary educational institution. It does not include payments for room and board.

There are a few restrictions for this deduction. The first and major restriction is that you can't take this if you also claim one of the education tax credits (i.e., The HOPE Credit and The Lifetime Learning Credit). Also, if you are taking this deduction for tuition and related fees that you pay for your child's education, you can only take it if you claim a personal exemption for that child (see the discussion above in this Chapter for more on personal exemptions). Finally, this deduction begins to decrease as your AGI reaches $65,000 for single folks and $130,000 for married taxpayers filing jointly. It's completely phased-out when your AGI reaches over $80,000 for single folks and $160,000 for married taxpayers filing jointly.

**Pointer 21: Form 1098-T**

You should receive *Form 1098-T, (Tuition Payment Statement)* from any institutions to which you pay tuition. Use this form to figure out your tuition expenses for the year. You do not need to attach this form to your tax return, but you should keep it for your tax files for at least three years.

## EDUCATOR EXPENSES

If you teach for a living, you may be able to deduct some of your educator expenses. Educators can deduct up to $250 for expenses spent on qualified educations expenses, like: books, supplies, equipment, computer software, and any other materials used in the classroom.

What counts as teaching? Anyone who teaches Kindergarten through 12th grade can qualify for this deduction. Classroom aides, principals, coaches and other administrative staff may also qualify if they work for more than 900 hours during a school year.

Of course, many of you are tirelessly dedicated educators and you spend a lot more than $250 on education related expenses. In such cases, there's more good news. You can take the excess over $250 as a miscellaneous itemized deduction. Also, these educator expenses are not subject to the 2% limitation for most miscellaneous itemized deduction. This means, they can be deducted without looking at your AGI. For more on miscellaneous itemized deductions, see Chapter 6: Itemized Deductions Part II.

### HEALTH SAVING ACCOUNTS

Similar to the contribution to an IRA discussed above, you can also deduct contributions made to a health savings account ("HSA"). You may be able to deduct up to $2,650 for single folks and $5,250 for married taxpayers filing jointly for your contributions to an HSA. Also, you have up until the date your tax return is due (i.e., April 15th, unless you file for an extension) to make contributions to an HSA and have it count on your tax return. So, if it looks like you owe taxes, it might make sense to set up an HSA and take a tax deduction to limit or completely get rid of your taxes. For more on setting up an HSA, see, Chapter 3: Side Businesses Part II. Also, see *IRS Publication 969, Health Savings Accounts and Other Tax-Favored Health Plans.*

### Pointer 22: Form 8889

You should receive a *Form 5498-SA, HSA, Archer MSA, or Medicare+Choice MSA* from your employer with your HSA contributions. Use this to calculate your deductible contribution on *Form 8889, Health Savings Accounts*. Transfer this amount to Line 28 (Form 1040). You must also attach Form 8889 to your tax return.

## MOVING EXPENSES

Do you like to "move it, move it" (aka, Reel 2 Reel style, "I Like To Move It," 1994)? Moving to a new home can be very exciting and nerve-wracking all at the same time. But, did you know you can also get a tax benefit for some of your moving expenses? If you have to move because of a new job, you may be able to deduct your moving expenses.

There are, of course, a couple of restrictions you must keep in mind with this deduction. First, you can deduct only reasonable moving expenses such as mileage (at 15 cents per mile for 2005), packing, storage and shipping costs, and costs for connecting and disconnecting utilities. It does not include your meals or costs of moving new furniture that you buy for your new home. Nor does it include any costs related to selling your home or money you lose from breaking a lease, including any lost security deposit.

Also, you must meet a 50-mile distance test before you can take this deduction. Your new job must be at least 50 miles farther from your old home than your old job was to your old home. Sound confusing? It's really not. Think of it as a test to see how much farther you have to drive now, thanks to your new job. If it's over 50 miles, then the IRS understands why you had to move, and you get this tax deduction. Here's how it works: First, take the distance from your old home to your old job; call this the Old School Distance. Then, take the distance from your new job to your old home: call this the New School Distance. Your New School Distance must be greater than your Old School Distance by 50 miles.

### EXAMPLE 1.7

Bill (or Tasty Taste, his stage name) and his wife, Bridgette, make quite a couple. She's a tall blond, striking model and he's a short, not so striking man. But, like Paula Abdul said, "Opposites Attract," (1989). They lived in a beautiful home in Santa Barbara, California with three of their closest friends, and worked for a company called Has-Been Productions. They only had a 5-mile commute to work. In late 2003, Bridgette got a new job teaching Italian to other Hollywood has-been actors who are trying to make a comeback. Bridgette was happy about the new job, but not about her new commute; which she calculated at over 110 miles from her Santa Barbara house to her new job. So Tasty Taste and Bridgette moved to a new home in Calabasas, California and cut her commute to the new job down to 20 miles. Bridgette meets the 50-mile test because her New School Distance (110 miles) is at least 50 miles greater than her Old School Distance (5 miles). Note: The distance from her new home to her new job, which is 20 miles, is irrelevant in meeting the 50-mile test.

Finally, you must generally work full-time in your new job for at least 39 weeks to take this deduction. For self-employed folks, the test also includes another hurdle. You generally must work 78 weeks over a 2-year period. However, there are a few exceptions that allow you to ignore these time rules. For example, because you have been laid off from your new job or left due to a disability, you can take this moving deduction even if you haven't met the time test when you file your tax return. You simply must expect to meet the test. What happens if it turns out that you didn't meet the test? You can either file an amended return or report the previous tax deduction that you took as income on your next tax returns. For more information on moving expenses, see *IRS Publication 521, Moving Expenses*. Also, check out the For The Love Of Money Top 10 For New Homeowners in the Appendix.

### Pointer 23: Form 3903 and 8822

Calculate your moving expenses on *Form 3903 Moving Expenses*. Then, report the total amount of moving expenses on line 29 of Form 1040 and attach Form 3903 to your tax return. Also, don't forget to send the IRS your new address by filing *Form 8822, Change of Address*.

**Pointer 24: Calculating Mileage for the 50-Mile Test**
Use websites like http://www.mapquest.com to calculate the mileage between your old house and your new job, and your old house and your old job. You should print out the mileage and keep a copy of this in your tax files. You do not need to send this to the IRS, but it's a good idea to keep the records for at least three years.

## SELF-EMPLOYMENT TAX & DEDUCTIONS

As a self-employed person, there are several deductions that you can take. First, you can deduct one-half of your self-employment taxes. For more on self-employment taxes, see the discussion below in this Chapter under Taxes and see Chapter 3: Side Business Part II.

Next, you may also be able to deduct up to 100% of the self-employed health insurance payments that you make for you, yourself and your children. You can take this deduction even if you can't take an itemized deduction for your medical expenses. However, the amount of the deduction cannot be greater than the net profit from your side business, less one-half of your self employment tax and your contributions to retirement plans (i.e., Keogh plans, SEP IRA and SIMPLE IRA). Also, any self-employed health insurance premiums that you can't deduct under these rules may still be deductible as itemized deductions. For more on the medical expense deduction, see Chapter 5: Itemized Deductions Part I.

Finally, you may also be able to deduct payments made to retirement plans, such as **SEP IRAs** and **SIMPLE IRAs**. For more information on self-employed retirement plans, see the discussion in Chapter 8: Investments, Education and Estate. Also, see *IRS Publication 560, Retirement Plans for Small Businesses*.

**Pointer 25: Calculating Self-Employed Deductions**
Use the worksheet in the instructions to Form 1040 to calculate your self-employed health insurance. Enter the result in line 32 of Form 1040. Use *Schedule SE, Self Employment Tax (Form 1040)* to calculate your self-employment taxes, take half of this number and include it on line 30 of Form 1040.

### ALIMONY

Alimony is included in the income of the spouse receiving the payments, but the spouse making the payments gets an equal tax deduction. See the discussion above for more on what payments count as alimony. Note: Payments (including property taxes) for a mortgage on a jointly owned house, but in which only one spouse lives, may not completely count as alimony. In many cases, only half of the mortgage and interest payments count as alimony. The other half of the interest may be deducted as an itemized deduction. For more on alimony and other tax rules in the case of divorce, see *IRS Publication 504, Divorced or Separated Individuals*. If you are going through a divorce, you should contact a tax advisor for specialized assistance.

**Pointer 26: Line 34 (Form 1040)**
Report all the alimony you paid on line 34(a) of Form 1040. Keep in mind, you must also include your ex-spouse's social security number on line 34(b). If you don't include this you may have to pay a $50 penalty tax and risk having the IRS disallow your deduction.

# Taxes & Credits

Now that you've figured out your total income and your adjusted gross income, it's almost time to finally get down to the amount of your tax. But first, you must take some more deductions. Once you are through with these deductions, you will have the amount of your taxable income. Next, take your taxable income and figure out your tax using tax rates. Finally, once you have your tax, you can then subtract certain credits to help you come up with the amount of income tax that you owe for the year. The following equations help illustrate the rules.

> **AGI − Below the Rim Deductions = Taxable Income**

> **Taxable Income X Tax Rate = Tax**

> **Tax − Credit = Tax Owed**

Check out the discussion below for an overview on the Below The Rim Deductions, Tax Rates and Credits.

### BELOW THE RIM DEDUCTIONS

In arriving at how much federal income tax you will owe, there are a number of other deductions that will reduce your taxable income dramatically. Each year, you are allowed to claim one of two common deductions when you file—standard or itemized. These deductions are sometimes referred to as "below-the-line" deductions, because they are deducted after you compute your line (i.e., AGI). In keeping with the basketball theme, I call them "Below the Rim Deductions."

Either deduction method will cut your tax bill. Which deduction you use depends on your personal circumstances. As a rule of thumb, if your itemized deductions are greater than the standard deduction, you are almost always better off choosing the higher amount, which will give you the larger write-off. Note: In addition your itemized deductions (or standard deduction) you will also deduct your personal exemptions here to arrive at taxable income.

## STANDARD

The IRS gives everyone a standard deduction "Just Because" you're you (Anita Baker, 1988). For 2005, the basic standard deductions are as follows:

| | |
|---|---|
| Single | $ 5,000 |
| Head of Household | $ 7,300 |
| Married, filing a joint return | $10,000 |
| Married, filing a separate return | $ 5,000 |
| Qualifying Widow(er) | $10,000 |

Unless your itemized expenses are greater, you will take the standard deduction. Note: If you are blind, or 65 years or older, you may be eligible for even a higher standard deduction and other deductions not covered in this book. Please see your tax advisor if this applies to you.

## ITEMIZED

Itemized deductions are a group of special deductions that you can take, if large enough, instead of the standard deduction. They include things like medical expenses, taxes, interest expenses, charitable contributions, casualty and theft losses and miscellaneous expenses. Many of these deductions are subject to their own limitations and restrictions. Also, unlike the Above the Rim Deductions, these Below the Rim Deductions may be further limited as your AGI increases (i.e., up to 80% reduction). For more on itemized deductions, see Chapter 5: Itemized Deductions Part I and Chapter 6: Itemized Deductions Part II.

## PERSONAL EXEMPTIONS

As explained earlier in this Chapter, you can take a $3,200 deduction for each person who qualifies under the personal exemption rules. For more on these rules, see the discussion on personal exemptions earlier in this Chapter.

## TAX RATES

In calculating the amount of your tax based on your taxable income, you will need to use several tax rates. For example, see the 2005 chart—Apply the appropriate tax rate when your taxable income is over the following:

| IRS Tax Rates | Single | Married filing jointly or Qualifying Widow(er) | Married filing separately | Head of Household |
|---|---|---|---|---|
| 10% | $0 | $0 | $0 | $0 |
| 15% | $7,300 | $14,600 | $7,300 | $10,450 |
| 25% | $29,700 | $59,400 | $29,700 | $39,800 |
| 28% | $71,950 | $119,950 | $59,975 | $102,800 |
| 33% | $150,150 | $182,800 | $91,400 | $166,450 |
| 35% | $326,450 | $326,450 | $163,225 | $326,450 |

Luckily, most folks can look up the amount of their tax on the IRS tax tables (see the IRS website or the back of the instructions booklet for your tax return) without having to actually calculate them using tax rates. The IRS provides tax tables that tell you the exact amount of your tax based on your filing status and the amount of your taxable income shown on line 42 of your tax return. Also, there are numerous computer software programs that will do this for you at the click of a button. Note: This discussion focuses on your regular income taxes. If you are unlucky enough to have any alternative minimum taxes, add them, right after you calculate your regular tax. For more on alternative minimum taxes see Chapter 7: Alternative Minimum Taxes.

**Pointer 27: Resources to Calculate Tax Rates**
There are numerous websites that will help you calculate your effective tax rate and marginal tax rate. Here are a couple of them:
- Yahoo Finance Center— http://taxes.yahoo.com/calculators

- Smartmoney.com—http://www.smartmoney.com/tax
- Mile High Accountancy (a product of CCH Tax & Accounting)—http://www.execusite.com/clmjr/tools.html

## CREDITS

In addition to tax deductions, there are several other "Goodies" (Ciara, 2004), known as tax credits, that you may be able to use to reduce your taxes. Credits may not be as good as making "a dollar out of fifteen cents (a dime and a nickel)" ("I Get Around," Tupac, 1993), but they can reduce your taxes on a dollar-for-dollar basis. This means for every dollar of tax you owe, a credit can decrease that tax by the same dollar; which is about as good as it's going to get in tax land. Remember, tax credits are often more beneficial than some tax deductions, because deductions only reduce the amount of your income subject to tax while the credit reduces the actual tax. Below, get the 411 on these tax credits:

➤ Child and Dependent Care Expenses Credit
➤ Child Tax Credit
➤ Adoption Credit
➤ Education Credits

For more on other tax credits, see *IRS Publication 17, Your Federal Income Tax (Individuals)*.

### CHILD AND DEPENDENT CARE EXPENSES CREDIT

You may be able to take a tax credit for some of your daycare expenses. This credit runs from $600 to $1,200, based on an IRS formula that looks at the amount of your daycare expenses.

To qualify, you must have daycare expenses for a child who is under 13 years of age. However, if you have a child or other dependent who is physically or mentally disabled, the age rule is waived. Also, dependent care expenses for an elderly parent or other relative can also count for this credit. For more on figuring out who qualifies as your dependent, see the discussion above in this Chapter under personal exemptions.

Next, you must be paying for the daycare because you are at work or looking for work. So, babysitting while you go run errands does not count. Also, you must have earned income to claim this credit (i.e., from salary, wages, side businesses, etc). Finally, you cannot use expenses that are reimbursed to you under an employer dependent care assistance plan.

But you can't take this credit if you participate in your flexible spending account for dependent care expenses at your "9 to 5" job. Remember, with a flexible spending account, you are putting away tax-free dollars, up to $5,000 a year, from your paycheck and then handing in receipts to get reimbursed for the amount you actually spend on daycare expenses. This money is not included in your wages as reported on your Form W-2. You must use all the money in the account by the end of the year or you lose it. Practically speaking, if you spend all of the money in your flexible spending account, it will probably give you a better tax savings than you can get with using this tax credit. For more on the child and dependent care expenses credit see *IRS Publication 503, Child and Dependent Care Expenses.*

### Pointer 28: Form 2441

Compute your child and dependent care expenses on *Form 2441, Child and Dependent Care Expenses.* You must include the social security number or employee identification number of the person or company that you pay to watch your child or dependent on this form. Then enter the amount of the credit on line 47 of Form 1040. Also you should attach this form to your tax return.

### Pointer 29: Divorce or Separation

In the case of divorce, this credit generally goes with the custodial parent (i.e., the parent with whom the child lives). This is the case, even though custodial parent can't claim a personal exemption for the child.

## CHILD TAX CREDIT

Parents love their children, no matter what. The feeling may best be summed up by the lyrics in the Billie Holiday classic, "God Bless The Child," (1939). But, did you know the IRS loves your children, too? That's right—there are tax credits just for having a kid. You may be able to deduct $1,000 for each child, but the child must be younger than 17. Also, the credit begins to phase-out when your AGI gets too high (i.e., $75,000 for an individual and $110,000 for married taxpayers filing jointly). For more on the child tax credit, see *IRS Publication 972, Child Tax Credit*.

**Pointer 30: Line 49 (Form 1040)**
This is one of the easiest tax credits to take. No additional forms or schedules are needed for the basic child credit. Simply calculate your child credit on line 49 of Form 1040.

## ADOPTION CREDIT

You may be able to deduct up to $10,390 of the costs associated with adopting a child. Expenses that may qualify for this credit include: adoption fees, court costs, attorney fees, and travel expenses. But if your AGI is higher than $199,450, you can't take this credit. For more on this credit, see *IRS Publication 986, Tax Benefits For Adoption*.

## EDUCATION CREDITS

Still trying to get that college degree? Wondering how you can afford to send your child to college? I may not have all the answers to these questions, but there are two tax breaks that sure can help ease the pain. With the Hope Credit, you may be able to take up to $1,500 in education tax credits for each eligible person. This means for a family of four where everyone is in college, the credit may be up to $6,000 (i.e., $1,500 x 4). With the Lifetime Learning Credit, you may be able to take up to $2,000 in tax credits on your tax return.

There is a catch. You can't take both credits for the same person in the same year. So for example, if you're taking a credit for tuition and fees that you paid for your child in 2005, you can either take the Hope Credit or the Lifetime Learning Credit. But you may be able to claim both credits on your tax return if you have more than one child in school, or when you and your spouses are taking classes. Also, both credits are phased-out when your AGI gets too high (i.e., $53,000 for an individual and $107,000 for married taxpayers filing jointly). For more on education credits, see Chapter 8: Investments, Education and Estate. Also see *IRS Publication 970, Tax Benefits for Educations*.

## Other Taxes

Now that you've figured out your income taxes, you're almost done, but you must also add certain other types of taxes to figure out the real deal on the most common ones, including, Self-Employment Taxes and Nanny Taxes. For more on other taxes that must be added on your Form 1040, see *Publication 17, Your Federal Income Tax (Individuals)*.

### SELF-EMPLOYMENT TAXES

If you operate a business, either full-time or on the side, you will probably have to pay self-employment taxes. Self-employment taxes are the same as the FICA and Medicare taxes paid by employees on their "J-O-B." But the self-employed person pays double the amount of an employee. So while an employee pays these taxes at 7.65%, a self-employed person pays 15.3%. However, as discussed earlier in this Chapter, self-employed folks can take a credit for half of their self-employment taxes (i.e., as an Above the Rim Deduction). For more on self-employment taxes, see *IRS Publication 533, Self Employment Tax*.

 **Pointer 31: Schedule SE**
Calculate your self-employment taxes on your net profit from your business using *Schedule SE, Self-Employment Tax (Form 1040)* if your net profit is greater than $400. Then, enter the amount of the tax on line 57 of Form 1040. Also you should attach this form to your tax return. Note: A husband and wife must complete separate a Schedule SE for their separate businesses. Also, several websites have free calculators that will let you estimate the amount of your self-employment tax such as:

- ✓ Turbotax's™—
  http://www.turbotax.com/articles/TheSelfEmploymentTax.html
- ✓ Commerce Clearing House's—
  http://www.finance.cch.com/tools/calcs.asp

### NANNY TAXES

Anyone with children knows the struggles of finding quality daycare. Some families choose traditional daycare centers while others opt for a babysitter or a nanny. If you employ someone to watch your children, even on a part-time basis, please read on.

You are required to pay employment taxes (i.e., nanny taxes) on income that you pay to a nanny or babysitter to watch your child, if you pay this person more than $1,400. This is called nanny taxes. You've probably heard of them, as they come up from time-to-time when someone is running for public office and news surfaces that they never paid employment taxes for their long-time nanny. Nanny taxes are made up of Social Security tax, Medicare tax (both of which are called FICA for short), and federal unemployment tax (or FUTA for short). FICA taxes are calculated at 7.65% of your wages, and both the employee and the employer have to each pay this same percentage.

FUTA taxes work out to be about .8% of your wages, and are calculated on the first $7,000 of wages. So, it's about $56 ($7,000 x .08). The employer

46 • For The Love Of Money

must pay the FUTA taxes. There may also be state or local nanny taxes (i.e., state unemployment taxes). This leaves the largest amount of employment taxes; the FICA taxes. You can either withhold the nanny's portion from her paycheck or pay her share of the FICA taxes. Practically speaking, good nannies are hard to find. Thus, many people wind up paying these taxes on behalf of the nanny so the nanny can have more money in her take-home pay.

### EXAMPLE 1.8

Brandi is a famous writer and mother of four-year old Ray, Jay. With her coast-to-coast book tour, she's on "Top of the World," (Brandy, featuring Mase 1998). Her book tour schedule keeps her busy and often away from home. To help with taking care of little Ray Jay, she hires Monika as her nanny. Of course after reading *For The Love Of Money*, Brandi knows all about paying nanny taxes. If Brandi decides to withhold FICA taxes from Monika's paycheck, she must withhold $7.65 in FICA taxes for every $100 she pays Monika (i.e., she will pay her $92.35). Brandi will also owe $7.65 as the employer. Keep in mind, this $7.65 is not Brandi's money—it's the IRS's money. Brandi is merely giving the IRS a helping hand. She can pay both amounts ($15.30) on Schedule H of Form 1040 when she files her tax return.

On the flip side, if she decides to pay Monika's employment taxes, she will pay Monika the full $100 and then pay the entire $15.30 in FICA taxes from her own funds. Again, she will pay this on Schedule H of Form 1040. Remember, Monika will have income of $107.65 (not $100) for tax purposes because Brandi paid the $7.65 on her behalf.

For more on nanny taxes, see Chapter 10: FAQ #14. Also, see *IRS Publication 926, Household Employer's Tax Guide*.

## Payments

Will you owe money or get a refund? That will depend on how much you paid to the IRS during the year. One of the biggest payments that you make to the IRS comes from your income tax withholdings at your J-O-B. You can find the total amount of income taxes that you withheld during the year on Box 2 of Form W-2. Also, if you have a side business and you made estimated tax payments during the year, make sure to include them here. Finally, did you know that you pay social security taxes on the first $87,900 of wages that you earn? But, if you change jobs during the year, your new employer has to start your social security withholding clock all over again. Your new employer will start withholding social security as if you haven't made a dollar. The result may be that you have had too much social security withheld from your paycheck. You can treat these excess social security payments as another tax payment. Note: Payments include other things, like the earned income credit for low income taxpayers. For more on these payments see *IRS Publication 17, Your Federal Income Tax (Individuals)*.

## Refund

Congratulations! If your Taxes are less than your Payments, you are getting a refund.

> **Taxes  <  Payments  =  Refund**

What are you going to do with the money—Pay off some bills? Go on a well deserved vacation? Buy some new clothes? Save for retirement or your kid's education? The options are endless. Maybe you'll follow Jadakiss and Mariah Carey's lead and give it to your income tax checks to your boo. ("U Make Me Wanna," Jadakiss, featuring Mariah Carey, 2004).

Whatever you do with it, promise yourself that you will try to do more tax planning this year so that next year you have an even smaller refund or close to none at all. No, I'm not trying to bring you down off your "Natural High," (Bloodstone, 1973), but getting a refund means that the IRS had your money for the year. Sure they'll give it back to you, but wouldn't you rather have had a little more in your paycheck each week. Even further—consider the fact that while they hold your money, it's not earning any interest. With good tax planning you can change this result.

Now that I'm done preaching, let's get to how you can get your money back now. Be thankful that you live in a time when even the government has high speed computers. You can now get your IRS refund check fairly quickly (i.e., 7 to 10 business days) and have the amounts deposited directly in your bank account. One of the quickest ways to get your return to the IRS, and, in turn, get your money is to e-file (i.e., electronically file your tax return). Be sure to ask your tax advisor about electronically filing your tax return.

Unless you've been living under a rock, you know you can get your tax refund on the spot (i.e., Rapid Refund™, tax refund loan, refund anticipation loan, etc.). You may get your money right away, but at what cost? Many of these programs charge high fees for their services. Think about it like this: Assume you have a new pair of $200 shoes (Air Jordan's, Jimmy Choo, Payless (if that's even possible)) and you got someone who offers to buy them from you but they will actually give you the money in 1-2 weeks. Then someone else comes along and offers you $150 today. Would you take the money? The answer will probably depend on how desperately you "need" the money. This same principle applies to tax refund loans. If you take one out, make sure you know that how much money you are giving up. Emergencies may happen, but hopefully with good tax and financial planning you will not be in the position where you feel pressured into needing a refund loan. For more on tax refund loans, see Chapter 10: FAQ #5.

# Amount You Owe

If your taxes are greater than your payments, then you will owe taxes.

> **Tax > Payments = Taxes You Owe**

After getting your work-out with this tax return, you figure out that you actually owe taxes. Cheer up. Take a spin through the rest of *For The Love Of Money* for ways that you can help avoid this situation for next year. But first and foremost, you must pay your taxes. There are no "ifs, ands, or buts" to this. Check out the Reasons To Pay Your Taxes in the Appendix.

What if you simply can't pay? What should you do? You should always, always, always file your tax return. Why? Because there are two major penalties that come with not filing a tax return: failing to file and failing to pay. By filing your tax return, you at least get rid of the non-filing interest and penalties. Also, keep in mind, every month that you don't file or pay, you rack up additional penalties and interest on top of the original penalties. By the time you finally settle your tax bill, you're paying over 10 times the amount of your original tax!

If you truly can't pay, then apply for an installment payment plan with the IRS. Don't just take your chances by ignoring the problem. If you think it's an audit lottery—think again. The IRS will find you just when you least expect it. For more on paying your taxes and installment payment plans, see Chapter 9: IRS Audits.

### Pointer 32: Extensions

You can file for an automatic four-month extension to file your tax return. Use *Form 4868, Application for Automatic Extension of Time to File US Income Tax Return*. Remember this is just an extension to FILE the tax return, not to PAY your taxes. You will still owe the money. So to avoid the "non-payment" interest and penalties, you have to pay these taxes by April 15th. If you fail to file on April 15th and you don't ask for an extension you will also be hit with the "non-filing" interest and penalties.

## REMIX

Here's the remix of what we learned in this Chapter.

1. Know the basic parts of Form 1040: Filing Status, Exemptions, Income, Adjusted Gross Income, Taxes and Credits, Other Taxes, Payments, Refunds, Amount You Owe.

2. Know your filing status: single, head of household, married/filing separately, married/filing jointly, qualifying widow(er). Your filing status is important because many of your tax benefits are based on this. Also, your actual tax rate will depend on this.

3. Personal exemptions are deductions that you get for yourself, your spouse and your dependents; to the tune of $3,200 for each person. But similar to Below the Line Deductions, these can be completely phased-out for big ballers and shoot callers

4. Dependents include your children, but can also be a relative that you support. In addition to getting a personal exemption, you may also be able to take other tax deductions (i.e., medical expenses) and tax credits (i.e., child and dependent care tax credit) for these people.

5. Your income includes more than your wages and salary from your J-O-B. Don't forget to include items like: dividends and interest, state tax refunds, alimony, side business income, capital gains and losses, rental real estate income and losses, gambling income, and prizes. You don't have to include: employer-provided educational assistance or gifts and inheritances.

6. Above the Rim Deductions are those that are deducted before the line (your AGI) and include items like: IRA deduction, student loan interest deduction, tuition and fees deduction, educator expenses, health saving accounts, moving expenses, self employment tax and deductions, and alimony.

7. Your income, less your Above the Rim Deductions equals your Adjusted Gross Income (AGI). Your AGI is important because many of your tax benefits, credits, reductions and phase-outs are based on this number.

8. You can either take a standard deduction (the set amount determined by the IRS) or itemized deductions (i.e., a group of deductions blessed by the IRS, such as certain medical expenses, interest deductions, state tax deductions, charitable contributions, casualty thefts and losses and miscellaneous deductions). I call these Below the Rim Deductions (aka, below the line deductions) because you take the after computing your line (i.e., AGI).

9. Unlike Above the Rim Deductions, Below the Rim Deductions can only be taken if you beat the standard deduction. Also, they are subject to significant phase-outs (i.e., reductions up to 80%) for certain big ballers and shoot callers (i.e., high-income taxpayers).

10. Once you calculate your tax, you can further decrease it by taking tax credits like: the child and dependent care expenses credit, child tax credit, and education credits.

11. You're not finished yet. In addition to the income taxes you just calculated, you might also need to add in items, like self-employment taxes, additional tax on IRAs and nanny taxes.

12. Now that you know how much you owe in taxes, it's time to see if you're getting a refund or if you owe taxes. This will depend on how many taxes payments you've made during the year, such as the tax payments withheld from your paycheck and shown on your Form W-2, estimated tax payments you made for your side business, and FICA tax overpayments.

13. If you're getting a refund, make sure you consider e-filing to get your money even quicker and deposited directly into your bank account. This typically takes 7 to 10 days. Things like Rapid

Refunds™, refund loans or refund anticipation loan, may get your money to you quicker, but the fees and costs are very expensive; so be wary.

14. Always file your tax return; even if you owe money and can't pay it. You can try to get an installment payment plan to pay your taxes. Also, you can avoid the penalties for failing to file your tax return. Remember, like President Bush said, "You can run, but you can't hide." The IRS will eventually find you. Better to file and work out a plan than to beg for a tax settlement later.

# Chapter 2

# Side Business
*Choosing Your Side Business*

> *Bet you got a chick on the side*
> *Sure you got a chick*
> *I know you got a chick on the side*
> *(Love bandit, love bandit)*

**"Chick On The Side (Remix)," Salt 'N' Pepa (1987)**

---

You've "Heard It All Before," (Sunshine Anderson, 2001). Go into business for yourself; Be in control of your own destiny; Small businesses drive the American economy. Sound advice told by friends, family, colleagues, and anyone else who had a dream like Diana Ross, to be "The Boss" (1979). But, being in business for yourself is much like life and love—you'll certainly experience ups and downs, but there is nothing else like it.

According to the U.S. Small Business Administration, there are more than 22.9 million small businesses. Many of these small businesses are started by people who also have "day jobs"—from the at-home catering business to selling ethnic greeting cards on-line. Your side business becomes like a "Chick on the Side"—it may one day blossom and become a full-time business, or it may stay in the shadows forever.

Whatever the case may be, for most people one of the key ways to building your net worth will be to start and run a side business. This Chapter will give you the 411 on basic business types you will need to consider when opening your side business, or changing your business tyep for an existing business. Chapter 3 continues with side businesses, giving you the scoop on common tax issues in operating your side business, like determining your salary, expensing assets, common automobile expenses, and tax benefits with health insurance options.

Chapters 2 and 3 are called "side business" to address the overwhelming number of people who slowly begin businesses while they are still otherwise gainfully employed with a "day job." Of course, much of what is discussed in these Chapters applies to those who in fact have taken the plunge and are running their side business full-time.

## Choice of Business Entity

Many important decisions begin long before the first dollar is collected for your services or products, and months or years before you declare to the world that you're open for business. Perhaps no decision is as crucial in the initial planning stages than what type of business entity is appropriate and most beneficial for your side business.

Choosing the appropriate type of business entity for your business has legal, operational, accounting and tax implications. The decision should be made based on both legal and financial considerations viewed from a long-term perspective. I've gotten questions, like:

- Should I incorporate?
- What is an LLC?
- How do I become an S-Corporation?
- Do I have to become anything at all to be a business owner?
- Do I have to do anything formal to have a partnership?
- With so many choices, what should I do?

Although the choice will depend completely on your facts and circumstances, here are a few observations to consider: The basic "C" Corporation is the time-honored business entity. The LLC, or limited liability company, is the new kid on the block and is fast becoming the popular business type for many new businesses. The Sole Proprietorship is the easiest type for one person to start, while a regular partnership is the easiest type for two or more people to start.

Below, get the 411 on each of these business entities. Remember, as I talk about these choices, "simplicity" is the key word. You should keep your business entity as simple as possible, until and unless facts and circumstances indicate more complexity should be contemplated.

**Pointer 1: Annual Business Type Check-up**
The following discussions will go over the various pros and cons of each type of business entity. There are tax costs involved with switching entities, but there are also situations where it may make sound business sense to switch. Please check your business type with your tax advisor on a regular basis. See the Appendix, Check-Up List for Side Businesses, for other issues to review with your tax advisor.

### SOLE PROPRIETORSHIP

The Sole Proprietorship is the easiest, least complex and least costly of the business entities that you may choose.

### FORMATION

Many start-up businesses and folks who call themselves "consultants" really have sole proprietorships. Once you begin to provide services or products to the public, or securing clients or customers, you're in business as a sole proprietorship. That's all that is needed. There are no major forms or paperwork to file (aside from a business license and similar forms that are primarily required by state and local laws and regulations). Also, as a sole proprietor, you own the business by yourself. In fact, the sole proprietor and the sole proprietorship are the same and legally "Inseparable" (Natalie Cole, 1975).

**Pointer 2: Tax Identification Number, Form SS-8**
You can get a taxpayer identification number (TIN) for your business by filing *Form SS-8, Determination of Worker Status for Purposes of Federal Employment Taxes and Income Tax Withholding*. Unlike any of the other business types discussed in this Chapter, as a sole proprietorship, it is not necessary for you to get a separate TIN. However, you may consider doing so because your bank may require a TIN instead of your Social Security Number. Also, you may need a TIN if you will have employees, since you will then be required to make tax deposits and file employment tax returns and reports.

## LIABILITY

What are some of the potential downsides of a sole proprietorship? One answer is unlimited liability. It is important to remember that your entity choice can expose your personal assets to any business legal matter. As a sole proprietor, if you have liabilities from your business, these creditors may also come after your personal assets (i.e., your house, your car, etc.) to satisfy their claims.

## EXAMPLE 2.1

Makehla has been an aspiring singer for many years, but she works as a sales associate at a local department store to make ends meet. She never forgets her real dream—to be the next big gospel superstar. Although she often sings in the shower, she has never shared her voice with anyone; that was until her cousin Shirley's wedding. At the wedding, she sang a stirring rendition of "Move on Up a Little Higher," that tore the house down, and she was suddenly in hot demand. After much encouragement from her friends and family, she decided to follow her dream and start a wedding singing business—which she appropriately titled "Queen of Gospel." She started performing everywhere from weddings to graduations, baptisms, church events, parties and other social gatherings. She was booked almost every weekend.

Because Makehla didn't set up any formal entity and just began by performing her services, her business is a sole proprietorship. This means she is personally responsible for any business debts. One of her business creditors, Ma Rainey, owner of "Mother of Blues Rentals," is suing her over non-payment of sound equipment that Makehla rented. If guilty, and Makehla's business assets aren't enough to cover the claim, her personal assets may be at risk—including, her house, car, and anything else of value.

### TAX ISSUES

However, it's not all bad (or should I say it's all good). With a sole proprietorship, you still have total responsibility for all aspects of the business, from selling products to paying taxes. The sole proprietorship pays taxes on the sole proprietor's tax return—*Schedule C, Profit or Loss from Business (Form 1040)*. This means that the profits of the business only get taxed one time and not twice, as may be the case with a C Corporation. Also, sole proprietors may be able to take advantage of special tax incentives, like deducting health insurance premiums or retirement plan contributions. Finally, there are potential alternative minimum tax issues (or AMT) that sole proprietors must be concerned about. See Chapter 7: Alternative Minimum Tax for more on this.

**Pointer 3: Types of Businesses Using Sole Proprietorships**

Small businesses that provide services are great candidates for sole proprietorships; like plumbers, exterminators, consultants, home appraisers, computer consultants, real estate investors, construction contractors and other such businesses where it is relatively easy to begin offering your service, and the risk of being sued isn't a major concern. Also many professionals (like lawyers, accountants, architects, or doctors, or appraisers) may start out as sole proprietorships before becoming more formal entities.

### Pointer 4: State Tax

If you plan to operate your sole proprietorship in more than one state, you may have to pay income or business taxes in each of those states (often called franchise taxes). Each state has different criteria for whether you will be required to file and pay state taxes. Some states base this on the volume of revenue generated or the volume of work conducted in that state. Other states pro-rate income and expenses, and still others require full tax payments that may be offset by a tax credit in your home state. Check with your tax advisor to help determine if your activities require paying taxes in more than your home state.

### Pointer 5: Schedule C

If you have a sole proprietorship, report this income on *Schedule C, Profit or Loss from Business (Sole Proprietorship) (Form 1040)*; then include it on line 12 of Form 1040. For more on expenses and deductions you may take for your sole proprietorship, see Chapter 3: Side Business Part II.

## C CORPORATION

The plain vanilla C Corporation is perhaps the most well-known of all business entities. You see the terms used for this entity everywhere; such as 'corp.,' 'corporation," or 'Inc.' In fact, you almost can't listen to a song by Ja Rule without hearing a shout-out to "Murder Inc."

## ARTICLES OF INCORPORATION

A C Corporation is a formal business entity that is created under a specific state statute or law. To legally start your business, typically articles of incorporation must be filed with your appropriate state office (in many cases, it is the office of the Secretary of State or State Corporation Commissioner) along with a small filing fee. These articles of incorporation contain very basic information about your business, such as the name of the corporation, name of the incorporators (many states require at least three people), purposes of the corporation, addresses, and a person who can serve as a registered agent for the company and whom the state may contact in formal proceedings (many folks use a registered agent company to serve this role).

### Pointer 6: Check the State's Incorporation Website

In this age of technology, every state has step-by-step information and examples on how to incorporate within their borders. Moreover, there are companies that can incorporate you for the low price of something that ends with 99 cents. You should start with the Small Business Administration's website (http://www.sba.gov), then search for your specific state's Secretary of State or similar office for more information.

### Pointer 7: Incorporating in Multiple States

Remember that song, "Area Codes," by Ludacris, featuring Nate Dogg (2001), where he talks about having pros in different area codes (at least this is what the song should state if you prefer the Wal-mart version of songs, as I do)? I've always wondered, does he really do business in all those states, and if so, has he registered? That's right, if you plan to operate your side business in more than one state, you may need to register as a "foreign corporation" in the states beyond your home state. The same issue applies if you choose any of the pass-through business entities discussed in the next section. Check with your tax advisor to help determine if your activities in the other state(s) give rise to requiring you to formally register.

## BYLAWS

You must also develop bylaws, which serve as your company's governing document. The bylaws include basic information on how your business will be run and what decisions will be made, such as:

- ✓ Board of Directors—number, how chosen, duties, meetings and voting requirements.
- ✓ Officers—how appointed, duties.
- ✓ Committees of the Board of Directors—general or specific provisions for standing committees and *ad hoc* committees.
- ✓ Financial Management issues—such as fiscal year and accounting method.
- ✓ Indemnification of officers and directors.
- ✓ Miscellaneous other provisions, including amendment provisions.

**Pointer 8: Sample Bylaws**
In addition to starting with the Small Business Administration's website (http://www.sba.gov), there are many other resources and books with sample bylaws. Also, check with your Secretary of State or similar office for more information. Of course, as your governing documents are extremely important to your corporation, you should confer with your tax advisor on drafting your final bylaws.

## OTHER FILINGS

In addition to these initial documents, the corporation must hold formal meetings with the directors and shareholders and maintain corporate minutes from meetings. Also, each state will have its own filing requirements, business licenses, etc. Although the state-by-state requirements are beyond the scope of this book, you can obtain a wealth of information from the Small Business Administration, and your state's corporate websites and offices. The important point is that you know where to get the information and you are aptly educated on these matters before you talk to your tax advisor.

## KEY PLAYERS

A sole proprietorship may be considered your alter ego, but a corporation is treated as a legal entity; separate and distinct from its owner(s). A corporation is a much more formal type of business entity, with various forms that must be filed and many more people involved in the day-to-day operations and decisions of the business.

There are three primary players to consider if you want your side business to be a corporation: the corporation itself, the shareholders and the board of directors.

- Corporation—The corporation is required to comply with various state law provisions for annual meetings, state law filings, and other business licenses and fees.
- Stockholder—You, as the owner of the corporation, are known as the stockholder and you must decide if there will be other owners besides yourself. Your ownership in the corporation is evidenced by stock certificates that indicate the portion of the company actually owned by you and each of the other owners.
- Board of Directors—The Board of Directors is responsible for policy-making and governance over the business. The shareholders select and appoint the board of directors, who in turn select and hire the management and staff. In reality, especially in a small business, the owner will normally function to some degree as the shareholder, director, manager and staff.

## LIABILITY

With all of these formalities, why choose a corporation as your business entity? One of the major reasons for becoming a corporation is limiting your liability. As a corporation, the stockholder's liability for business debts is limited to the amount he or she has invested in the business. As a stockholder, your personal assets will not be at risk. It's your investment in the corporation that may be lost. Keep in mind, however, that if you also work for your business (as is the case with most side businesses), you will still be liable for your own acts of negligence or malpractice. This liability cannot be waived and that is why professional liability insurance exists. However, your personal assets may be protected from negligence and malpractice caused by other employees and owners of the business.

**EXAMPLE 2.2**

Robyn and Eddy opened a side business, "Stank Beautiful," (a C Corporation) selling a line of perfume (under the same name) made to rekindle the romance in any relationship. Initial sales were very promising, which the company attributed to their famous spokesperson, Kitty Kat, and her commercials showing men some twenty to thirty years her junior, fawning over her after a whiff of her Stank Beautiful. But then, the company began receiving complaints that Stank Beautiful really began to stink if worn for more than four hours without washing. Then, even more women began to complain about unsightly rashes that developed from Stank Beautiful. The final straw was when noted actress and singer, Grace Robinson, was shooting her Slave to the Sound of Music video, and her entire crew broke out into hives. Grace, apparently an ex-girlfriend of Eddy's, had given Stank Beautiful as gifts to her band.

The company pulled Stank Beautiful from the market due to numerous lawsuits. Eventually they settled all claims for $1 million. Since the company only had $100,000 left in assets and cash and with product liability insurance of $500,000, they still owed claimants $400,000. If it can be proven that Robyn and Eddy were personally negligent for the defective product, the claimants may sue them personally for the remaining $400,000. If only one of them was negligent, say Eddy, then he would be personally liable.

Robyn's personal assets would remain protected thanks to limited liability.

**Pointer 9: Personal Liability for Payroll Taxes**
Not even the corporate business entity can protect you from personal liability for payroll taxes. As far as the IRS is concerned, "Thou Shalt Pay Employment Taxes." The responsibility to withhold and pay payroll taxes to the IRS is absolute. The IRS will come after your personal assets if you don't make these payments. See the discussion regarding payroll taxes in Chapter 3: Side Business Part II.

## TAX ISSUES

The corporation is called a "C" corporation (or regular corporation), because the tax laws that cover this area can be found in Subchapter C of the Internal Revenue Code. Under these laws, C Corporations are subject to a concept known as double taxation. This means that the corporation itself pays income taxes on its tax return (known as "at the entity level") and the stockholders also pay taxes on their tax return when they receive a dividend (your return on your investment). But, the corporation does not get a deduction on its tax return when the dividend is paid out to you. This means the dividend is subject to "double taxation." The corporation paid a tax on this money with no deduction, and you pay a tax on your tax return when the money is received.

## EXAMPLE 2.3

Ray Ray Jones loves everything in doubles—from his name, to his twin sons' names Lil' Ray Ray, Jr. and Lil' Day day, down to his business passion, Ray Ray's Double Dutch Studio. He was so inspired by the 1981 hit single "Double Dutch Bus" (by Frankie Smith), that he took up the sport at the tender age of 12 and was the world's double dutch record holder for 15 years straight. But he lost his throne in 2003. So he decided to give back to the sport that brought him so much popularity and opened a studio to train the world's best double dutch teams. Given his love for doubles, he opened this business as a C Corporation. In addition to being a shareholder in the corporation, he also serves as the President, and he personally trains the children. He also employs a small staff of trainers. In his first year, the studio made $400,000 and had expenses of $300,000 (including Ray Ray's $50,000 salary), giving a net profit of $100,000. Here's how double taxation works:

The Corporation will pay a tax on the net profits of $100,000 equal to $22,250. Assume Ray Ray wants to take some money out of the business, and the corporation pays him a dividend of $20,000; leaving $80,000 in the corporation. This $20,000 will also be subjected to tax on Ray Ray's tax return. At the current maximum capital gains rate of 15%, his tax on the dividend would be $3,000. Keep in mind that the corporation has also already paid a tax of $22,250 on the entire $100,000, which included the $20,000 dividend. The corporation does not get a deduction for the dividend that it pays Ray Ray.

The double taxation only applies to the dividends that are actually paid out to a stockholder. Also, it does not apply to the salary or wages that a stockholder earns from the corporation. This means, Ray Ray's $50,000 salary is not subject to double taxation (e.g., the corporation took a deduction for his salary in arriving at the $100,000 net profit amount).

---

Another thing to keep in mind is that a C Corporation can make more money than a sole proprietor or pass-through entity before it is subject to a higher tax rate. Why? Because of the way the tax rates are applied to the income made by each entity. C corporations only pay 15% on the first $50,000 their income, 25% on the next $25,000 of income, and increasing up to 39% for income over $100,000, and the dropping to 34% for income exceeding $335,000. On the flip side, a single individual pays 10% on the first $7,150 of income, 15% on income up to $29,050, and the rate keeps increasing all the way to 35% for income over $319,100.

Moreover, you may pay fewer taxes on retained earning with a C Corporation—money that you keep in the business to be used for reasons like: expanding markets or a new product line. Why? Because as mentioned above, C Corporations often have lower tax rates. A sole proprietor or pass-through entity pay higher taxes on this same money, whether or not it's retained in the business. But remember, when the stockholder takes the money out for personal reasons, there could be double taxation. Note: Taking money out does not include the money you receive for your salary as an employee of the business. Instead, it means the money you take out in return for being a stockholder in the company (i.e., the return on your investment).

## EXAMPLE 2.4

Tyrone operates "Ty's Answering Service," which he aims at single professional women who want their calls screened. Believe it or not, his business has been booming ever since Erykha Badu's 1998 smash, "Tyrone." Ladies from all over the world have been calling him and signing up for his services. Tyrone opened his business as a C Corporation in 2004 and netted $75,000 after expenses (including the salary that he paid to himself). He decides to keep the entire $75,000 in the business as retained earnings and not to pay himself a dividend. The corporate tax on this $75,000 is $13,750. If Tyrone opened his business as a sole proprietorship, the tax on that same $75,000 (assume Ty is single) would have been $15,627.

Now assume that Ty decides to keep the first $50,000 in the corporation and takes out $25,000 as a dividend to pay for a Caribbean vacation. The corporation would be taxed on the entire $75,000, equaling a tax of $13,750. Ty will also have to pay a tax on the $25,000 dividend equal to $3,393. This makes his total taxes equal to $17,134 ($13,750 + $3,393). In this case, Ty would pay less taxes if his business is a sole proprietorship (i.e., $15,627), and he can still take out the money to use for an island vacation.

Practically speaking, many small corporations avoid double taxation altogether by paying out most of the corporation's profits for business expenses, including to stockholders for salaries. For more on corporations, see *IRS Publication 542, Corporations.*

**Pointer 10: Retained Earnings**
The amount that can be kept as retained earnings depends on your corporation's facts and circumstances. As a general rule of thumb, $250,000 or less is a reasonable amount for retained earnings. Keep in mind, you still need to be able to justify what the money will be used for (such as: working capital, marketing or product expansion, customer/supplier needs or concerns, or paying off debts). Saving taxes is certainly a reason, but it shouldn't be your motivation for accumulating earnings. This is an area where I strongly suggest that you work with your tax advisor.

**Pointer 11: IPOs**
If you are planning to have that side business lead to an Initial Public Offering (IPO) and trading on a stock exchange, you should probably start your business as a C Corporation. Why? Because it's easier to sell "interests," or stock, in a C Corporation to investors based on federal securities laws. Practically speaking, it is nearly impossible to sell your interests in pass-through entities like limited liability companies. These interests aren't freely transferable, meaning you have to get approval from the owners before you transfer them; which is not the case with stock in a C corporation.

**Pointer 12: Form 1120 and 1099-DIV**
Corporations report income and losses on *Form 1065, US Partnership Return of Income*, which is known as an information return because all it does is record information. Each stockholder is given a *Form 1099-DIV, Dividend Income* to report any dividends.

### PASS-THROUGH ENTITIES

Pass-through entities are formal businesses that do not pay income taxes at the business or entity level, but make payments or distributions to owners who pay the income tax on their individual tax returns. Put simply, a pass-through entity is a business that doesn't pay income taxes on its income; but the money is not tax-free. Instead it "passes" the income through to its owners, who each pay their share of the business' income on their personal tax returns. Perhaps a more unique way to think about this may be from The Pharcyde's 1993 Top 40 Single, "Passin Me By." Similar to the lyrics in the song that talks about a girl who keeps walking by and treating the singer like he doesn't exist, the IRS treats a pass-through entity like it doesn't exist, as the income and losses pass by and get reported directly on the owners' tax return.

### EXAMPLE 2.5

Kingdom Come is a pass-through entity that is owned equally by Kleeofus (pronounced "clee—o-fuss) and Kiara King (they are first cousins on their daddy's side). Kingdom Come had a net profit of $3,000 this year (after paying expenses), but the King's decided to keep the money in the business to use for next year. When Kingdom Come files its information tax return to show the $3,000 net profit, it doesn't have to pay any taxes. Instead, the taxes are paid on the King's individual tax returns. As equal owners, they

> will both include $1,500 from Kingdom Come's profits on their personal tax returns.

There are three common pass-through entities: partnerships, S Corporations and limited liability companies.

## PARTNERSHIPS

A partnership is a pass-through business entity in which there are a least two owners. Each owner is called a Partner. There are two types of partnerships that can be formed: a general partnership and a limited partnership, or a limited liability partnership.

### Formation

General partnerships are often formed without filing anything with the state. They exist when at least two people come together with a business purpose and began to actively pursue their business. So if you own a sole proprietorship and decide to bring in another owner, you become a partnership simply by adding the additional owner. In the music world, think of some of the greatest musical duets as partnerships, like Tammy Terrell and Marvin Gaye, Ashford and Simpson, Donnie Hathaway and Roberta Flack, and even Bobby and Whitney (Okay, maybe not this last one). You will recognize a general partnership because it's usually followed by the word "Partnership."

Limited partnerships, or limited liability partnerships, are more formal and require filing of articles of organization with your appropriate state agency. You will recognize this business type because it's usually followed by the letters "LP" or "LLP."

A partnership's governing and management document is called a partnership agreement. This agreement includes details on how profits and losses will be allocated and distributed among the members of the partnership. Unlike a corporation or a limited liability company, a general partnership is managed and governed by the partners themselves. This means that business decisions are usually voted on by all the partners. This vote may be based on one of numerous methods, such as partnership interest percentages, unanimous consent, or majority consent. Limited partnerships are managed by a general partner (see more on this below under the key players section).

In addition to these initial formal documents, partnerships must also hold formal meetings with the partners and maintain minutes from meetings. Also, each state will have various filing requirements, business licenses and other regulations to which your partnership may be subject. Although the state-by-state requirements are beyond the scope of this book, you can obtain a wealth of information from the Small Business Administration, and your state's business entities websites and offices. The important point is that you know where to get the information and you are educated on these matters before you talk to your tax advisor.

**Pointer 13: Draft a Formal Partnership Agreement**
Although no formal written agreement is needed, it's highly recommended that you write out your business arrangement, including things like how profits should be divided and how to terminate the partnership. Without this formal agreement, your partnership will be governed by state statutes, which often won't give you the result that you and your partners desire. In addition to starting with the Small Business Administration's website (http://www.sba.gov), there are many other resources and books with sample bylaws. Also, check with your Secretary of State or similar office for more information. Of course, as your partnership agreement is extremely important, I suggest that you confer with your tax and legal advisor for assistance with drafting this agreement.

## Key Players

In a general partnership, the key players are the partnership and the general partners themselves. The partnership may be required to comply with various state law provisions for annual meetings, state law filings and other business licenses and fees. The general partners are the owners of the partnership and they own partnership interests. The partners are also responsible for the management of the partnership.

In a limited partnership, there are three players: the general partners, the limited partners and the limited partnership.

- General Partners—Owners of the limited partnership. Responsible for the overall management of the limited partnership.
- Limited Partners—Owners of the limited partnership with limited liability for the partnership's debts.
- Limited Partnership—As a formal entity, the limited partnership will be required to comply with various state law provisions for annual meetings, state law filings and other business licenses and fees.

## Liability

A general partnership is very similar to a sole proprietorship when it comes to liability. In fact, you may think of it as two sole proprietorships who join together to form an alliance. As you may have guessed, all of the partners in the general partnership have unlimited liability.

With a limited partnership or a limited liability partnership, all of the limited partners have limited liability, much like the stockholders in a corporation. Remember the general partner still has unlimited liability. Many partnerships are formed as limited partnerships or limited liability partnerships, primarily because of liability issues.

**Pointer 14: Types of Businesses Using LPs**
Many professional service providers opt for partnerships, and in particular, limited partnerships, like lawyers, doctors, architects, accountants and other professions that require licensure. However, with the advent of limited liability companies, LLPs aren't as popular as the business entity of choice. See the discussion below on limited liability companies.

## Tax Issues

Each partner has an account called a "capital account," which reflects the partner's equity or ownership in the partnership. Your capital account includes things like your cash contributions to the partnership and distributions from the partnership, your share of the partnership's net profit or net loss, and your portion of partnership's debt. Calculating your contributions and your share of the partnership's debts is typically straightforward. The most difficult part is figuring out your share of the partnership's net profits or losses.

Remember, as pass-through entities, partnerships don't pay taxes themselves. The individual partner is responsible for his or her share of the partnership's net profits and losses, often based on some reasonable method; known as an allocation. Common allocation methods to divide partnership net profits and losses include those:

➢ based on the percentage of each partner's capital account
➢ based on the amount or value of the services provided by the partners
➢ based on the cash contributions made to the partnership by the partners
➢ based on any combination of the three above methods

### EXAMPLE 2.6

The Fu-Tang Clan, was best known for its rapping style, mixed with martial arts dance moves. They decided to open a martial arts studio, just in case the rap thing didn't work out. So, in late 2003, all nine members put in $10,000 each to open the Fu Tang Clan Martial Arts Work-It-Out Studio. Before they even opened the doors to teach the first lesson, seven of the members had started solo rap careers and were too busy to deal with the day-to-day classes at Work-It-Out. This left two members, Dirt McGirty and Methodology Man to deal with running the business full-time.

> In their original partnership agreement, they decided to base their partnership allocations of any net profit or net loss from Work-It-Out on each partner's capital account, which was equal to $10,000 for each partner (i.e., the equal amount that they all contributed). But in 2004, they decided to change their partnership allocations, since only Dirty McGirty and Methodology Man were actually working on the business full-time. Their new allocations were based on the services each partner provided. This means the two working partners will add the allocations for Work-It-Out's net profits to their capital accounts. The other seven partners will not receive any allocations since they did not provide any services.

How best to allocate net profits and losses can be quite simple, such as using capital accounts. It can also be quite complex, because the larger the partnership and the more partners or various types and involvements, the more consideration that has to be given to equitable treatment amongst the partners. As demonstrated in example 2.6 above, it may not be fair to have an allocation method based solely on capital accounts, when only some of the partners provide all of the services. Partnerships should have their tax advisor conduct an analysis of the partnership's overall capital account, and then an analysis of each of the partner's capital accounts to determine ownership percentages. The amount of salary, payments and distributions taken by each partner can then become factors in the considerations, influenced by the partner's involvement and whether that partner is a general or limited partner.

Keep in mind, net profits are taxable to the partner, regardless of whether the profits were actually distributed out to the partners or just credited to their capital account and retained for working business capital. Moreover, partners who also work for the partnership are often paid salaries. These salaries are called "guaranteed payments," in tax talk, and mean that the partner will get this money, regardless of that partnership's income. In fact, general partners are often required by state unemployment laws to be considered employees and paid a salary. These guaranteed payments are typically subject to self employment tax on the partner's individual tax return. For more on self-employment taxes and tips on determining your salary, see Chapter 3: Side Business Part II.

But, guaranteed payments are not the same as withdrawals made by partners. These withdrawals are similar to a dividend issued to a stockholder. They are in return for the partners being an owner in the partnership and not for compensation of services in the employment context (i.e., no self employment taxes). However, unlike with a dividend, the partner does not have to pay a tax on the cash withdrawal. Remember this partner already paid taxes on this money when she paid taxes on her share of the partnership income.

What does this all mean? Practically speaking, limited partners who aren't involved in the day-to-day activities of the partnership can take advantage of receiving withdrawals without having to pay self-employment taxes. Why? Because only those partners who are actively engaged in the partnership, such as the general partner or certain limited partners (i.e., those who spend over 500 hours a year working in the business), are required, under the tax rules, to treat any withdrawals or distributions from the partnership as income subject to self-employment tax. This means for general partners and active limited partners, most, if not all, of the payments they receive from the partnership are subject to self-employment taxes.

In addition to the very brief discussion above, you may also be able to deduct other expenses on your tax return that you may have in connection with the partnership but that are not, in fact, paid by the partnership (See *Schedule E, Supplemental Income and Loss (Form 1040)* to report these expenses). As you can see, the tax issues around partnerships are extremely complex and depend heavily on your facts and circumstances. I've only given you the basic 411 on partnership tax; certainly not enough to get your Ph.D. Please contact your tax advisor (who should have this Ph.D. knowledge) for more on partnership taxation. For more on partnerships, see *IRS Publication 541, Partnerships*

**Pointer 15: Determining a Reasonable Allocation Method**

The IRS allows the partners to determine the allocation, because the facts and circumstances vary so greatly in pass-through entities. Remember, you should strive for equitable treatment of partners, not equal treatment; as equal treatment may not accurately reflect each partner's relationship with the partnership (i.e., you have tow other partners so you each get one-third even though one partner does nothing with the business). Your tax advisor should advise the partnership and calculate each partner's capital account annually.

**Pointer 16: Form 1065**

Partnerships report their income and losses on *Form 1065, U.S. Partnership Return of Income*, which is known as an information return because all it does is record information. Each partner is given a *Schedule K-1, US Return of Partnership Income (Form 1065)* which reports the partner's share of the partnership's profits and losses. Take the amount listed as income or losses from this form and include it on line 21 of *Form 1040*. Note: You do not need to attach *Schedule K-1* to your tax return, but you should generally keep it in your tax records for at least 3 years.

## S CORPORATION

Another type of pass-through entity is the S Corporation. As you've probably guessed by now, the "S" Corporation also got its name because the tax law provisions that apply to it can be found under Subchapter S of the Internal Revenue Code.

### Formation

An S Corporation is also a formal business entity that begins its legal existence by filing articles of incorporation with an appropriate state agency. But it's initially formed with the state as a C corporation. Once it's formed, the stockholders must then "elect" to be treated as an S Corporation. You must file *Form 2553, Election by a Small Business Corporation* requesting S Corporation treatment with the IRS. S Corporations use the same designations as C Corporations behind their names such as "Inc., Corp. or Company."

**Pointer 17: File by March 15<sup>th</sup> or within 75 Days**
For an existing C Corporation looking to change to an S Corporation, you must file Form 2553 by March 15<sup>th</sup> in order to be treated as an S corporation for the entire year. Newly formed corporations (including those that are successors of a sole proprietorship) must file Form 2553 within 75 days from when the business is started (by looking at when it acquired assets, issued stock to shareholders or otherwise began business).

An S Corporation also has Bylaws that govern its management and operations. In addition to these initial formal documents, the corporation must hold formal meetings with the directors and shareholders and maintain corporate minutes from meetings. Also, each state will have various filing requirements, business licenses and other regulations to which your corporation may be subject. Although the state-by-state requirements are beyond the scope of this book, you can obtain a wealth of information from the Small Business Administration and your state's business entities website. The important point is that you know where to get the information and you are aptly educated on these matters before you talk to your tax and legal advisor.

**Pointer 18: Sample Bylaws**
In addition to starting with the Small Business Administration's website (http://www.sba.gov), there are many other resources and books with sample bylaws. Also, check with your Secretary of State or similar office for more information and your tax/legal advisor for drafting your bylaws.

### Key Players

The key players for the S Corporation are the corporation itself, the stockholders and the board of directors.

- S Corporation—The S Corporation is required to comply with various state law provisions for annual meetings, state law filings and other business licenses and fees.
- Stockholder—The number of stockholders or owners of an S corporation are limited to 75 (100 for 2005). Note: A husband and wife count as one stockholder, and this amount is increased to 100 for tax years after 2004. Moreover, the stockholders must be U.S. citizens or permanent resident aliens.
- Board of Directors—. S Corporations also have board of directors who are responsible for policy making and governance over the business.

There are several other restrictions that apply to S corporations, such as one class of stock and how much income the corporation can earn from investment type activities (i.e., rental real estate). Although there are more restrictions on S Corporations, many small businesses can still utilize this business entity. The point is to recognize that for many small businesses, S Corporations can offer the best of both worlds—a corporate form with pass-through tax treatment.

**Pointer 19: Types of Businesses Using S Corporations**

Many folks use S Corporations where they plan on having losses early on or want to take low salaries, but also want to take some money out of the business in the form of dividends. Almost any type of business can be an S Corporation. Examples include: computer equipment and hardware firms, accountants, real estate developers, doctors, management consulting firms, and financial advisors. However, with the advent of limited liability companies, S Corporations aren't as popular as the business entity of choice. See the discussion below on limited liability companies.

## Liability

Like the stockholders of a C Corporation, the shareholders of the S Corporations have limited liability for the S Corporation's debts and claims.

## Tax Issues

An S Corporation is treated like a partnership for tax purposes rather than as a separate entity like a C Corporation. So the income is "passed-through" to the shareholders for purposes of computing tax liability. This means a stockholder's individual tax returns will report the income or loss generated by the S Corporation.

Allocations made by S Corporations are generally based on the ownership of the stock in the company. Also, withdrawals from the company typically aren't subject to self-employment tax. Translation: The stockholders can avoid or reduce FICA/Medicare tax obligations (to the tune of 15.3%). This is a huge advantage for stockholders of S Corporations who also actively work in the business. There is no presumption in the tax laws that taints this income and makes it subject to self-employment taxes; unlike as the case described above with general partners in partnerships (or described below with Members in an LLC). Of course, the salary that the stockholder earns will still be subject to employment taxes; and practically speaking, many folks who own S Corporations try to pay themselves little to no salary to avoid employment taxes.

But beware—the IRS is hip to folks claiming that they have no salary, such that any money they take out of the S Corporation will be treated as withdrawals or dividends. Also, some states require owners who also work for their S Corporation to be considered as employees for any money that they take out of their S Corporation. This is why it is very important to come up with a reasonable amount for your salary with the help of your tax advisor. See Chapter 3: Side Business Part II for more on determining your salary.

## EXAMPLE 2.7

BBD is an S Corporation that provides environmental clean-up services, with a specialty of cleaning up "Poison" (Bell Biv DeVoe, 1990). There are 2 equal stockholders, who both work in the company; one as the Service Manager, the other as Marketing Manager. The Marketing Manager does not take a salary in the first year because cash flow is devoted to expanding operations. The Service Manager takes a salary of $10,000.

BBD has a net profit of $50,000 (which is computed after paying the Service Manager's $10,000 salary). Also, BBD withheld federal employment taxes for the Service Manager's salary—about $765 for FICA and Medicare ($10,000 x 7.65%) and paid the employer's matching amount, again about $765. Note: BBD also had to do similar payments and withholdings for state taxes.

BBD must allocate this net profit to the stockholders based on the amount of stock owned, or in this case 50/50. When the stockholder's receive their K-1's, each will have $25,000 of BBD income to report on their personal tax returns. None of this will be subject to self-employment taxes.

If the Marketing Manager then decides to pay himself $10,000 because there was sufficient cash in BBD, he would avoid having to pay any employment taxes, or the $765 that the Service Manager had to pay. Also, BBD would save, too, because it would not have to pay the employer's matching amount; again $765. Keep in mind, both stockholders got $10,000. But the Service Manager had to pay employment taxes on his $10,000.

### Pointer 20: S Corporation Losses

Many new businesses experience losses in the early years of operations, for this reason, new businesses should consider becoming an S Corporation. Why? Because net losses from the S Corporation can be used on the stockholder's personal tax return to reduce your overall income (i.e., wages from your 9 to 5 job). But in order to take the S Corporation losses your tax return, you must have enough invested (i.e., money and property) in the S Corporation to cover the loss. If you take a loss for more than your interest in the S Corporation, you could have taxable income. Note: Any unused losses can be taken as deductions on subsequent tax returns.

### Pointer 21: Form 1120S

S Corporations report their income and losses on *Form 1120S, US Income Tax Return for an S Corporation*. Each stockholder is given a *Schedule K-1, US Income Tax Return for an S Corporation (Form 1120S)*, which reports each stockholder's share of the corporation's profits and losses. Take the amount listed as income or losses from this form and include it on line 21 of Form 1040. Note: You do not need to attach *Schedule K-1* to your tax return, but you should generally keep it in your tax records for at least 3 years.

## LIMITED LIABILITY COMPANY

The Limited Liability Company (referred to as LLC) is a relatively new type of business entity. However, what it lacks in terms of time, it makes up for in terms of popularity. Why? Because even more than an S Corporation, an LLC can come closer to the best of both worlds. It has many of the corporate attributes of a C Corporation and the pass-through tax treatment. But it offers all of this without the restrictions on ownership and income placed on S Corporations (i.e., number of stockholders, limits on passive investment income, etc.).

## Formation

An LLC is also a formal entity that is formed by filing documents, called articles of organization with the appropriate state agency. You will recognize this business type because it is usually followed by the letters "LLC."

The LLC's governing and management document is called an operating agreement. This agreement is rooted in both the corporate world (i.e., Bylaws) and the pass-through world (i.e., partnership agreement). Similar to what you might find in a corporation's Bylaws, the Operating Agreement provides details on the LLC's managing group called the Management Committee or Managers, such as: number of managers, how they are chosen, their duties, types of meetings and voting requirements. The Operating Agreement also includes details on how profits and losses will be allocated and distributed among the members of the LLC; much like a partnership agreement.

In addition to these initial documents, the LLC must hold formal meetings with the members and management committee, and maintain minutes from the meetings. Also, each state will have filing requirements, business licenses and other regulations that your LLC may be subject to. Although the state-by-state requirements are beyond the scope of this book, you can obtain a wealth of information from the Small Business Administration, and your state's business entities website. The important point is that you know where to get the information and you are educated on these matters before you talk to your tax advisor.

**Pointer 22: Draft a Formal Operating Agreement**
Although no formal written agreement is needed, it is highly recommended that you write out your business arrangement including things like: how profits should be divided, how to terminate the LLC, etc. Without this formal agreement, your partnership will be governed by state statutes, which almost never give you the result that you and your partners desired.

In addition to starting with the Small Business Administration website (http://www.sba.gov) there are many other resources and books with sample bylaws. Also, check with your Secretary of State or similar office for more information. Of course, as your Operating Agreement is extremely important, I suggest that you confer with your tax and legal advisor for assistance with drafting this agreement.

## Key Players

The key players for an LLC are: the limited liability company, the Members and the Managers.

- LLC—As stated above in the previous section, the LLC may be required to comply with various state law provisions for annual meetings, state law filings and other business licenses and fees.
- Managers—An LLC is governed by its Managers or a Management Committee (like the Board of Directors or a General Partner).
- Members—The Members are the owners of the LLC (like shareholders or partners), and they own "Units" (like stock or partnership interest) in the LLC. However, unlike with a partnership where you need at least two partners, in most states an LLC may be formed by a single member. While a single member LLC is a legal entity recognized by the state, it is not recognized by the IRS for tax purposes. Unless the single member LLC elects to be treated as a corporation, for tax purposes, it will be treated as a sole proprietorship, and is required to report its operations as part of the owner's personal tax return (e.g., using *Schedule C, Profit or Loss From Business (Form 1040)*.

### Pointer 23: Types of Business Using LLCs
All types of professionals, service providers, and everything else have been formed as LLCs. In particular, many folks are using LLCs for their rental real estate investments.

## Liability

As with the stockholders of a C Corporation and an S Corporation, members of an LLC also have limited liability for the LLC's debts and claims.

## Tax Issues

An LLC is a pass-through entity for tax purposes. Similar to a partnership, the LLC doesn't pay income taxes directly. Instead its members pay income taxes on their share of the LLC's income. Allocations from an LLC to its members can be based on any reasonable basis on which the members agree. This means allocations, like partnership allocations, don't have to be based on ownership of units. (See Example 2.6 above describing partnership allocations).

In addition to income taxes, members must also be concerned about employment taxes. Much like with a partnership, many members of the LLC must pay self-employment taxes on their share of the LLC's income (i.e., to the tune of 15.3%). This includes any withdrawals where the member is actively engaged in the business of the LLC. Actively engaged typically means where the member spends significant time on the business (i.e., over 500 hours per year), the LLC offers professional services (i.e.., law, health, consulting, accounting, architecture, engineering, or actuarial service), or the Member is a manager of the LLC (i.e., a Managing Member). Members who aren't actively engaged in the business of the LLC may be able to avoid employment taxes on their withdrawals. But remember all members are subject to employment taxes when it comes to their salary.

**Pointer 24: Form 1065**

Limited Liability Company's, like partnerships, report their income and losses on *Form 1065, US Partnership Return of Income.* Each member is given a *Schedule K-1, US Return of Partnership Income (Form 1065)* which reports the member's share of the company's profits and losses. Take the amount listed as income or losses from this form and include it on line 21 of Form 1040. Note: You do not need to attach *Schedule K-1* to your tax return, but you should generally keep it in your tax records for at least 3 years.

**Pointer 25: Single Member**
If you set up a single member LLC, you must report the LLC's income on *Schedule C, Profit or Loss from Business (Form 1040)* and not on *Form 1065, US Partnership Return of Income.* But beware. Businesses that report income on *Schedule C* may have a higher chance of being audited by the IRS than those that report on Form 1065. Why? There is no definite answer, but one theory is that it is easier for one person to commit abuse (i.e., under-reporting income) than it is for a business run by two or more persons. Many folks solve this by forming their LLC with a friend or their spouse.

## REMIX

Here's the remix on what we learned in this Chapter:

1. Choose the side business entity that will be best for your operation, keeping in mind that simplicity is best.

    ### Sole Proprietorship

    | *Pros* | *Cons* |
    |---|---|
    | Easy start-up | Unlimited liability |
    | Single level of tax | |

    ### C Corporation

    | *Pros* | *Cons* |
    |---|---|
    | Graduated Tax rates | Double Taxation |
    | Limited Liability | More complex administration |

### S Corporation

*Pros*  
Single level of tax  
Limited Liability  
Earnings not subject to  
self-employment tax  

*Cons*  
Formal limits number of owners  
More complex administration  

### LLC

*Pros*  
Single level of tax  
Limited Liability  

*Cons*  
Earnings subject to self-employment tax  
More Complex administration  

### Partnership

*Pros*  
Some limited liability  
Single level of tax  
Easy start-up  

*Cons*  
Unlimited liability for general p-ships  
Earnings subject to self-employment tax

# Chapter 3

# Side Business Part II
*Operating Your Business*

> *I'm taking square biz to you baby*
> *Square, square biz*
> *I'm talkin' love that is*
> *That is, that is, that is, square biz*
>
> "Square Biz," Tenna Marie (1981)

---

You've also probably heard that if you run your own business, you can deduct anything and everything. While this is a gross exaggeration, as you can never deduct expenses which are truly personal, there are many expenses that you can take with proper tax planning. Now that's square biz! I'm about to "Get Low" on some of the hottest tax issues for the small business owner (aka, Lil' Jon & The East Side Boyz, 2004—the clean lyrics version, of course).

## Operating Your Side Business

Before I get into the specifics of the many tax issues you will encounter with your side business, I must make sure what you're doing will count as true business. If it's not (i.e., it's a hobby), you won't be able to take advantage of many of the tax benefits available to business owners.

Merriam-Webster's dictionary defines a hobby as the "pursuit outside one's regular occupation engaged in, especially for relaxation." I compare it to the feeling you get when you are relaxing, like: "Just Kickin' It," (Xscape, 1993), "Just Coolin," (LeVert, 1989) or (just) "Funkin' for Jamaica," (Tom Browne, 1980). There's nothing wrong with absolutely loving what you do and getting a truly ecstatic, glorious and yet relaxing feeling from running your side business. But, your work must be devoted to more than that; I'm talking about a side business that is trying to make cold hard cash, the greenback, the "dollar, dollar bill y'all" ("C.R.E.A.M.," by Wu-Tan Clan, 1994).

Having your business treated like a hobby is like the one-two punch. First, any income from your hobby is taxable—it's reportable on line 20 of Form 1040 as other income. Second, the expenses related to the hobby are difficult, if not impossible, to deduct. If you use a standard deduction, you can forget taking these expenses. Even if you itemize, you can only take these as miscellaneous itemized deductions which are deductible once they reach more than 2% of your adjusted gross income. In essence, you report all the revenue like a true business but you get none, or very few, of the expenses. The point is simple—your side business must avoid hobby characterization at all costs. See Chapter 6: Itemized Deductions Part II for more on miscellaneous itemized deductions.

Confused? You are not alone. Many people mistake what is truly a hobby for a side business.

### EXAMPLE 3.1

Aunt Sarah is always starting a new business. Three years ago, she approached you with her wonderful idea of selling hot combs that get hot by putting them in a boiling hot cup of water; no more stove or electric comb oven. This magic hot cup just needs hot water, and you can travel anywhere in the world with it; after all, you never know when you might need your hot comb. You knew

Aunt Sarah would never make any money doing this. Five years later, you're wondering why she still continues to try and sell her hot comb with hot water cup combo when it's a clear money loser. You are not alone in your bewilderment. The IRS happens to agree and probably won't recognize this as a true business enterprise. What Aunt Sarah runs is called a hobby, and at this rate, she will never give Dudley's™ a run for their money.

Keep in mind, although hobbies make us feel good, and indeed many folks hope they will someday turn into a booming enterprise, a hobby won't pay the rent. The tax law states that to be considered as a business venture your business has to be operated to make a profit. This does not mean that if your side business never becomes profitable, it is a hobby. The IRS uses the three-out-of-five-year rule. If your business can not show a profit in three-out-of-five years, IRS will typically presume that you are not operating a business, but you are running a hobby. The key word here is "presume." If, through records and activities, you can show that your intention was to operate a profitable business, that IRS presumption can be overcome. You should keep good records, because as with everything in tax law, the facts and circumstances will be extremely important in making this determination.

Now that you know your labor of love is truly a business, let's get down to business on the following:

- Start-up expenses
- Determining your salary
- Employee vs. Independent Contractor
- Payroll Taxes
- Self Employment Taxes
- Estimated Quarterly Taxes
- Expensing & Depreciating Assets
- Leased Assets
- Home Office Expense
- Meals and Entertainment
- Employee Fringe Benefits
- Health Insurance
- Key Person Policy

### START-UP EXPENSES

Beginning a new business is an exciting and wonderful time for the business owner. It's sort of like the feeling that you get when the dance floor is empty and the DJ starts playing a song to get the crowd on their feet, like the 1984 jam "Set it Off," by Strafe (originally mixed by Walter Gibbons).

Of course, you can't set anything off without paying money. As a new business, you will inevitably have numerous beginning costs. Expenses such as advertising, office supplies, equipment, travel, and utilities are all examples of expenses that you will have, and can be deducted against your business income. But, the tax laws treat all pre-operating costs, known as start-up expenses, and organizational expenses, a bit differently than other business expenses that you may have once your business is up and running.

Generally, start-up expenses and organizational expenses cannot be deducted in full in the first year of your business. You may elect to spread them out, or "amortize" them, and take them as deductions over a 5-year period (but, see the tax law change below for expenses after October 22, 2004).

The IRS specifically states that start-up expenses include: advertising costs, inspection fees, supply expenses, pre-opening payroll expenses, professional fees, and other miscellaneous expenses paid or incurred prior to opening day. Also, organizational costs include things like legal fees and accounting fees to set up your business, filing fees with the state, and any other expenses to set up your business.

### EXAMPLE 3.2

Pamela decided to open a new club in her hometown, "Boogie Wonderland," appropriately named after her favorite 70s jam by Earth Wind and Fire. She decides to hire a lawyer to incorporate her business and paid him $1,000.

Pamela also paid $1,000 to advertise and market the grand opening in local newspapers and radio stations. Finally, she spent another $500 on flyers and advertisements. In all, she spent a total of $2,500 in start-up and organizational expenses. Unfortunately, since she incurred these expenses before the business was open and operating, she can not deduct the $2,500 as a current expense for tax purposes. She must spread the deduction over 5 years, taking $500 each year until the full $2,500 is deducted.

However, these same expenses are fully deductible once your business is officially open. How do you determine when your business officially begins? As a general rule of thumb, when your business is ready to receive customers, provide services, or sell products, it is officially operating. These are very subjective measurements, which you should document; especially when you have significant expenses in connection with the opening of your business.

## EXAMPLE 3.3

Pamela, from example 3.2 above, being a cautious person, decided to open her club three weeks before her planned "Grand Opening" as a way to test the water before her big day. Much to her surprise, her pre-grand opening event had over 500 customers, and her guest list for the Grand Opening rose to over 2,000 people. So, when did Pamela's business start—on the first night it was open or not until the grand opening?

The first night Pamela opened Boogie Wonderland to the public, (i.e., the pre-grand opening event) is when she officially began business. She can deduct all of the expenses she spent on her pre-grand opening event, such as food, drinks, security, bartenders, etc. Also, if she had spent some of the costs from Example 3.2 above after the grand-opening event, they, too, could be fully deductible on her first tax return. For example, she could have probably waited to spend most of the $1,500 on radio advertising and flyers after the pre-grand opening event. If so, she would be able to deduct the entire $1,500 now and not have to wait to spread it out over 5 years. Note: She will still have to spread out the legal and incorporation fees over 5 years, as they are organizational costs.

### Pointer 1: Form 4652
Make the election to spread out (called amortize, in tax talk) your start-up and organizational expenses on *Form 4562, Depreciation and Amortization*. You must also attach a statement to Form 4562 on your business' first tax return that includes a description of your business, a description of you start-up costs, and organizational costs (including, the amount and the date), the amount of money you started your business with, and how long you have to amortize the expenses. Keep in mind, once you make this election you cannot change it.

### ALERT: TAX LAW CHANGE—START-UP & ORGANIZATIONAL EXPENSES
Under a new change to the tax laws, you can elect to deduct up to $5,000 of any start-up and organizational expenses you have after October 22, 2004. You make the election by simply taking the deductions on your first business tax return. Anything over $5,000 can be spread out and deducted over 15 years. Thus, for 2004 tax returns, any start up expenses before October 22, 2004 can be spread out over 5 years. Any expenses after that date are subject to the new rules (i.e.., $5,000 up front and the rest over 15 years).

### Pointer 2: Minimize Start-Up Expenses
Since start-up expenses may be deducted over a 5-year period (or after October 22, 2004, 15-years for amounts over $5,000) try to minimize these costs and accelerate the opening of your business. For example, instead of

initially ordering 1,000 business cards you may consider a smaller order (maybe 100 cards) to get you started, and then order 900 cards once your business is open.

## DETERMINING YOUR SALARY

Pay yourself first! This and other similar concepts have been championed by several popular finance self-help books, most notably *"The Rich Dad Poor Dad"* series of books by Robert T. Kiyosaki, and Sharon L. Lechter, *"The Millionaire Next Door,"* by Thomas J. Stanley and *"Sister CEO,"* by Cheryl D. Broussard. But, how do you know how much to pay yourself? This is the hard part, and being savvy about tax laws can go a long way.

The IRS looks for you to come up with, what's called, "reasonable" compensation. In fact, this is an area that receives a significant amount of attention from the IRS because of the potential for abuse; which will often depend on what type of business form you choose as your side business.

With C Corporations the game is to go "so high" (aka, "How High" style by Method Man and Redman, 1995 and the remix featuring Toni Braxton, 2001). The IRS is looking for folks who will try to have higher salaries so they can avoid dividend treatment (i.e., double taxation) when they take money out of the company. The issue is a bit different with an S Corporation where folks are trying to "Get Low" (Lil' John and the East Side Boyz, featuring the Ying Yang Twins, 2003). The concern is that owners of S Corporations will come up with low salaries to avoid, or significantly minimize, employment taxes.

There will always be discussions about what is considered a reasonable salary for tax purposes, and a reasonable salary for state unemployment purposes. The rule of thumb should be what other similarly situated companies are paying their officers and employees for similar duties. Can you pay yourself more or less? Certainly, but document the industry and regional norms, and then your criteria for making your salary higher or lower.

**Pointer 3: Salary Surveys**
There are several salary surveys you can use to help in determining your salary. Documentation is important in justifying your compensation and can help in proving that it is reasonable. As always, document your compensation decision with your tax advisor. You may try starting with these:

- Robert Half—http://www.roberthalffinance.com/FreeResources
- Manpower—http://www.manpower.ie/employers/main_salary.asp
- Salaryexpert.com—http://www.salaryexpert.com

## EMPLOYEE VS. INDEPENDENT CONTRACTOR

Now that you have determined how much to pay yourself, it's time to decide what to pay those who work for you or those who help your side business. It's one of those quintessential decisions that every successful side business must make time and time again. It's sort of like asking; "Do you like east coast or west coast rap better?" Deciding whether to hire employees, independent contractors, or both, is a question that has no clear answer.

Knowing the differences can be significant in whether or not your side business will have to pay employment taxes. In a nutshell, if you hire employees, you will be liable for withholding employment taxes and paying them over to the IRS. You must also pay a similar amount from your own pocket to the IRS. If, instead, you hire independent contractors, those individuals remain responsible for their own employment taxes. All you have to do is give them a summary tax form detailing their earnings (i.e., *Form 1099-MISC, Miscellaneous Income*). See the next section for more employment taxes.

At this point, you might be thinking that every side business should hire independent contractors to avoid employment taxes. Not so fast. No matter how hard you try, the facts may support that your staff should be treated as employees, and nothing you call them or try to put in a written contract or consulting agreement will change that conclusion.

There is no black and white test for employee or independent contractor status. It's truly a facts and circumstances test. In general, someone will probably be an employee when you control or have the right to control how the job is done, where the job is done, when the job is done or provide the means for doing the job.

The following factors may tend to indicate that someone is an independent contractor:

- Working for more than one company or person
- Having her own place of work and tools of the trade
- Advertising her skills and availability to the public
- Having business cards, letterhead, brochures or other signs of being in business
- Providing proposals for services and contracts for engagements
- Paying her own business costs; including commuting, expenses, insurance, benefits and taxes

## EXAMPLE 3.4

Maria was an artist at heart. You could find her every weeknight salsa dancing at her favorite club, "The West Side Story." She wants to become a performer, and sing and dance with musicians like Wyclef Jean and Carlos Santana. Alas, it was all a dream; just like reading Word-up Magazine ("Juicy," Notorious BIG, 1994). In order to pay her "Bills, Bills, Bills" (Destiny's Child, 1999), she works three days a week as a contractor doing drawings for Refugee Inc, an architectural firm. These drawings are done in her home-office, using her supplies and materials, and are delivered when completed, but in a pre-agreed time-frame. She sends Refugee a bill for her time and they pay her as an independent contractor.

Maria also works 2 days a week doing mark-ups on other folks' drawings for Solo Inc. She goes to Solo, where they provide her with an office, a computer and software to do the mark-ups. Although she fills out a time sheet, Solo also pays Maria as a contractor.

Is Maria an independent contractor for both jobs? Probably not. The facts tend to support that she is a contractor in the drawing job with Refugee because she is fully in control of her work and work method. She is probably not a contractor in the mark-up job with Solo because Solo seems to be in control of her work and work method. So, the same person can be classified two different ways, even when providing similar types of services.

For more on determining employee and independent contractor status, see *Form SS-8, Determination of Employee Work Status for Purposes of Federal Employment Taxes and Income Tax Withholding.*

**Pointer 4: Hiring an Employee or Independent Contractor**

You must verify that each new employee is legally eligible to work in the United States. Have the employees you hire fill out *Form I-9, Employment Eligibility Verification* and *Form W-4, Employee's Withholding Allowance Certificate.* If your employees qualify for and want to receive advanced earned income credit payments, they must give you a completed *Form W-5, Earned Income Credit Advanced Payment Certificate.* You are also required to get each employee's name and Social Security Number (SSN), and enter them in the personnel record you maintain for them. These same procedures should be followed for hiring an independent contractor, even if that person is using a DBA (doing business as or a fictitious business name). You should collect both the SSN and Taxpayer Identification Number (TIN), and maintain a contractor's file with a copy of the independent contractor agreement.

Please talk to your tax advisor for more information on hiring employees and independent contractors.

## PAYROLL TAXES

If you've ever had a "J-O-B," you've certainly felt the impact of payroll taxes (also called employment taxes). When most people talk about payroll taxes, they are referring to Medicare taxes and social security (or FICA). These are taxes that all employers are required to withhold from the employee paychecks. The employer also has to match this payment out of her own business revenues.

Medicare taxes are calculated at 1.45% of wages and the money collected is used to provide medical benefits for certain individuals when they reach age 65. Social Security taxes are calculated at 6.2% of wages, and covers benefits for retired workers, the disabled, and their dependents. Together, these taxes equal 7.65%; which is the figure you see most people use when referring to payroll taxes.

Employers are required to withhold this 7.65% from an employee's pay checks and also make a matching 7.65% payment to the IRS. Note: You only have to withhold FICA taxes on the first $87,900 of wages ($90,000 for 2005) that an employee makes. After that, there is no more FICA withholding. Thus, the maximum amount that you have to withhold in one year for a single employee is $5,450 ($5,580 for 2005); and the maximum amount that you as the employer would have to pay out of your profits is also $5,450 ($5,580 for 2005). However, you must still withhold Medicare taxes, regardless of your employee's wages.

If you are the only person working on your side business, it's pretty straightforward. You pay the entire amount of the payroll taxes; both the employee and the employer's portion (i.e.., 15.3%). These are actually called self-employment taxes and will be discussed in more detail in the next section of this Chapter.

When there are other people you pay to help with this side business, you must decide if they are employees (and hence, you have payroll tax withholding obligation) or independent contractors (you have no payroll tax withholding obligation). See the discussion in the previous section of this Chapter for more on employees and independent contractors.

As a small business owner with employees, you are required by law to withhold the employee's share of FICA/Medicare and pay an equal amount as the employer's share of these employment taxes. The IRS requires that you deposit these taxes at least monthly, using *Form 8109, Federal Tax Deposit Coupon* and file a report to reconcile your payments on a quarterly basis, using *Form 941, Employer's Quarterly Federal Tax Return*. Note: The IRS now requires tax deposits to be filed electronically with an authorized financial institution. Please see *IRS Publication 966, Electronic Choices for Paying All Your Federal Business Taxes* for more on this or your tax advisor.

Too many well-meaning businesses simply neglect paying these taxes, particularly when cash flow is weak (it's the "Rob from Peter to pay Paul" syndrome). The result can be catastrophic for a small business. The IRS has all but declared war on small business owners who don't pay employment taxes for their employees. It's almost tantamount to stealing. Why? The withholdings don't belong to the small business owner. You are simply holding the government's money and it's your duty (and also the law) to timely and fully make these deposits.

In addition to FICA and Medicare, there are also unemployment taxes that employers must pay on behalf of their employees; federal unemployment taxes (or FUTA) and state unemployment taxes (or SUTA). These taxes are raised to help with the administration of federal and state unemployment insurance programs. However, FUTA and SUTA are both paid from the employer's own funds and are not withheld from employee's paychecks. They are calculated as a percentage of a base salary, generally on the first $7,000 of an employee's wages, with SUTA at 5.4% and FUTA at .8%. The employee wage base and percentage of tax vary widely between states, and the federal government provides a range of tax credits for timely payments made to your state.

Please check with your tax advisor for your specific payroll obligations. Also, see IRS *Publication 15, Circular E, Employer's Tax Guide*

**Pointer 5: Calculating and Paying Payroll Taxes**

You will need to use your employee's Form W-4 to help calculate how much to withhold from their paychecks for payroll taxes. Also, the deposits are reported and paid with *Form 8109, Federal Tax Deposit Coupon and Form 941, Employer's Quarterly Federal Tax Return*. These deposits must be made electronically (i.e., not with a check in the mail to the IRS). Use *Form 940, Employer's Annual Federal Unemployment Tax Return* to report your FUTA payments. Also you should consider hiring a payroll processing company to calculate payroll withholdings and to make the required tax deposits. These companies will handle the entire process for you. Your tax advisor should be able to recommend an established credible local or national company.

### SELF-EMPLOYMENT TAXES

Self-employment taxes are the same as the FICA and Medicare taxes paid by employees; they are just doubled. For the self-employed, which can include sole proprietors, partners, LLC members, this tax ensures that you pay into the Social Security system. The tax is 15.3% (i.e., 12.4% for FICA and 2.9% for Medicare) of your net profit from your side business that exceed $400. Only the first $90,000 of wages is subject to FICA taxes. After that, there is no more FICA payment to be made. Thus, the maximum amount that you have to pay in FICA taxes is $5,580 for 2005.

There is some good news. You can take a deduction equal to half of your self employment taxes. The net effect of all of this is that you only pay that portion that would've been withheld from your wages had you been treated as an employee of your business. See Chapter 1: Tax Basics for more on the self employment tax deduction. Also, these self-employment taxes often have to be paid to the IRS on a quarterly basis. See the next section in this Chapter for more on estimated quarterly tax payments.

Note: Self-employment taxes apply to income you earn from running an active trade or business. If you have a passive activity, like for many folks who serve as landlords with rental real estate, you don't have to pay self-employment taxes on your income. See the discussion at the end of this Chapter for more on rental real estate activities. Also, stockholders in C corporations and S Corporations typically aren't subject to self-employment taxes, but they do pay regular payroll taxes (i.e., 7.65%) like any other employees.

**Pointer 6: Calculating & Paying Self Employment Taxes**
Use form *Schedule SE, Self Employment Tax (Form 1040)*, to calculate self-employment taxes. You must file this form if your self-employment income is $400 or more. Remember, you may have to pay your self-employment taxes on a quarterly basis.

### ESTIMATED QUARTERLY TAXES

Even though you file your tax return once a year, if you own a side business the IRS wants its money during the year; once every "winter, spring, summer, fall," (aka, LeVert's 1990s song, "All Seasons").

Most businesses will have to make estimated quarterly tax payments on their net profit—in April, June, September and January. These quarterly estimated tax payments are required by any entity; whether a corporation, partnership, LLC or sole proprietorship. Also, the businesses are required to make regular payroll tax payments (i.e., FICA and Medicare).

Why does the IRS require business owners to make estimated quarterly tax payments? Because without this rule, self-employed folks wouldn't have to make these payments until they filed their tax returns. Keep in mind, most people who are employees are making tax payments every two weeks through their paycheck withholdings.

The key to whether quarterly estimated taxes are required is knowing at each quarterly period (i.e., April 15th, June 15th, September 15th and January 15th) whether or not your net profit from operations will result in an income tax liability. If the answer is yes, then the IRS wants its money in four installments; no waiting until you file a tax return. If the answer is no, you don't have to make an estimated tax payment for that quarter. Note: You may have to file *Form 2210, Underpayment of Estimated Tax by Individuals, Estates and Trusts,* with your tax return if you don't make equal estimated installment payments.

In general you must make these estimated tax payments if you will owe $1,000 or more in taxes beyond your payroll tax withholdings. The amount of your estimated tax payments must be at least 90% of the taxes you will owe this year, 100% of your taxes from the previous year, or if your adjusted gross income is over $150,000, 110% of the previous year's taxes. Luckily, there are software programs that will calculate your estimated taxes for you; for example:

- Intuit (Quarterly Estimated Taxes Calculator)— http://www.quicken.com/taxes/taxslashing/estimatedtaxes
- Commerce Clearing House (Self-Employment Tax Estimator)— http://www.finance.cch.com/tools/calcs.asp

Your tax advisor should be able to calculate this for you as well. Keep in mind, quarterly estimated income taxes paid on operating net profits are not the same as monthly payroll tax deposits payments on wages and salaries for employees discussed above under payroll taxes. For salaries, Uncle Sam wants those deposits monthly.

### Pointer 7: Form 1040-ES

Pay your estimated tax payments using *Form 1040-ES, Estimated Tax for Individuals*, to pay their estimated tax payments. The IRS highly recommends that you make these payments electronically. See *IRS Publication 966, Electronic Choices for Paying All Your Federal Business Taxes* for more on this. Also, as mentioned in Pointer 5, there are many payroll processing companies that can help with this. But always, deal with an established company and check with your tax advisor.

### Pointer 8: Set Aside Taxes From Your Revenues

Too many people forget, or simply don't make estimated payments. Perhaps they assume that they can make them up on April 15th. Even if you are getting a tax refund, you could still owe interest and tax penalties from failing to make estimated tax payments throughout the year. Keep in mind that estimated payments gives the IRS a steady stream of money throughout the year, so you may incur a penalty by paying them late (i.e., April 15th). Of course this is the IRS, so if they owe you money, as is the case with a tax refund, they won't pay you any interest for having your money all year. It's the "do as I say and not as I do" principle. To avoid this, you should set aside money throughout the year to make estimated tax payments. Treat these expenses just like some of your other fixed expenses (i.e., car notes, supplies, utilities, etc.).

## EXPENSING & DEPRECIATING ASSETS

The majority of your business expenses will come from your business assets. You can also deduct other business expenses, such as supplies, professional dues and costs for business-related services. In this next section, get the 411 on:

➢ Expensing
➢ Depreciation
➢ Mileage

### Pointer 9: Car Deductions

If you use your automobile in your business, you may be able to take an expense deduction, a bonus depreciation deduction, and a regular depreciation deduction; or you may decide to take the IRS standard mileage rate. For many, the car related deductions can be large and can have you singing, "Take That To The Bank" (Shalamar, 1979). Intrigued? Please, read on.

#### EXPENSING

You will buy many capital assets to start your side business. Things like computers, office furniture, fax machines, and fancy mobile phone/personal organizer combos are just a few essentials that every small business owner might have.

Did you know that you may not be able to take a tax deduction for the entire amount you spend on these assets; at least not all at once? Your business assets are thought to benefit your business for longer than just the first year in which you purchase them. In tax talk, this is called the useful life. The thinking is, these assets will have a useful life for many future years (i.e., five for many business assets). Any tax deduction for this asset should match the years in which it was useful. So, you can only deduct a portion of the asset's cost in the year in which you purchased it. The rest is spread out (i.e., depreciated) over the remaining useful life.

Thanks to a special tax exception for small businesses (i.e., those businesses making less than around $410,000), you may be able to take a current tax deduction (called expensing, 179 expensing, or first-year expensing exception, in tax talk) in the year that you actually purchase the assets.

You can generally expense up to $105,000 of your business assets in the year in which you purchase them. So thanks to this first-year expensing exception, your new $1,500 lap-top computer can be fully deducted in the year that it was purchased. Why is the tax law so generous? This exception is trying to provide an incentive to help businesses prosper. Expensing can provide both the cash flow and the tax break to make asset purchases possible and feasible for many small businesses. Here are the particulars:

The asset must be used by you in your business for more than 50% of the time. This means the personal use of the asset cannot be greater than 50%. But this is only part of the test. You must then back out your personal usage from the cost of the asset to come up with your actual deduction. So, you must multiply the cost of the asset times your business usage percentage to come up with the amount of your deduction. Finally, any amount over the $105,000 limit must be depreciated. Please see the next section in this Chapter for more on depreciation.

## EXAMPLE 3.5

Kristina was a very successful businesswoman. At the tender age of seven she got her big break in the TV show "Moon Search." This landed her a recurring role on a kid's TV show, "Donald Ducketeer." She had made millions by the time she became 18, but she always wanted to run her own business. So she decided to start a business teaching other young girls how to be "Ghetto Superstars," (Pras, featuring Ol' Dirty Bastard and Mya, 1998). She had always been fascinated by the TV show "Bewitched," and thus decided to name her new venture "Genie in a Bottle," (Christina Aguilera, 1999).

In 2004, Kristina bought an expensive $2,000 lap top computer to use for her new business. She also bought a new Sidekick (a cell phone/personal desk assistant) for $400 that was "Hot," (aka, Paris Hilton style). Kristina estimates that she uses her computer 100% of the time for business purposes, but she does take personal calls on her Sidekick. Assume that out of 20,000 minutes for the year on her cell phone, she spent 16,000 minutes on business calls and 4,000 minutes on personal calls.

> Kristina should be able to deduct the entire $2,000 she spent on her laptop on her under the first-year expensing exception. But she must back out her personal usage from the cost of her Sidekick. She should be able to deduct $320 (400 x 16,000/20,000 or 80%) for her Sidekick. The $80 for the personal use of the Sidekick cannot be deducted. Note: Kristina should also be able to deduct her cell phone costs and her internet service costs. Again, she can only take 80% of the cell phone costs since this is her business usage. See the discussion at the end of this section for more on deducting costs related to utilities.

No area has seen as much press, fanfare and criticism than expensing your car. Almost all small business owners use their automobile in some form or fashion to carry out their business. You can never deduct the personal use of a car as a business expense. This means that you must come up with a business use percentage or some other way to figure out how much of your deduction is related to the business use of the asset. Once you pass this hurdle, thanks to the first-year expensing exception, you may be able to deduct the entire cost of your car right? "No Can Do" ("I Can't Go For That," Hall & Oates, 1982).

Prior to 2005, there was a law (known by many as the SUV or Hummer tax deduction) that allowed you to expense the cost of certain cars that you used in your business. The special law applied to cars, particularly SUVs that weighed 6,000 pounds or more. Practically speaking, this only applied to big baller cars like the "summertime hangout-out" that looks like a "car-show," ("Summertime," Will Smith, 1991). Cars like the Porsche Cayenne, Cadillac Escalade, Hummer, Range Rover and Lincoln Navigator all qualified for this exception.

This all changed at the end of 2004. Any SUV or other large car purchased after December 31, 2004, can no longer be completely expensed. Now, you can only expense the first $25,000 for the costs of such cars, the rest must be depreciated. For cars that weigh less than 6,000 pounds (i.e. luxury sedan or sports cars), you can't expense any of it. Instead you must depreciate the cost under several IRS depreciation calculations.

Keep in mind that the above discussion focuses on expensing business assets (i.e., your fax machine, computer, etc.). You can expense the entire cost of your business supplies (i.e.., paper, pen, tape, etc.) in the year that you purchase them. The same holds true for other things, like: utilities, professional dues, magazines and subscriptions. Finally, when it comes to your car, you can also take current deductions for mileage, or the actual costs to operate your car (i.e., gas, repairs, etc.)

Note: These expensing rules do not apply to the real estate that you purchased for your side business. You must look to the depreciation rules, discussed below in this Chapter for help on how much you can deduct for your real estate.

### Pointer 10: Form 4562
You must make an election to use the first-year expensing exception on *Form 4562, Depreciation and Amortization*. This form should be attached to your tax return. This deduction only applies to the year in which you purchase the asset. If you miss making the election in first year, you will probably have to depreciate it (i.e., spread out the deduction) over the useful life of the asset.

### Pointer 11: Car Weight
There are several websites that will help you figure out the actual weight of your car. Here's a few websites:
- Car Max—http://www.carmax.com
- Edmunds—http://www.edmunds.com
- Kelley Blue book—http://www.kbb.com

Pointer 12: New to You

Any business asset, whether new or used, is eligible for the first-year expensing deduction. The asset does not have to be new (i.e., a 2005 model car). It just must be new to you (i.e., even a hooptie will count).

Pointer 13: Finance Charges on Auto Loans

Many folks will take out auto loans to purchase their business car. Whether you take out a loan or it's Paid in Full" (Erik B. and Rakim1987) is irrelevant to the amount of the deduction you may be able to take for the car. It will generally be a depreciation deduction based on the value of the car (with some expensing for those autos over 6,000 pounds. But, the interest amount on your auto loan is deductible as a current business expense and can be taken in the year in which you pay it. So, in addition to the car's costs, consider the impact of finance charges when deciding how to purchase your business auto.

## DEPRECIATION

When you purchase an asset to use in your business, you sometimes can realize the amount you paid for it as a current tax deduction; as explained above in the section on expensing. But, normally, most of your tax deduction has to be spread over several years under a process called depreciation. This depreciation allows a business to recover the cost of assets purchased over a period that the assets will be useful to the business.

Knowing how many years to use when calculating your depreciation will depend on the type of asset. Most small businesses will have assets with useful lives of either 5 to 7 yeas. Below is the IRS general guide for most business asset.

- 3 years for manufacturing equipment (i.e., for plastics, metal fabrication, glass)
- 5 years for business assets (i.e., cars, trucks, computers, copiers, typewriters, etc.)
- 7 years for assets, like: office furniture, other types of manufacturing equipment
- 20 years for some types of land improvement costs (i.e., sidewalks, roads, drainage facilities, fences and landscaping)
- 27.5 years for residential real estate
- 39 years for commercial real estate (buildings only)

There are two general depreciation methods that you can use: straight line depreciation and accelerated depreciation. Under the accelerated depreciation method (called **MACRS** or modified accelerated cost recovery system), you can take a higher depreciation deduction in the earlier years, when the asset is more useful to you and then it declines significantly towards the end of the assets life.

Under the straight line depreciation, you might think that it means you take the depreciation deductions in an equal straight line; but this is tax law and nothing is that simple. Straight line means you spread out the deduction equally over a period of time, such as 5 years. But, there are special depreciation rules that govern how much you can take the first year and the last year of the asset's useful life. This often means that in the first and last year, you only get half of the deduction (called the half-year convention). Confused? See the next example for more clarification.

### EXAMPLE 3.6

Using Kristina from example 3.5, let's now assume that she purchased a lot of business assets in the first year (i.e., more than $105,000) such that she now is over the first-year expensing exception. Also, assume these remaining assets total $10,000 and have a useful life of 5 years. Under the straight line depreciation method, she can deduct $1,000 in the first year, $2,000 each in years 2-5 and the final $1,000 in year 6.

Keep in mind, whichever depreciation method will end up getting to the same total depreciation amount over time. Some methods allow you to take more depreciation deductions in earlier years, while others provide more steady deductions. Note: Depreciation differs from intangible assets that are amortized (i.e., like the start-up costs mentioned earlier in this Chapter, or franchise costs discussed later in the Chapter). Under amortization, you spread out the costs equally over the time period.

If that's not enough to make you start pop-locking and dancing like "Planet Rock," (Afrika Bambaataa and the Soul Sonic Force, 1982), or the new version "One Two Step" (Ciara, featuring Missy Elliot, 2004), you may also get an additional depreciation deduction known as bonus depreciation. You can take a depreciation deduction up to 50% of the cost of the car in the year that you purchased it. This is different than the first-year expensing deduction described in the previous example. Why is one called expensing and the other called bonus depreciation? Who cares? Just keep in mind that you may be able to take all of these extra deductions the first year in which you purchase an asset. But this was a "Goodie" (Ciara, 2004), because there is no more bonus depreciation for tax returns after 2004.

Luckily, the IRS provides depreciation tables in the instructions to Form 1040 where you can look up various depreciation amounts on a chart, and there are many computer programs that will calculate depreciation for you (i.e., Turbotax™). Also, check with your tax advisor. See *IRS Publication 946, How to Depreciate Property* for more information.

### Pointer 14: Form 4562

Report your depreciation deductions on *Form 4562, Depreciation and Amortization*. This form should be attached to your tax return.

### Pointer 15: Depreciation Recapture

There may come a time when you sell your business assets after several years of depreciation, or after it has been fully depreciated or expensed. If you have a gain on the sale of that asset, you may have to pay ordinary income taxes. Why? The tax laws treat you as having recaptured or reclaimed the previous tax deductions that you took (i.e., depreciation) in the form of this new gain.

## MILEAGE

You've seen the cars on the highway with business logos painted on the side and catchy phrases like, "Paul's Detailing, The Best in Town," with phone numbers and e-mail addresses. Even more common are the signs and logos you see on cars used by popular businesses like Domino's™, Molly Maid™ and Kinko's™, to name a few. Some of the cars are actually owned by the company or business. While others, as with many pizza-delivery services, are owned by the employee.

When starting your side business, you will undoubtedly use your automobile in conducting your business affairs. But there are many questions around how to best use a car for business purposes. Will you purchase the car outright or lease it? Will you also use it for personal use? Will you just use a car you already own? Will you ask employees to use their personal car? The answer will depend on many non-tax things, like whether or not you can afford a new car or just use an existing car. But knowing the tax impact can also be helpful in deciding the best course of action.

When it comes to your automobile, you have two choices for tax deductions: You can use your actual expenses; which can include first year expensing (i.e., for SUVs weighing over 6,000 pounds), double depreciation and regular depreciation (i.e., either straight line or MACRS). It can also include gas, repairs, lease payments, maintenance, licenses, registration fees, and insurance. Or on the flip side, you can choose to take a standard mileage rate of 40.5 cents per business mile driven. The 40.5 cent mileage rate is the amount that the IRS estimates will cover your actual expenses, such as expenses and depreciation. You can also deduct costs for parking and tolls under either method.

Choosing a method is important, because it may impact your depreciation method. For example, if you start with the standard mileage rate in year 1 and then switch to the actual expense method in a later year, you can't use the accelerated depreciation method for your car. You must instead use the straight line method.

Which method is better? This is a case where you will need to run the calculations. In many cases, if you can expense your car, and take bonus and accelerated depreciation, the actual expense method will be higher than the standard mileage rate. The result may be the same with leased vehicles. For more on leasing business assets, see the discussion in the next section. As each situation is different, please contact your tax advisor for your specific fact pattern. For more on actual expenses and the standard mileage deduction, please see *Publication 463, Travel, Entertainment, Gift and Car Expense.*

**Pointer 16: Tracking Your Auto**

Business auto expenses must be well documented. You should keep timely and accurate auto records. This sounds easier than it actually may be. When you get into your car and go to an appointment, remembering to jot down the mileage may not be top on your list of things to do. Here are a few suggestions: Retain two auto repair receipts that show the automobile's mileage, one dated very close to the beginning of the year and the other dated very close to the end of the year. Identify the clients you visit often and make sure you know the mileage to their offices, in case you have to reconstruct your business mileage. Try to use one credit card for all business auto expenses; preferably the credit card will provide expense summaries of all your costs. To minimize the commuting miles to and from work arrange for your first or last business stop to be closer to your home. Generally, self-employed business owners who have a home office do not incur commuting mileage, but certainly have personal mileage just like everyone else. Read more on the home office expense later in this Chapter.

## LEASED ASSETS

Many side business owners also lease their business assets, such as computers, fax machines, photocopiers, etc. Typically, lease payments are treated like any other regular business expenses; you can deduct them in full when you pay them. Thus, the rules that I discussed earlier in this section regarding expensing and depreciating assets do not come into play when you're talking about your lease payments.

As long as you're paying a true bona fide lease, you take the deduction in that year that you pay them. Again, keep in mind you can only deduct that portion that represents your business usage. If you lease a vehicle, but only use it for 80% for business and 20% of the time to run personal errands, you can only deduct 80% of the lease payments.

In the case of a business automobile, the decision to lease or buy will depend on a lot of other factors beyond tax issues, such as financial concerns like your business cash flows. Keep in mind that if you buy a car, you are looking at primarily taking depreciation deductions and maybe some expensing (i.e., up to $25,000 for certain SUVs). You also may get some interest deductions if you take out a loan to purchase the car. Finally, in some cases, it may be better to take the standard mileage rate (i.e., 40.5 cents per mile) instead of actual expenses.

On the other hand, if you lease, you are looking at deducting lease payments each year (subject to an IRS calculation that reduces it slightly from the amount of your actual lease payments, which is known as the "inclusion amount"). You have to choose between taking the actual lease payments or taking the standard mileage rate. Typically, the lease payments, along with other deductions (such as gas, oil, repairs, etc.) will be higher than the standard mileage rate.

Whichever method will give you the greatest tax deduction (purchasing vs. leasing) will depend on your specific facts. Just make sure to run the comparison or have your tax advisor help you on this.

This brings up another important point with leasing. The lease must be a true business debt. When you lease property that was previously owned by you, hence personal property, the IRS will scrutinize this. For example, if you are leasing a car and then you start a side business and decided that the car is now business property, you need to make sure that you have some document to reflect this transfer. At a minimum, you will probably need a lease agreement between you and your company that is a true contract, with fair and reasonable lease terms. This is an area where I highly recommend that you talk to your tax advisor.

## HOME OFFICE EXPENSES

A very popular deduction for many side businesses, is the home office deduction; the cost of having an office in your home. However, thanks to a lot of abuse with this deduction, the IRS will also scrutinize this deduction, so you better make sure you've done your "homework."

> **Requirements to deduct home office expenses:**
>
> ➤ Exclusive use—the office area must be identifiable and separate. The area must not also be used for personal and/or entertainment.
> ➤ Regular use—must be consistently used, not just occasional or incidental.

> ➤ For a trade or business—business is conducted and managed at the home
> ➤ Either your principal place of business, place to meet and deal with clients, vendor, or a separate structure to the home.
> ➤ If you are an employee, for the convenience of your employer

Most people who run their side business full time and have no other office should be able to meet these rules. To strengthen your case, you should also document the business meetings that you have in your home office and make sure they occur on a regular basis. Also, make sure that you don't use the room for personal purposes (i.e., hanging out on the weekend to watch videos).

If you run your business full-time but still have an office somewhere else outside of your home, you will need to prove that your home office is your principal place of business. You should be able to show things like:

✓ Conducting most of your client meetings at your home office
✓ Keeping your business files at your home office
✓ Conducting most of your administrative business activities at your home office (e.g., bookkeeping, faxes, computer work, and other secretarial duties).

The home office expense includes deducting the business portion of your home expenses for things, like: rent, leases, mortgage payments, insurance, utilities, general repairs, home owner association fees, trash removal, cleaning services, snow removal, grass and lawn maintenance. Also, your business usage is often determined by looking at the square footage of your home office and comparing that to the total square footage of your house. So if you live in a 3,000 square foot house and your home office is 300 square feet, you should be able to take 10% of many of your home related costs listed above and list use them in calculating your home office expense. But, you can use a reasonable method to come up with your business percentage: For example, when the rooms in your house are all about the same, size you can base it on the number of rooms. If you have four rooms and use one of them for your home office, your business percentage is 25% (i.e., 1/4).

Because you can also deduct your mortgage interest and real estate taxes as itemized deductions, you must make sure to back out the amount that is attributable to your home office expense. Remember to claim these itemized expenses on *Schedule A, Itemized Deductions (Form 1040)*. However, the amount for your home office expenses is added on *Form 8829—Expense for Business Use of Your Home*, and then transferred to Schedule C along with your other business expenses.

Finally, the home office expense also includes the full value of many costs that are only for your home office, such as painting or repair work to your office only. Your tax advisor should be able to help you calculate this deduction. Also, there are several websites that can help you calculate your home office expenses including, Commerce Clearing House, http://www.toolkit.cch.com/text/p07_2740.asp.

For more on the home office deduction when you are an employee and taking the expense under the convenience of your employer rule, please see Chapter 10, FAQ # 8. Also, see *IRS Publication 587, Business Use of Your Home*.

### Pointer 17: Form 8829

Use *Form 8829—Expense for Business Use of Your Home* to calculate the home office deduction. The home office expense calculated on this form is then transferred to *Schedule C, Profit or Loss from Business (Sole Proprietorship) (Form 1040)*.

### Pointer 18: Storing Inventory or Samples

If you use a part of your home to store inventory or samples, you may be able to take the home office deduction; even if you use that room for other things. For example, if you sell hair products and you store them in your garage, you may be able to write off the home office expenses associated with your garage even those you also park your car in there. Note: To use this rule, you cannot have another office located outside of your home.

### Pointer 19: Proof for the Tax File

Home office deductions are still an area that could trigger an IRS audit. If you plan on taking a home office deduction, I suggest that you take pictures of your home office along with clients and vendors visiting your office. Also, make sure that all of your business cards, flyers and other information describing your business include your home address for the contact information. Finally, keep a notebook, calendar or use a computer spread sheet to track visits to your house and the amount of time you spend in your office. Remember to keep these files for your tax files; you don't need to attach them to your tax return. Also, be sure get in the habit of doing them throughout the year, and by all means before you file your tax return. This will give more credibility to the fact that they are real documents and not done to fight an IRS audit.

## MEALS AND ENTERTAINMENT

Entertainment and business meals are often required to help you run your side business, but the tax laws don't necessarily agree. You can typically only deduct 50% of your meal and entertainment expenses. Entertainment includes things like: nightclubs, athletic events, theatres, and any other venue where you entertain your clients. Meals include the costs of the food, beverages, tips and sales taxes. Note: When you are attending a conference or convention, the registration fees, lodging and transportation remain fully deductible. Make sure to get a breakdown of how much of your fees went to entertainment and meals so that you only deduct 50% for these expenses.

If you get audited, the IRS may ask you to prove the amount of your meals and entertainment; particularly where these expenses are large. Thus, you should have receipts, a log book, a computer spreadsheet, or something in your tax files that backs up your numbers. Also, remember that many business credit cards will give you a year-end list that summarizes details of the meals. This is another good way to help you gather your business expenses. Make sure your documents include things, like the following, to help prove your expense was business related:

- Date of the expense
- Place of the meal or entertainment
- Amount for the meal or entertainment
- Names of everyone present
- Description of the business discussed

### EMPLOYEE FRINGE BENEFITS

An employee fringe benefit is an incentive provided to any employee in connection with job performance or as an incentive. As business owners, you should look for fringe benefits that complement your compensation, ownership or succession. These can be as simple as use of the company car or as complex as key-person insurance policy.

The value of these fringe benefits may be included in the employee's wages. But there are many fringe benefits that are specifically excluded from tax and do not have to be included in the employee's wages. A full listing of these excluded fringe benefits can be found in *IRS Publication 15-B, Employer's Tax Guide*, but the include things like: Group life and disability insurance policies, Commuting and parking benefits to certain levels, Staff lunches, Educational assistance, and Employee stock options.

## HEALTH INSURANCE

This section reminds me of the words to a Whitney Houston classic (featuring Jermaine Jackson), "Take Good Care Of My Heart," (1985). Side business owners must make sure that they have appropriate health and medical insurance for themselves and their employees. But too many Americans don't have health insurance. A major portion of this number is self-employed business owners and the employees of these small businesses. With the high cost of traditional health insurance policies, which are increasing significantly annually, small business owners are finding it difficult to pay for health insurance plans for themselves and for their employees. Small business owners should consider:

➢ Traditional Health Insurance Plans
➢ Health Savings Accounts
➢ Health Care Flexible Spending Accounts.

Traditional health insurance plans cover hospitalization and physician visits in some form and varying cost levels. Most have a deductible amount for which the employee is responsible and is normally required to be paid before the insurance coverage becomes effective.

Balancing the costs of the health insurance can be a tricky thing, because they are shared between the employer and the employee. As the cost for insurance premiums goes up for the employee, the cost of the policy goes down for the small business owner. If the costs are too high, it may be hard to keep employees. On the other hand, if the small business owner pays higher costs for the policy (meaning lower premiums for the employee) this could severely impact the business' cash flows.

One solution for the small business is to obtain traditional health insurance coverage through a "Group Insurance Plan." An example of a group insurance is that offered by the National Association of Self-Employed (NASE) (http://www.nase.org), whose health and disability policies are offered to members at significantly reduced prices. Any self-employed person can become a member of NASE; membership fees are low, with numerous health insurance options.

As the backbone of the Nation's economy, small business owners must explore novel ways to acquire and provide health insurance; especially to "Baby-boomers" and young families. In addition to traditional health insurance, you should consider, Health Savings Accounts (HSA).

In many ways, HSAs are like 401(k)s. Employees can make tax-free contributions to an account (up to $2,650 for individuals and $5,250 for families). They can choose how this money is invested (stocks, bonds, mutual funds), and as the money grows, they aren't taxed on any gains. When employees have a medical expense, they pay for it first, submit a receipt and get reimbursed from the HSA. If they don't spend the money, it rolls over and can be used in future years (making it a much better alternative then the money put away by an employee in a flexible spending account discussed below). Also the premiums are often cheaper than other traditional health insurance plans. The HSA moves with the employee as she changes jobs. In fact, all of the contributions, investments earnings, and withdrawals from the HSA are tax free; "Hip Hop Hooray," (Naughty By Nature, 1993). For more on the tax deduction for HSA contributions, see Chapter 1: Tax Basics.

So what's the downside? Your deductible with an HSA is often very high. Some plans require you to pay from $3,000 to over $5,000 before your traditional health insurance kicks in. On the flip side, traditional health insurance plans have deductibles in the $500 to $1,000 range.

Finally, small business owners should consider Health Care Flexible Spending Accounts. Again, as with a 401(k), plan, employees can make tax free contributions to an account up to $1,000. The money is used to reimburse the employee's medical expenses. Unlike an HSA, the money in the flexible spending account is not invested. Also, any amount not used by the end of the year is forfeited. For more on health savings accounts, see *IRS Publication 969, Health Savings Accounts and Other Tax-Favored Health Plans.*

**Pointer 20: Employee Deduction for Health Insurance**

Employees can take a tax deduction for their contributions to HSAs on *Form 8889, Health Savings Accounts*. For more on this deduction, see Chapter 1: Tax Basics.

## KEY PERSON POLICY

Remember the chorus from the 70s disco hit by Yvonne Elliman, "If I can't have you, I don't want nobody baby?" For many side businesses, this song echoes on and on as the business itself would have trouble surviving if something happened to the business owner. Succession planning is vital to the business continuing. This planning often focuses on identifying the right person(s) to continue the legacy of the business. It also includes important financial planning for the future. A key person policy is just as the name implies; a life insurance policy for your key man or woman. For a sole proprietorship, this is easy because there is only one owner. For other business entities (corporations, partnerships and limited liability companies), the key man policies may be for the owners and/or key employees.

Typically, the life insurance policy is purchased by the business. The business pays the premiums and is the beneficiary of the policy. If the key employee dies, the proceeds from the policy can be used to help the business stay afloat while the business searches for a successor, or can be used to wind up the business, and pay creditors and investors.

From a tax standpoint, the key person has no tax liability because of the key man policy. This is because the key person does not directly benefit from the proceeds of the policy and neither does his or her family members. The business gets all of the proceeds from the policy. Moreover, the premiums paid by the business have no tax impact on the key person's personal tax return. In many cases, the premium payments should be treated as a deductible expense by the business on its tax return.

# Popular Side Businesses

There are many types of side businesses in which you may engage. Here is the All-Star List of some of the more popular types of side businesses.

- Arts and crafts
- Franchises
- Home Based Businesses
- Rental Real Estate
- Service Consultant
- Sales Consultant
- Investment Club

### ARTS AND CRAFTS

Folks who sell arts and crafts products (i.e., paintings, gift baskets, kente clothes, dolls, stationary products, etc.). often operate this side business as a sole proprietorship. Since this is typically a cash business, your risk of an audit may be greater. You also run the risk of being accused of operating a hobby. To help against this you should consider the following:

- ✓ Have a separate business bank account.
- ✓ Keep a log, note book, or computer spread sheet detailing your business activities (especially for your cash receipts).
- ✓ Show a profit in at least three out of five years.
- ✓ Consider making a room in your house your home office, but make sure you can meet all of the tax law restrictions (i.e., use it regularly, meet potential clients there, have a dedicated space, etc.). Note: If your arts or crafts can qualify as inventory, you may be able to use this deduction; even if the room in your home 'dubs' for something else (i.e., your garage).
- ✓ Don't forget to deduct all of your business expenses such as: flyers advertising your arts and crafts, printing costs, booth set-up, internet, cell phone, and car and other transportation costs).
- ✓ Also, you will be subject to paying self-employment taxes and making estimated tax payments to the IRS throughout the year.

## FRANCHISES

Franchises are fast becoming one of the most common types of side businesses that people decide to open. The advantages of buying a franchise are numerous. They allow you to purchase a business that has been proven, and thus lowers your risk of failure. They also provide you with an instant network of other franchisees that are available to help mentor you in your business. As with most things, there are disadvantages, such as: the franchise business structure and rules may be too rigid or there are significant yearly franchise fees that you have to pay.

If you decide to purchase a franchise, be sure that you have an understanding of some of the possible tax issues. Many of the business set-up issues (discussed in Chapter 2: Side Business Part I and this Chapter) also apply in the case of a franchise. You will still need to decide what type of business form to purchase your franchise business (i.e., corporation, partnership, LLC, etc.). You will also need to decide how many employees and independent contractors to hire and what type of benefits you must give. You may have some self-employment tax issues. You will need to determine how best to expense and depreciate your assets. Finally, you will also need to track all kinds of business expenses. Typically, the franchisor will be able to help you with many of these issues. After all, you are buying into part of a team that has proven itself in business before.

When trying to make the decision whether or not to buy a franchise, you will certainly rack-up some expenses. Keep in mind that most of these expenses are treated as start-up costs. As explained earlier in this Chapter, you can typically deduct the first $5,000 of start-up expenses. The rest has to be spread out or amortized over a 15-year period. (Note: If your start-up expenses are before October 22, 2004, you may elect to amortize your costs over a 5-year period).

The cost for buying a franchise is often large. Depending on the franchise, you could be looking at $25,000 to several hundred thousands or even millions, so it is important to understand how much of that cost you can deduct right away, and what portion you will have to amortize. In addition to start-up costs, when you buy a franchise you will amortize the purchase price and related things over a 15-year period—like goodwill (i.e., the value of the name or reputation of the business) or a covenant not to compete (i.e., an agreement between the seller and buyer where the seller agrees not to start a competing business within a certain period of time). Finally, when buying an existing franchise, make sure you do your homework; particularly looking at the tax obligations of that business (i.e., are they current on their payroll tax withholdings and deposits). The last thing you want to do is inherit someone else's tax problems.

This is a brief overview of some of the tax issues involved with purchasing a franchise. If you are considering purchasing a franchise, either new or existing, getting your tax advisor involved early is a must.

### Pointer 21: Form 4562

Report your amortization deductions on *Form 4562, Depreciation and Amortization*. This form should be attached to your tax return.

## HOME-BASED BUSINESSES

If you happen to be at home during the day, you can't help but notice all of the commercials advertising the next great home business that will make you thousands. By home-based business, I don't mean selling a product, like Amway™, Tupperware™, etc. (see the discussion below on sales consultants for more on these side businesses). Instead, I mean a business that is run out of your home where you are providing some type of service; for example, medical transcription, computer-repair, massage therapy, etc.

I'm not passing judgment on these businesses and in fact, many can be very credible ways for you to make money. However, I strongly encourage you to be educated about the business and the true realistic prospects for you to make money. For example, take a look at Ms. Cleo and the "Call ma Now" commercials done in her best Jamaican accent (when she was straight out of Compton). Being a fortune teller may not be the best home-based business. There are a lot of scams out there, so do your homework.

Most people run their home-based businesses as sole proprietorships. This is primarily because of the ease of starting the business, since there are no formal set-up requirements. Typically, the company that runs the services you're providing will treat you as an independent contractor and will give you a *Form 1099 MISC, Miscellaneous Income*, showing the income that you earned for the year. You are responsible for tracking your business expenses, which for a home-based business may include things, like: the home office deduction, meals, transportation, telephone, internet, and supplies. You will report all of your income and losses on *Schedule C, Profit or Loss from Business (Form 1040)*. Also, you will be subject to pay self-employment taxes and you should make estimated tax payments to the IRS throughout the year.

Note: It is possible to set up another business entity, like a single member LLC, to run your home-based business. This is not too typical, given the extra costs and complexities for up-keep. For more on types of business entities, see Chapter 2: Side Businesses Part I.

**Pointer 22: Do Your Due Diligence**
Become familiar with the various resources to determine if an opportunity is legitimate. Some websites that might help you include:
- Work-at-home Moms—http://www.wahm.com
- Stay at Home—http://www.homewiththekids.com
- Federal Trade Commission—http://www.ftc.gov

Also check with the Better Business Bureau (http://www.bbb.org) or your state's Attorney General's Office for more information and help in this area.

### RENTAL REAL ESTATE

Thanks in part to an unprecedented real estate market from coast-to-coast, many people are buying and renting real estate as their side business. There are so many flavors of rental real estate activities. There are the part-time landlords, who often take a home that they previously used as their primary home and rent it out. This is often the case for people who have traded-up to a new house, but also for people who are downsizing. They realize a good opportunity; they can rent out their old house for an amount that more than covers their mortgage and pocket the difference. In some cases, they may be taking a loss (the rental payments are less than the mortgage), but they keep the house as a rental because perhaps they plan to eventually return to the house, and some money is better than having to cover the mortgage entirely. Then there are the people who buy a few properties, renovate them, and then rent them out for extra income. Even, further yet, there are the people who buy duplexes and rent out units.

If you've got the rental real estate fever, keep in mind the following tax issues. First, make sure you charge enough rent to cover your mortgage and related costs, at least, so as to provide you with either a positive cash flow or so you will break even. Next, understand the tax break for rental real estate. This comes from the fact that you can take depreciation on your rental property. Because depreciation is a tax deduction and not an actual dollar expenditure, it can result in lowering the taxable amount on a rental property. This means you can use losses from rental real estate to reduce income from other sources, such as your wages from your 9 to 5 job.

Sounds good right? Well, what Uncle Sam giveth, he also taketh away. You can only take up to $25,000 in losses from your rental real estate. Also, the $25,000 limit must be reduced (and eventually completely eliminated) as your AGI (adjusted gross income reaches) over $100,000 and becomes higher than $150,000. What happens if your loss is greater than $25,000? You can carry the loss over into subsequent years and deduct it when you have other rental income. Also, typically as you continue to rent the property, you will probably eventually be able to take these deductions. Why?

In time, you will probably charge more for rent, and this added income will allow you to take bigger deductions, including those losses carried over from previous years. Note: In such case, you may have to file *Form 8582, Passive Activity Loss Limitations.*

If you spend a lot of time on your rental real estate side business, there is one exception that may help you take all of your losses. Under special provisions called "Material Participation," the $25,000 loss limit can be exceeded; meaning you can ignore it and take your losses over $25,000. The definition of Material Participation is quite complex; you must prove that you devote significant time and energy to the management and operation of your rental property (i.e., over 750 hours per year), and that time is considerably more than anyone else devotes to this business. In my experience, meeting the Material Participation rules while running another business or working a 9 to 5 job is seldom accomplished.

Moreover, unless you are a full-time rental real estate playa, the IRS considers this to be a "passive" business activity. The IRS considers you to be running a business and not a hobby, but because your business is deemed less demanding than a full-fledged active business it's called a passive activity. This typically means that your losses can only offset gains from passive income and not from things, like your active salary income, from your 9 to 5 job. Luckily, there is an exception for rental real estate, as described above with the $25,000 loss rule. Also, since your activity is "passive" you don't have to pay self-employment taxes (to the tune of 15.3%) on your rental real estate activities.

Keep in mind that if your rental real estate business turns into a full time job, it's probably time for you to consider setting this up under a formal business entity. Remember many people are managing and owning real property through an LLC. That's because of the limited liability feature of an LLC that can shield the owner from liability exposure involving the property. Also, these folks are setting up a series of LLCs, each holding a single property rather than putting multiple properties in one entity. This helps to protect one property from any litigations or debts of the other properties that you own. They typically use one holding company (i.e., the parent) that owns all of the interests in the multiple LLCs (i.e., the subsidiary).

Finally, when you sell your rental property, you may have to pay taxes on the amount of depreciation that you deducted in previous years. For more on rental real estate, see the discussion in Chapter 1: Tax Basics.

### Pointer 23: Schedule E and Form 1065

Whatever the flavor of your rental real estate activities, if you're doing this truly as a side business to your 9 to 5 job, you must report these activities on your personal tax return, using *Schedule E, Supplemental Income and Loss (Form 1040)*. If you manager your rental properties through LLCs with their friends, families, co-workers, etc. Use *Form 1065, US Partnership Return of Income* and make sure each member is given a *Schedule K-1, US Return of Partnership Income (Form 1065)* which reports the member's share of the LLC profits and losses.

## SERVICE CONSULTANT

Whether you're a lawyer, engineer, doctor, a handyman, freelance writer or any other professional service provider, when you get paid for you business knowledge and know-how, you are a service consultant. Many service consultants are sole proprietorships. As a sole proprietor, in many cases you will receive a *Form 1099 MISC, Miscellaneous Income* showing the compensation for your services. You will report all of your income and losses on *Schedule C, Profit or Loss from Business (Form 1040)*. Don't forget to include your business deductions, such as professional dues, magazines and subscriptions, depreciation, transportation, meals, and utilities. Also, you will be subject to pay self-employment taxes and make estimated tax payments to the IRS throughout the year.

Service consultants who want to pair with a friend or many friends have to decide if a C corporation is best or if they are interested in a pass-through entity. If you choose the C Corporation, some states will require that you form as a professional corporation. However, as a professional corporation, the service consultants may still opt to be treated as a pass-through entity by electing to become an S Corporation.

If a pass-through entity is what you're looking for, many services consultants are opting for the ease and flexibility of setting up a limited liability company. These consultants often receive a salary or wage from the LLC, which is reported on a *Form W-2, Wage and Tax Statement*. They also must include their share of the entities profit or losses on their tax return. They will receive a *Schedule K-1, US Return of Partnership Income (Form 1065)*. For tax tips geared to the self-employed consultant see the Appendix for the For The Love Of Money Top 10 For The Self-Employed.

### SALES CONSULTANT

A sales consultant is obviously someone who sells products. This is different from a service consultant, because here you are selling a product and not just your knowledge. Examples of sales consultants include: Avon™, Amway™, and Tupperware™, just to name a few, but it also includes the person who sells items, like: computer equipment or pharmaceutical products. All of these sales consultants get paid for reselling a product that someone else makes.

As a sales consultant, you will have many business expenses related to travel, cell phone, internet, meals, and transportation. You have to keep in mind that you can't have so many expenses year after year that you never show a real profit. If this happens the IRS is likely to say you are running a hobby and not a true business. If declared a hobby, you will not be able to take a full deduction for your expenses. They will be treated as miscellaneous itemized deductions and must be greater than 2% of your adjusted gross income before you can deduct them. Also, you have to pay taxes on the full value of your hobby income. See the discussion earlier in this Chapter on hobbies.

Also, be sure that costs to attend regional or national meetings of your fellow sales consultants have real business substance. Hanging out with the other sales consultants cannot be the primary purpose of the meeting. In other words, if most of your time is spent singing "Where The Party At?" (Jagged Edge, Featuring Nelly, 2001) or "Fiesta," (R. Kelly 2001), you won't be able to deduct your costs for attending the meeting. For tax tips geared to the self-employed consultant, see the For The Love Of Money Top 10 For The Self-Employed.

## INVESTMENT CLUBS

You and your friends just got done reading "The Millionaire's Club: How to Start and Run Your Own Investment Club, and Make Your Money Grow," by Carolyn Brown and you're ready to start your own investment club. Here's the quick 411 on some tax issues involved with investment clubs:

Many folks start their investment clubs as a general partnership. Why? This is the easiest business entity to form. In most states when you pool all of your money together to make investments, you have a partnership without ever filing any forms. Remember, with a general partnership, all of the partners have unlimited liability. Some investment clubs form as LLCs. State filing fees for LLCs are often more expensive, and there is often more complexity with running an LLC. For an example of a model partnership agreement for investment clubs, see National Association of Investors Corporation at http://www.better-investing.org/articles/web/3462.

Remember the partners in the investment club must pay their share of the club's income on their personal tax returns. The investment club must complete a *Form 1065, US Partnership Return of Income* and make sure each partner is given a *Schedule K-1, US Return of Partnership Income (Form 1065)* which reports the partner's share of the LLC's profits and losses.

What type of income can you expect on the Schedule K-1s? The investment club will typically have interest and dividend income, and capital gains or losses when investments are sold or exchanged. Any expenses that you have related to the investment club can be deducted as miscellaneous itemized deductions. Keep in mind, these expenses are subject to a 2% limit; (i.e., you must spend more than 2% of your adjusted gross income before you can deduct them). For more on miscellaneous itemized deductions, see Chapter 6: Itemized Deductions Part II.

Finally, for most investment clubs where all you are doing is investing in stocks and collecting dividend and interest income, the individual partners do not have to pay self-employment taxes on their share of the partnership's income.

**Pointer 24: Employer ID Number**
Your investment club must have an Employer Identification Number (EIN). Do not use the social security number of individual members when filling out the tax return for the investment club. Use *Form SS-4, Employee Identification Number (EIN)* to get your EIN.

# REMIX

Here's the remix on what we learned in the Chapter:

1. Your business must eventually show a profit or else you are running a hobby. The general rule of thumb is the three-out-of-five-year rule. If your business can show a profit in three-out-of-five years, it will typically be presumed that you are not running a hobby. Of course with everything in tax law, the facts and circumstances will be extremely important in making this determination.

2. Taxes, taxes and more taxes. If you operate a side biz, make sure you are educated on the various taxes you will encounter—payroll taxes, income taxes, and self-employment taxes. They are all discussed in this Chapter. Also make sure you pay these taxes

throughout the year (i.e., monthly for payroll taxes and quarterly for everything else).

3. Never, never, ever miss a payroll tax deposit. Remember, it's not your money. If you don't have the cash, you should forego your salary for that period. Then, become more aggressive in collecting your outstanding receivables, and go back and do a cash flow management plan with your tax advisor.

4. Evaluate all of your workers to determine if they are employees or independent contractors. Be able to provide agreements and other documents that support your position. Just because you call your worker an independent contractor doesn't mean it is so. If she's your "secretary, working everyday of the week," (i.e., like "Not Gon' Cry," Mary J. Blige, 1995), she's probably an employee.

5. At some point, you are going to have to pay yourself a salary, and it must be reasonable. You should talk to your tax advisor to help support your actual amounts.

6. You may not be able to take all of your expenses in year 1. So, keep in mind that start-up expenses and costs for some of your business assets will need to be spread out (i.e., depreciated or amortized) over several years.

7. There are many business expenses that you can take in the first year, such as, home office deductions, internet, telephone charges and supplies. Keep in mind that you can only deduct the portion of the costs that can be attributable to your business. You must back out any personal costs. For example, if you use your phone for business and personal reasons, you must come up with the percentage of business usage.

8. You should keep accurate records of auto use for your business. You don't have to record every mile traveled and every cent spent, but the records should be able to substantiate (e.g., prove) any deductions claimed. A comparison of business miles driven to the

total miles driven for the year will determine the percentage of business use that can be applied to any depreciation, expense or mileage deduction. So, keep good records.

9. Work with your tax advisor to compute your auto deduction using the actual expense and the standard mileage computations to take the method that results in the highest tax deductions. Normally, a leased vehicle can realize higher tax deductions using the actual expense method because of the increased cost of insurance and maintenance, and the limitation on miles driven. A purchased car (less than 6,000 pounds) can realize a higher deduction using the standard mileage rate, especially if the business miles are relatively large. With an SUV or similar vehicle, you may be better off with the actual expense method. Either way, only a comparison of allowable methods will reveal the best deduction.

10. You can only deduct 50% of your meals and entertainment. Also you will need receipts for these expenses, such as: the date, place, amount, who was there, and what you discussed.

11. There are many tax advantaged fringe benefits that you may offer your employees, such as group life and disability insurance policies, commuting and parking benefits (to certain levels), staff lunches, educational assistance, and employee stock options. Also there are many health insurance options that you may choose for your side business, such as Traditional Health Insurance Plans, Health Savings Accounts and Health Care Flexible Spending Accounts. Contact your tax advisor for help on figuring out what mix is good for you, and how to set these up.

12. In addition to the general rules for side businesses, there are particular tax rules to look out for in specific industries. Make sure that you also dig deeper and talk with a qualified tax advisor with experience in dealing with other folks in your industry. For tips on how to choose a tax advisor, see Chapter 10: FAQ #10. Also, check out the Appendix for the Top 10 lists for various professions.

# Chapter 4

# Capital Gains
*Capital Gains Strategies That Work*

>*Cash Rules Everything Around, Me,*
>*C.R.E.A.M*
>*Get the money*
>*Dollar, dollar bill y'all*
>
>"C.R.E.A.M." Wu-Tang Clan (1994)

---

The song focuses on cash, and there's no mistaking that cash is very important to obtaining financial freedom. But if you really want to have the American dream, the white house with the picket fence, the Volvo and the 2.2 kids, you will need more than cash. You've heard over and over that capital gains are subject to special tax rates. Capital gains tax rates have been covered in much of the tax legislation over the last five years. In fact, President George W. Bush has signed some of the most sweeping capital gain tax decreases in modern history. This furthers the point that if you're going through life trying to make your money only through a "9 to 5," you'll have a hard time accumulating wealth. You must look at building net worth through things like Capital Gains.

Yet, with all of this exposure, many people aren't hip to this and don't understand how to calculate their capital gains, let alone how to take advantage of capital gains investment strategies. Don't Worry, Be Happy

(Bobby McFerrin, 1988); *For The Love Of Money* has an entire chapter dedicated to giving you the scoop on using capital gains to build your net worth.

First get the basics of what a capital asset is and how to calculate a single capital gain or loss. Next, breeze through the concepts of holding periods and netting, which are both crucial in calculating your capital gains tax or, in the case of a loss, the amount that can be used to offset your other income. Finish by getting the lowdown with tips and strategies on how to use your capital gains. Note: This book focuses on federal individual capital gains/loss issues. It does not cover the capital gains rules on the state level or the capital gains rules for businesses and/or corporations. Please consult your tax advisor for more on these subjects.

## Capital Assets

Let's start with the premise that the best way to accumulate wealth is to put your money into assets that have the potential to increase in value. Almost everything you own, whether it's for personal pleasure or investment purposes, is considered a capital asset.

| Examples of capital assets: | |
|---|---|
| ➤ House | ➤ Clothes |
| ➤ Car | ➤ Stocks & bonds |
| ➤ Furniture | ➤ Jewelry |
| ➤ Computer (for personal use) | |

| Capital assets are NOT: | |
|---|---|
| ➤ Business equipment | ➤ Musical or artistic compositions. |
| ➤ Inventory | ➤ Business supplies |
| ➤ Copyrights | |

When you sell, trade or transfer a capital asset, you will need to calculate the amount of your capital gain or loss. To calculate this capital gain or loss, you will need to pinpoint two items: Sale Price and Basis. The formula to remember is:

> **Sales Price − Basis = Capital Gain or Loss**

Your capital gains is the difference between the selling price (or amount realized) and your basis (or cost) in the capital asset. If your basis is greater than the selling price, you have a capital loss. On the flip side, if the basis is lower then the selling price you have a capital gain.

### SALES PRICE

The first component in calculating your capital gain or loss is the sales price. Calculating the sales price is simple enough. For most types of capital assets, the sales price is the "agreed-upon" figure between you and the buyer for the property.

### EXAMPLE 4.1

Nia needs money and is forced to sell an original signed picture by the Gap Band on eBay. She hates to sell it because she's sure the Gap Band will be doing another "Party Train" (1983), any day now. She values the picture at $300. But the eBay bidders don't agree. She ultimately gets a bid of $120 and decides to take the deal. For purposes of calculating her capital gain, is her sales price $300 or $120? The answer is $120. That's what the market place will pay and this is what she agrees to. The fact that she believes the true value is higher is irrelevant.

### Pointer 1: Form 1099-B, Sales Price for Stock and Bonds

At the end of the year, your broker will send you a *Form 1099-B, Sales Price for Stock and Bonds* that shows the gross sales price for any stock or bond sales for the year. You will need to put this amount on *Schedule D, Capital Gains and Losses (Form 1040)*. Keep in mind that Form 1099-B is not a reflection of capital gains or profit and loss. It is your responsibility to calculate any capital gain or losses. It is very important for you to keep accurate records of your stock and bond purchases throughout the year. One suggestion for a quick and inexpensive way to do this is to use a three-ring binder/notebook to store all of your stock purchase confirmations. When it's time to calculate your capital gain or loss, simply take the gross sales prices from Form 1099-B and subtract your cost basis (which you can find in your three-ring binder). Please see the section below for further details on calculating your basis and capital gains.

### Pointer 2: Sales Price for House

When selling a house, you will need to compute a 'net sales' price. Take your actual sales price and deduct any selling costs (such as: title fees, sales commissions, transfer fees, survey fees, document recording fees and related legal fees). The result is your net sales price. The selling costs will be reflected on your closing statement. You will use this statement to calculate several tax deductions so keep a few copies; giving one of them to your tax advisor.

## BASIS

As a general rule, think of your basis as what you paid for the capital asset. But it's probably easiest to think of basis in terms of the type of capital asset you are selling.

## PROPERTY OTHER THAN STOCKS AND BONDS

For capital assets other than stocks, your basis will start with the cost of the property. Next, add things that increase the value of the asset, like: sales commissions you paid or improvements that are not cosmetic. Basis is not increased by routine repairs and maintenance; for example, with a care this would be like oil changes or tire replacements. You also need to deduct things that decrease the value of the property, like: depreciation or amortization.

### Pointer 3: Basis for a House

When calculating the basis for your home, start with your home purchase closing statement. Take the actual purchase price of the house, but also include any other costs paid to gain ownership reflected on the closing statement (such as, agent commissions, appraisal costs, and option premiums paid). Add any improvements that you have made to the house since you bought it, then subtract any depreciation that you claimed (i.e., which you may have taken because you had a home office, or rented all or part of the house to a tenant). Improvements that increase the basis of your home include things like costs for completing an unfinished basement, or conversion of a garage into a home office. Do not include the following: Points, or the loan origination fees, real estate taxes, and/or interest paid the year the mortgage was obtained or refinanced.

### Pointer 4: Basis for Gifted or Inherited Property

When someone gives you property (called the donor), you have to determine two values—the donor's basis, just before you received it, and how much it is worth the day you received it (fair market value). If the fair market value is less than the donor's basis, your basis depends on whether you have a gain or loss when you get rid of it. If you are selling the property for a gain, your basis would then be the same as the donor's on the date you received the property. If you are selling the property at a loss, your basis is the fair market value the day you received it. For example, assume

Big Momma gives you her 50 shares of Disney stock that she purchased in 1950 for $10 per share. Your basis in the Disney stock would be either what she paid for it ($500) or the current stock price listed on the stock exchange on the date she gave the stock to you.

## STOCKS AND BONDS

The basis for stocks & bonds also starts with the cost (i.e., what you originally paid for them). Cost, in this instance, is calculated as the price per share times the number of shares of stock that you purchase. Also, increase the basis by any commissions you pay.

### EXAMPLE 4.2

Jarrett buys 100 shares of stock in Zulu Corp when it is trading at $55.98 per share. His basis in his Zulu stock is $5,598 ($55.98 X 100 shares).

That was the easy math. Things get a bit more complicated when you do things like purchase additional blocks of the same stock at different times of the year. Each purchase needs to be tracked, so if you sell shares from two different blocks of purchases, the gain or loss can accurately reflect the proper basis for each stock.

**Pointer 5: Tracking Your Stock Basis**
This information could get complicated and time consuming; when you make several purchases during the year. The better your organization and record keeping, the easier the calculation. Luckily, your tax advisor or financial professional should be equipped to help you do all of this. Also, for people with significant stock trades and transactions, there are computer programs designed to help track this, such as:

- GainsKeeper™—(http://www.gainskeeper.com)
- Intuit™—(http://www.intuit.com)
- TradeLog™—(http://www.armencorp.com/tradelog)

# The Holding Period

Now that you know the basics of calculating a capital gain or loss, you're well on your way to figuring out if you have to pay a capital gains tax. The second important item that needs to be determined is whether you have a "short-term" or a "long-term" gain or loss; because this will impact the amount of taxes that you might have to pay. You figure this out by knowing your "holding period."

Your holding period is based on how long you owned the capital asset. If you hold the capital asset for over 1 year, any gain or loss will be long-term. On the flip side, if you hold it for 1 year or less, any gain or loss will be short-term. It begins on the date after you purchase the asset. For example, if you purchase a house on November 22$^{nd}$, your holding period will begin on November 23$^{rd}$. Your holding period ends on the date you actually sell or dispose of the property.

### Pointer 6: Home Purchase
You are deemed to have purchased a house on the date you actually acquired title to the property, not the first day funds were transferred as a deposit, or the first day escrow.

### Pointer 7: Exclusion for Inherited Property
If you sell property that you inherited, you should report the gain or loss as long-term, regardless of how long you personally held the property.

Holding periods become very important, after you have calculated all of your capital gains and losses, because you will need to put them in categories (known as "netting"), based on whether they are short-term or long-term. Only after doing all of these steps will you be able to apply the proper tax rate to your gain, or use your loss to offset other income. The next section discusses how this netting is done.

## Netting Capital Gains and Losses

Now that you know how to calculate a capital gain or loss, and how long to hold the capital asset, you're getting closer to figuring out how to calculate your actual tax. The next step is a process called "netting." Think of netting as a matching game, like Uno™. In fact, I was thinking of pitching the "Capital Gains Netting Game" as a new cable TV game show to MTV, BET, TV-One, The Black Family Channel or VH-1. Read on for the rules of the slammin' Capital Gains Netting Game and 'holla back' "Young'in" (Fabolous, 2001) if you think I've got a shot.

1. **Get your dancing shoes together**

    If you're like me, you're always searching for that missing shoe to those hot boots you bought two seasons ago, but only wore once because they hurt your feet. The Capital Gains Netting Game is basically the same concept—you're looking for a match, even though you know the process may be painful. Take each of your capital gains and capital losses, and categorize them by holding period. List the short-term capitals gains under one section, short-term capital losses under another section, long-term capital gains under still another section, and long-term capital losses under a final section.

2. **New kids on the block go first**

    You're trying to get in the party mood and can't decide if you want to listen to the latest jam, or take it back to your favorite old school 70s or 80s jam. Start with the new stuff. Net your short-term capital gains and losses (in other words subtract your short term capital losses from your short-term capital gains). This will either give you a net short-term loss (because your losses were greater than your gains), or a net short-term gain (because your gains were greater than your losses).

3.  **Old school time** ("Old School Lovin'," Shante Moore style, 1994)

Now that you finished with "getting your freak on" ("Get Ur Freak On," Missy Elliot 2001), it's time to "Slow Down" (Brand Nubian, 1990) and get funky. Whatever your cup of tea, it's time to bring it back old-school style. Net all your long-term capital gains (meaning subtract your long term capital losses from your long-term capital gains). This will either give you a net long-term loss (because your losses were greater than your gains) or a net long-term gain (because your gains were greater than your losses).

4.  **Get Jiggy With It** ("Gettin Jiggy Wit It," Will Smith style 1997)

Now that you've done a little 'old school, new school, no school rule' ("Keep Risin' To The Top," Doug E Fresh and the Get Fresh Crew, 1988), it's time to take whatever results you got in step 2 and 3 and net those together. So you are taking your short-term capital gain or loss and netting that against your long-term capital gain or loss. The result can be a net gain—either short-term or long-term. It can also be a net loss—again, either short-term or long-term.

5.  **Net Gains—"Pay Your Taxes"**

Got a net gain? This means you got a tax. But how much of a tax will depend on if the net gain is short-term or long-term. (See the next section in this Chapter on calculating the capital gains tax.) Keep in mind, having a gain isn't necessarily a bad thing, particularly a gain that is taxed at a lower tax rate than your salary and wages. After all, it's often better to pay taxes on some money than have no money at all.

6. Net Losses—"Game Over"

Got a net loss? "It's Over Now," (Luther Vandross, 1985). You don't have to pay any taxes, but you probably won't be able to deduct that much of your net loss; at least not this year. You are limited to a maximum deduction of $3,000 for net capital losses each tax year. This means you can deduct the first $3,000 of you net capital losses against your other income, but for the rest, you must "Hold On" (En Vogue, 1990). These remaining net losses are held and carried forward to be used on your future tax returns. The good news is that these losses may be carried forward indefinitely until the balance is zero.

I hope you enjoyed the Capital Gains Netting Game. You are required to play this game once a year when you fill out your tax return. For those of you who are heavy hitters, big playas, ballers and shoot callers, you should play it once a quarter; of course with the help of your favorite tax advisor.

## EXAMPLE 4.3

Tawana read an advance copy of *For The Love Of Money* and got her groove back by playing the Capital Gains Netting Game. She started by getting "Head Sprung" (LL Cool J, 2004) while putting together her short-term capital gains and losses; which were $6,000 and $10,000 respectively. This gave her a net short-term capital loss of $4,000.

Not wanting to "disturb her groove" ("Don't Disturb This Groove," The System, 1987), after calculating her long-term capital gains, Tawana had to "give it up" ("Got to Give It Up," Marvin Gaye', 1977) because she did quite well. She had $32,000 in long-term capital gains and only $2,500 in long-term capital losses; making a combined total of $29,500 in net long-term capital gains.

When the dust settled and it was time to put it all together she had a $29,500 net long-term capital gains, minus her $4,000 net short-term capital loss; resulting in a $25,500 net long-term gain.

## EXAMPLE 4.4

Jackie also played the Capital Gains Netting Game, but with different results. Jackie started out doing her best "Lean Back" (Terror Squad, featuring Fat Joe & Remy, 2004), and netted her $15,000 short-term capital gain against $7,000 short-term capital loss. This gave her a net short-term capital gain of $8,000.

Then she slowed it down and decided to play another "Slow Jam" (Midnight Star, 1983); only this time it wasn't sweet. She had a long-term capital gain of $5,000 and netted this against her $22,000 long-term capital loss. This gave her a net long-term capital loss of $17,000.

Feeling a bit confused and in a losing mood, for her freestyle round she picked "Lose Yourself," by Eminem (2002). She deducted her net short-term capital gain against her net long-term capital gain, and still had $9,000 of her long-term capital loss left. She can use $3,000 of this loss on her current tax return as a deduction against her other income. The remaining $6,000 will have to be held and used on future tax returns.

**Pointer 8: Capital Loss Carryover Worksheet**
Because you can carry forward capital losses indefinitely, good record keeping is important. Commerce Clearing House ("CCH") has an excellent and free capital loss carryover worksheet you can use to calculate your capital loss carryovers for future years. Check out CCH's "Financial Planning Toolkitä" on their website at http://www.finance.cch.com.

# Calculating Capital Gains Tax & Handling Capital Losses

You're almost there. Now that you know what a capital asset is, how to calculate any gains or losses, and how to net those capital gains or losses based on your holding period, you're finally ready to calculate the capital gains tax.

First, a little bit of information on why you're going through all of this trouble. Besides the fact that it's the law, net long-term capital gains receive a significant tax benefit. Your actual capital gains tax rate depends on your tax bracket. For example, for those single taxpayers whose income level exceeds $28,000, and those married couples filing jointly and have income levels exceeding $56,000, their long-term capital gains are taxed at 15%. When you compare this to your "9 to 5" salary income which would be taxed at 25% this is quite a bargain. Even further, the maximum rate you use for your net long-term capital gains 20%; which is significantly less than the maximum tax rate for your "9 to 5" money which is 39.6%

As mentioned earlier in this Chapter under step 6 the Capital Gains Netting Game, only $3,000 of your net capital losses can be used in any given year to be deducted against your other income. Any remaining losses must be carried forward to other tax years.

### Pointer 9: Schedule D
These calculations can be extremely complicated. Please use *Schedule D, Capital Gains and Losses (Form 1040)* to calculate your capital gains and losses. Luckily, there are many software programs that will make these calculations for you such as, Investment Software found at http://www.investmentsoftware.com. For those with numerous capital gains and losses, particularly from the sale of stock or bonds, you should consult with a tax advisor. Please see, Chapter 10: FAQ #10 for tips on choosing a tax advisor.

# Special Exclusions and Rules

As with other areas in tax law, there is ALWAYS a special exclusion, an exception, an exception-to-the-exception, and on and on. The exceptions normally have specific time periods and criteria for how to apply.

Here's the "Scenario," (Tribe Called Quest, 1991) Listed below are some of the more common capital gain or loss scenarios that will impact most of us at some point in our lives. As you read the following scenarios, make sure to take note and discuss them with your tax advisor.

## HOUSE SALES

Over the last few years, home prices have soared to new heights from coast-to-coast. Will they come down soon? Nobody knows. After all, almost nothing is as "Solid" (...as a rock, Ashford & Simpson, 1984). Modern history has shown that if you own your home long enough, you will have a capital gain. For many lucky homeowners, this has resulted in new-found wealth when they cash in their house. Perhaps the area that I get the most confusing questions, hypotheses and conjectures is on how to handle capital gains from home sales.

## SALE OF PRIMARY HOME

Owning a home has many advantages; including many under the tax laws. It should come as no surprise, then, that there are special rules that apply to capital gains from selling your primary home. But, there is also a lot of confusion about how this capital gains exclusion works.

First, I want to clear up an overwhelmingly common misperception. You no longer have to take the capital gain from your house sale and roll it over into the purchase of another house to avoid a capital gain. So don't ask your tax advisor questions like, "How much does my new house have to be worth because of my capital gains from my old house?" Just don't ask, because for most folks it doesn't matter.

Under the newer rules (put into law under the Clinton regime), you can now exclude up to $250,000 for single-filing taxpayers and $500,000 for those married filing jointly of any capital gains from a home sale.

### EXAMPLE 4.5

Jada and Jordan bought their dream home in 2000 for $550,000. They made improvements valued at $50,000. Their basis in their home is $600,000. In 2004, they decided to cash in and take their money out of the house. Thanks to the real estate boom, they sold their home for $950,000. Their long-term capital gain is $350,000 ($950,000 sales price—$600,000 basis). Assuming they file a joint tax return, all of this gain is excluded, as it is less than $500,000.

Unfortunately, if you have a loss on the sale of your house you cannot deduct this loss. It is treated as a personal loss (see the discussion below on the next section of this Chapter regarding personal use property).

But there are a few rules you need to know about to take advantage of this exclusion. First, you must own your home for at least 2 years out of the last 5 years before you sell the house. However, if you are selling your home because of a significant change in circumstances such as a new job, health condition or other unforeseen circumstance, you can still use the exclusion; but you must pro rate the exclusion amount based on the time you actually owned the home. Unforeseen circumstances include many of the common reasons people decide to move from a home, such as:

- death,
- divorce or legal separation, multiple births (i.e., triplets, sextuplets, etc.),
- significant damage to the house from disasters such as earthquakes, hurricanes, etc.,

➢ being laid-off from your job such that you can no longer afford the mortgage payments and/or you start receiving unemployment compensation, or
➢ condemnation or seizure of the home.

### EXAMPLE 4.6

Brandon and Bridgette bought their dream home in January 2003 for $275,000. Bridgette was offered a significant promotion with her company, but taking it meant the family had to move to a new city. This city was over 350 miles from their home and much too far for Bridgette to commute. The couple decided to sell their home in July 2004, and thanks to a favorable real estate market, they got a whopping $400,000. Their net capital gain was $125,000 ($400,000 sales price-$275,000 basis). Although they did not own the home for 2 out of the last 5 years, they still took advantage of the capital gain exclusion by pro rating the exclusion based on how many months they actually lived in the house out of two years. In this case, assume they were in the house for 18 months out of 24 months. Their newly pro rated exclusion amount is $375,000 ($500,000 X 18/24). They excluded their entire $125,000 gain, since it was less than the partial exclusion of $375,000.

You must also use the house as your primary residence to qualify for the exclusion. A primary residence is the house in which you spend most of your time. It is not a vacation home, or your second home that you use seasonally or infrequently. Also a "house" includes most structures that you use as your dwelling (such as, a free standing home, duplex, condo, townhouse, mobile home, houseboat, a coop or a trailer).

Next, many people have home offices in their primary residence, or use part of their property to generate rental income. The good news is that you can still use the house exclusion when you sell this property. The bad news is that any depreciation that you took in previous years, when the property was used for business purposes, must be recaptured or claimed as income in the year in which you sell your primary residence.

## EXAMPLE 4.7

Joanna, a single taxpayer, bought her house in 2000 for $125,000 and lived in it for 3 years before moving out in 2003 to a smaller condo. She decided to keep the house and turn it into a rental property. But by late 2004, the tenant had moved out. Because of high real estate prices, she thought it would be best to sell the house. She promptly sold the home for $385,000. For purposes of this example, let's assume that she took total depreciation deductions of $7,500 while she used the home as a rental property.

Her long-term capital gain is $260,000 ($385,000 sales price less $125,000 basis). Joanna can only exclude $250,000 of her capital gain; thus, she will have to pay taxes on $10,000 of the gain that isn't excluded ($260,000 less $250,000). Also, she will have to pay taxes on the $7,500 of depreciation (treated now as a capital gain) that she previously deducted when her house was a rental property.

## EXAMPLE 4.8

Sharlita and Simon, a married couple filing jointly, bought a three-plex in 2002 for $670,000. They lived in one unit and rented out the other two. Assume they took a total depreciation deduction of $15,000 for their two rental units. In 2004, they decided to sell the three-plex for $1 million, making a gain of $330,000. However, this entire gain cannot be excluded. They must first allocate the gain between the personal use and the business use. In this case, 1/3$^{rd}$ of their gain is personal or $110,000. This amount can be completely excluded, as it is less than their $500,000 exclusion amount. The remaining $220,000 is treated as attributable to the rental property and is not subject to the exclusion. They also must treat the $15,000 in previous depreciation as a capital gain subject to tax.

## EXAMPLE 4.9

Lisa, a single taxpayer, bought her townhouse in 2001 for $250,000. She works from home, using her basement as a home office. She got married in 2004 and decided to sell her townhouse for $325,000. She bought a house with her new hubby. Assume she took $5,000 in depreciation deductions for the home office. Lisa can exclude all of her capital gain of $125,000, since it is less than the $250,000 exclusion amount for single taxpayers. However, thanks to the depreciation recapture rule, the $5,000 will be treated as a capital gain and is subject to tax.

Finally, you can only use this exclusion every two years. This prevents taxpayers who constantly sell homes (known as flipping) from using this exclusion to avoid capital gains, when they probably should be treated as in the business of selling homes.

**Pointer 10: Reporting House Sales**
You don't have to report capital gains that meet the home sale exclusion on your tax return. But if you receive *Form 1099-S, Proceeds from Real Estate Transactions,* you either do in fact have a capital gain (because your gain is larger than the exclusion amounts), or your real estate broker has made a mistake. If you believe this was in error, please notify your tax advisor.

## SALE OF VACATION OR SECOND HOME

We all dream of owning that vacation home on the beach or in the mountains. For those of you fortunate enough to have your island paradise, what happens to your second home? As discussed above, a vacation home is not your primary residence and thus does not qualify for the home sales exclusion. Any gains from the sale of a vacation home will be subject to capital gains tax. That's not all. In the true essence of "kicking you when you're down," any losses from the sale of a vacation home will not be deductible as they are treated as personal losses (see the discussion below in the next section of this Chapter regarding personal use property).

## SALE OF RENTAL REAL ESTATE

With the real estate boom of the 2000s, many people are buying rental real estate properties. As discussed in Chapter 3: Side Business Part II, rental real estate is treated as a passive activity. When you sell this property, it is not subject to the home sales exclusion. This means you must treat this sale like any other capital asset and calculate your capital gain or loss. Moreover, any depreciation that you claimed in previous years as deductions may have to be recaptured and treated as capital gains themselves in the year that you sell the rental real estate. For more on this, see Example 4.8 above.

However, "Somewhere Over the Rainbow" (take your pick as to which version you prefer, Judy Garland in the 1939 movie "Wizard of Oz," Patti LaBelle and the Blue Belles circa 1965, or Kimberly Locke's version in 2004 on American Idol), there is some relief due to another special tax provision for rental real estate, known as 1231 property. First, with respect to gains, any capital gains recognized from the sale of your rental real estate will be treated as long-term capital gains (except for amounts attributable to depreciation recapture, which are treated as short-term capital gains). Second, with respect to losses, rental real estate is not treated as personal use property. Thus, these losses may be used to offset other income. Moreover, these losses are treated as an ordinary loss and not a capital loss. This means they are not limited to the $3,000 deduction that applies for capital losses. Instead, these losses are completely deductible against your ordinary income (i.e., from your "9 to 5").

### PERSONAL USE PROPERTY

The beginning of this Chapter discussed categories of assets that are included in capital assets. It included just about everything you own, including items like your car. As an exclusion to the capital loss rules, you are not allowed to deduct capital losses resulting from the sale of certain personal use assets. This means, if you sell your personal car for a loss, which is common for most car sales, you cannot take this loss against your other income (i.e., salary or wages). It's also not a part of the $3,000 maximum net capital losses you can use to offset other income. It's treated as one of those losses that never existed and you don't need to report the sale on your tax return.

### EXAMPLE 4.10

Pinky, who thinks she was the inspiration for Boogie Boys' 1985 hit "Fly Girl," bought her 2000 BMW 325i convertible and paid $35,000. She put down $10,000 and financed the rest over 4 years. She just finished making her last payment in November of 2004. When she added it all up, she actually paid a total of $45,000 for the car. She decided to trade the car in for a new BMW 330i convertible. The dealer gives her $15,000 for her old car. As a car is a capital asset, Pinky calculated her capital loss, a whopping $30,000 ($15,000 sales price-$45,000 basis). However, because a car is a personal use asset, Pinky will not be able to use her $30,000 loss.

### EXAMPLE 4.11

Pinky's cousin, Pearl also bought a BMW 325i in 2000. But Gina's BMW is like no other. She "pimped" her car with 19" wheels, a spoiler kit, xenon lighting and sports package, TV screen in the trunk and pink and green leather inside. She even had it painted apple green. She, too, paid $35,000 for her car; although she paid cash and did not finance it. With all of the car's upgrades and improvements, she spent an additional $25,000 (making her basis on the car $60,000). This car has caught the eye of a famous rap producer who just has to have Pearl's car to use in his next video. He offers Peral $80,000 for the car, and she gladly sells it. Pinky tells Pearl that she probably doesn't have to report anything on her tax return from the sale. Not so fast. Pearl actually has a gain from her car sale. Her long-term capital gain is $20,000 ($80,000 sales price-$60,000 basis).

Any gains realized from selling personal use property are treated as capital gains and you will have to pay taxes on them. Who would likely have a gain from selling personal assets? Take a custom antique and rare vehicle or a rebuilt car with original parts (like those seen on the MTV show "Pimp My Ride"). It is likely that these cars can actually be sold at a gain. So, if you're a car buff and just restored your dream car, you may have to worry about this rule. The rest of us will continue to sell our cars and not report these sales on any tax returns.

## Tax Planning

As you increase your knowledge and understanding of capital gains, you will increase the likelihood of using strategies to minimize the net tax effect of your property sales. The best way to help capital gains and losses work for you is to have a good handle on your current tax position, *without* consideration of the potential capital asset sale. This advantage is the greatest if you think about it BEFORE you proceed with the sale. Admittedly, this tax planning works best as long as there's no pressure to dispose of the property quickly. So, when you are in a bind and you need cash fast, tax planning is probably not high on your list. In such situations, you should still confer with your tax advisor. You may be surprised at what you can do to minimize the tax bite; keeping more money in your pocket and building your net worth. Now that you've learned what a capital asset is and how to calculate your capital gains and losses, it's time to do some tax planning.

## INCOME TIMING

You may have heard that the general rule of thumb for making investment gains is to buy low and sell high. The tax law favors this by giving you a favorable tax rate for investments that you sell after holding them longer than 1 year. Two general rules to follow:

- If you have long-term capital gains, try to take these; they are taxed at the lower capital gains tax rate.
- Save your capital losses for subsequent years when you have short-term capital gains.

Of course, these are general rules that does not take into account every situation and circumstance. Remember Morris Day and The Times' smash hit "What Time Is It?" circa 1982? What you really need to remember is that timing is everything. With all other things being consistent from one tax year to another, a property sale can significantly increase or decrease your tax bill. But, you typically control the date of sale. There may be some years when it is better to have the gain, or you may need to generate a loss to help offset a gain that you must take. If you want to defer the sale date from one year to another, all you need to do is close the deal in January versus December.

## EXAMPLE 4.12

Angela, an investment novice, decided to take a chance on Soul Glow, a struggling company that produced a product known as the "Kerry Kurl". The company gained popularity with a Kerry Curl product back in the 80s, but due to some manufacturing glitches, the product was too oily and had to be taken off the shelf. After 10 years of research and development, this new Kerry Kurl product promised to be a hit. Angela purchased 10,000 shares of Soul Glow stock in January 2004 for a penny a share (a total of $100 which is also her basis). Much to her surprise (and the stock market's) Kerry Kurl became a hit after being featured as the product of choice by several hip hop artists.

By December 31, 2004, Soul Glow was trading at $20 a share! Her expected gain is $199,900 ($200,000 sales price less 100 basis). Angela was so happy with her investment that she decided to quit her $70,000 a year job to become a Soul Glow distributor in January 2005. She knows it may take her awhile to be profitable, so she plans to live off her gains from selling her Soul Glow stock. If Angela sells the stock in December of 2004 she will have a short-term capital gain. If she waits and sells her Soul Glow stock in January 2005 she will have a long-term capital gain. Her timing is probably better if she waits since she will have no salary income and her business net income will probably be lower than her previous 2004 salary of $70,000.

**MATCHING**

You will remember the matching concept from the Capital Gains Netting Game. In fact, matching is very important in your tax planning for capital gains. A general rule of thumb with matching is that you should try and match large capital gains (and by that I mean big money) with large capital losses in the same tax year. Why? Because large net capital gains will certainly increase your tax bill, even with a favorable tax rate, to an amount that is likely to shock even the savviest investor. I know of cases where corporate executives, who have been with their companies for 20+ years, decided to retire. They cashed in all their stock options and ended up with amazing gains (in the millions of dollars). They knew that their investments were growing and worth a lot. It's one thing to see it on paper. It's another to be sitting at that desk when your tax advisor shows you your gain, and then your huge seven-figure capital gains tax.

## EXAMPLE 4.13

Cantrell was a big muscular guy who could often be found spending his days working out on Venice beach. In the 80s, he had moderate success as a performer with the music group "Half Force," which he co-founded with four of his friends. But his real money came from writing the lyrics and producing the popular 80s R&B group "Tina Tina & the Fad Groove." Sensing the change in the music scene with the emergence of so-called gangsta rap, Cantrell decided to get out of the record business in the early 90s and used his money to purchase a gym in downtown LA; forming a partnership with two of his weightlifting buddies. He also tried his hand at the stock market and purchased 10,000 shares in a small start-up company called Black Curly Curl at $25 per share. Black Curly Curl was going to change how people got jerry curls by using a natural herbal extract instead of the chemicals that are so popular with competitor products. Plus, as an added bonus, the company sent free products to its shareholders every year; a perk which Cantrell took full advantage of. Unfortunately, Cantrell paid no attention to the stock market, and by 2000, the stock value had dropped to $6.50 per share.

In 2004, Cantrell wanted to move abroad for a couple of years to try to launch a reunion tour for Half Force and Tina Tina. He decided it was time to sell his partnership interest in the fitness gym. His partners agreed to buy him out for $450,000. Cantrell's adjusted basis in the partnership totaled $100,000. Cantrell's long-term capital gain was $350,000 ($450,000 - $100,000). When Cantrell consulted his tax advisor, he remembered that he still owned his shares in Black Curly Curl. The shares were now worth $1.50 per share. With this big gain, Cantrell, sensed that it was finally time to give up on the jerry kurl (and in fact cut his own) and decided to sell his losing stock. He took the long-term gain from the sale of the gym ($350,000) and reduced it by his long-term capital loss of $235,000 ($15,000 - $250,000). This gave him a net long term capital gain of $115,000 ($350,000 - $235,000). This is the matching tax strategy and it saved Cantrell $24,000 in capital gain taxes as well as increased his cash-flow by $15,000.

## REMIX

Here's the remix on what we learned in the Chapter:

1. Know what a capital asset is and isn't—Your house, yes; your inventory, no.

2. Calculate a capital gain and loss by using this formula:

    Selling Price-Basis = Capital Gain or Loss

3. When you sell stock or bonds, you will need to enter the selling price on, *Schedule D, Capital Gains and Losses (Form 1040)*. Please make sure the amount you put down matches the amount reported on *Form 1099-B, Sales Price for Stock and Bond*, which you should receive from your broker. The IRS will get a copy of Form 1099-B and their computers are sure to catch any discrepancies. In other words, you can bet you will at least get a letter from the IRS about this, which could lead to an audit. For more on audits see Chapter 9: IRS Audits. Also, check-out the appendix for the Top 10 Ways to Avoid an Audit.

4. Your basis is what you paid for the capital asset (less commissions and fees, plus improvements.

5. Your holding period is the amount of time you owned the capital asset. It will either be short-term (1 year or less) or long term (over 1 year).

6. You must organize all short-term and long-term capital gains and losses. Then, play the netting game to get to your net result. Use *Schedule D, Capital Gains and Losses (Form 1040)* for this calculation.

7. Remember all the special rules and exclusions for sales of houses, vacation homes, rental real estate, and personal use assets.

8. Tax planning is extremely important to get the most out of your capital gains and losses each year. Although you should review your investment portfolio on a frequent basis, for purposes of tax planning, you should start to really look at your net position by October of each year (or the beginning of the 4$^{th}$ quarter). This gives you a few months to decide if you need to sell some more capital assets to achieve your desired net position by year end.

9. As with most things in life, proper planning assists in making sound decisions. Getting a handle on your estimated current tax position will help you with your decision to sell now or later.

10. Keep in mind, the tax laws actually make it more advantageous for you to invest, hold and then sell capital assets at a gain than to strive for larger salaries. If you want to build your net worth, get hip to capital gains. Invest in capital assets and learn how to time and match your capital gains and losses.

# Chapter 5

# Itemized Deductions
*Itemize Your Life*

> *Things you seem to do divine (You look straight into my eyes)*
> *I know our love was meant to be (Because our souls touch tenderly)*
> *Love is life and life is living,*
> *It's very special*
>
> "Very Special," Debra Laws, featuring Ronnie Laws (1981)

---

Very special, may best describe the category of expenses known as itemized deductions. These are numerous expenses that you incur in your daily life, like: dry cleaning, day care costs, cable TV, phone bills, shoes, clothes, rent, mortgage, food; and the list goes on and on, like Janet Jackson sings in the Joni Mitchell remake of "Got 'Til It's Gone" (1997). The expenses that qualify as itemized deductions are given a special status by the IRS, because you actually get a tax benefit from making these expenditures.

As explained in Chapter 1: Tax Basics, one of the keys to taking control of your taxes is understanding how to get the most out of your deductions. Itemized deductions are a group of special deductions that you may deduct if they are higher than your standard deduction (i.e., married folks filing jointly use $10,000 and single taxpayers use $5,000). Generally, if you own a home, you will itemize deductions. Under current law, there are six kinds of itemized expenses:

1. Medical expenses
2. Taxes
3. Interest expenses
4. Charitable contributions
5. Casualty and theft losses
6. Job expenses and other miscellaneous expenses

This Chapter will give you the 411 on medical expenses, taxes, and interest expenses. Please see Chapter 6: Itemized Deductions Part II, for the 411 on charitable contributions, casualty and theft losses, job expenses, and other miscellaneous expenses.

**Pointer 1: Schedule A**

Use *Schedule A, Itemized Deductions (Form 1040)* to calculate and report your itemized deductions. In most cases, if the total itemized deductions on *Schedule A* are greater than the standard deductions, you are better off choosing the higher amount. Keep in mind you cannot take itemized deductions if you use Form 1040EZ or 1040A.

# Medical Expenses

Remember the song, "Go See the Doctor," by Kool Moe Dee (1986), or "Operator" ("...this is an emergency...") by Midnight Star (1984)? All conjure up interesting medical problems. Although I wish good health for everyone, medical expenses are unavoidable. In many cases they are necessary for the prevention of even worse things, and the tax laws actually treat them favorably.

Unreimbursed medical expenses for you, your spouse, and any dependents are deductible as itemized deductions to the extent that the expenses exceed 7.5% of your adjusted gross income. There are three things you need to focus on under this rule.

- Unreimbursed medical expenses
- Deductible medical expenses
- Greater than 7.5% of adjusted gross income

### UNREIMBURSED MEDICAL EXPENSES

First, the medical expenses must be unreimbursed. This means that if the medical expenses are covered by insurance (or in some cases paid for by the government), you cannot deduct them since, after all, you didn't pay for them. Arguments like "I'm a taxpayer and part of my money goes to pay Medicare and Medicaid and so I should get some benefit," will not work.

### EXAMPLE 5.1

Funkytown, USA is the home of the annual pop locking competition. Over the last few years, the competition has either been won by JJ Evans, or his arch rival Re-run Jones. This year, word on the street is that a newcomer, simply known as Pharrell, might give them both a run for their money. JJ had been practicing day and night. During one real grueling practice, where he practiced a spin move with a lead into twirling his practice partner, Ma Evans, he broke his arm. In fact, it almost tore in half just like a twig. He yelled out "dang, dang, dang," as he realized he would not be able to compete in the Funkytown competition.

JJ's gets good government benefits from his fulltime job at the post office, including health insurance. Although his medical expenses for his broken arm (including the hospital and doctor office visits) came to $5,000, he only had to pay a deductible of $100. He also pays $600 a year (deducted from his paycheck) in medical insurance premiums. JJ has $700 ($100 deductible and

$600 premiums) of medical expenses that may qualify as itemized deductions. JJ is not able to deduct the remaining $4,900 from his broken arm because he didn't pay for this.

---

Keep in mind, you can only deduct medical expenses for you, yourself or your dependents. A dependent is someone who lives with you, as a member of your household, for the entire year, is a US citizen or resident (or a resident of Canada or Mexico), and for whom you provided over half of their total support. Dependents can also include your family members (i.e., children, grandchildren, siblings, parents, grandparents, aunts, uncles, nieces, nephews, and in-laws) who don't live with you for the entire year, but for whom you provide over half of their support.

### EXAMPLE 5.2

Tanisha and her boyfriend, Sean, have been living together for several years. They have two children—Deon and Terrell, who live with them, and Tanisha pays for over half of their support. Sean got drafted to play professional football with the Washington Redskins. Unfortunately, Sean's football career was cut short after he tore his ACL during the first game of the season. Two years later, he's still trying to recuperate and work part time at a sports club to make ends meet. But Tanisha still provides over half of his support (i.e., she pays most of the bills, buys him clothes, pays for the food, etc.). They live in Tanisha's house that she purchased right after college.

Things have been a little better for Tanisha. She started a web-based business called How to Date a Playa Fo' Sho.' Through her company, Tanisha helps women all over the world find eligible athletes to date, and tells them how to weed out the losers and find the ones most likely to make the most money. She has been criticized by many media outlets as running a gold-digger service; but

Tanisha doesn't care, as all the controversy has her laughing all the way to the bank. She has over 100,000 subscribers paying $29.99 a year. In addition to Sean and her two children, Tanisha's friend Kiehsa also lives with them (for over 1 year now). Kiesha has fallen on hard times. She doesn't have a job and the baller that Tanisha picked for her, wound up being a big time loser. Kiesha never finished college. Tanisha agreed to let Kiesha live with her until she can get back on her feet. She also agreed to pay all of Kiesha's bills. Finally, Tanisha pays over half the support for her elderly parents, who live in their own house. Tanisha, Sean, Deon, Terrell, Kiesha and Tanisha's parents are all US citizens.

Because Tanisha provides more than half the support for Kiesha and Kiesha lived with her for the entire year, Tanisha can claim all of the medical expenses that she paid for Kiehsa. Next, Tanisha can claim the medical expenses that she paid for Deon and Terrell, as they are her children and she provides over half of their support. She can also claim any of Sean's medical expenses that she paid for on her tax return, since she provides half of his support and he lived with her for the entire year. Finally, Tanisha can claim any of the medical expenses that she paid for her parents. Although they don't live in her household, they are family members for whom she provided over half of their support.

### Pointer 2: Divorce and Separation

In cases of separation and divorce, it is important to make sure that you clearly detail who will handle various aspects of your child's life. This includes making sure that your financial arrangements and commitments are clearly spelled out. Make sure your separation agreement or divorce decree includes who will get to claim various deductions; such as, for your child's medical expenses. It's possible for a divorced parent to claim medical expenses paid for a child even if the other parent claims the child as a dependent. Consult your tax advisor for further details.

## DEDUCTIBLE MEDICAL EXPENSES

Secondly, you must focus on those expenses that are treated as true medical and dental expenses. The definition of what constitutes a medical expense is very broad and focuses on those expenses paid to diagnose, cure, mitigate, treat or prevent a physical disease or mental defect or illness. Examples of some common deductible medical expenses listed in *IRS Publication 502, Medical and Dental Expenses* are:

### Deductible medical expenses

- ambulance costs
- birth control pills
- child birth classes
- chiropractors
- contact lenses
- crutches
- dentist
- dentures
- doctor fees
- drug addiction treatment
- prescription drugs
- dyslexia (reading programs and tutors)
- eye examination and glasses
- guide dogs
- health insurance
- hearing aids
- hospital bills
- insulin
- laboratory fees
- long-term care insurance
- nursing home (if for medical treatment)
- optometrist
- osteopath
- physical therapy
- psychiatrist
- psychologist
- travel to medical clinics (auto, lodging, 50% of meals, etc.)
- vasectomy
- weight-loss program (if the expense is for a specific disease or medical condition)
- wheelchair

Medical expenses do not include things that are merely beneficial to your health. Over-the-counter drugs and other nonprescription drugs are not deductible as medical expenses. This is the case, even if your doctor prescribes nonprescription drugs such as Tylenol™, Advil™, aspirin, etc. Also, marijuana is not deductible, even if it's legally prescribed. Other examples of nondeductible medical expenses include: most cosmetic surgery, doctor prescribed travel for "rest", and expenses for the improvement of your general health such as a weight-loss food or health club fees.

## EXAMPLE 5.3

The Parker family, an average American family, had a particularly rough year. Daddy Parker ruptured a disc in his back in a 3-on-3 competition, and had to go to a physical therapist twice a week for 6 months. After watching the television show "The Swan," Momma Parker got her teeth whitened and had liposuction done on her thighs. Little Bebe Parker took dancing and swimming lessons because the family doctor suggested that this may help her coordination. Parker, Jr. had a real bad case of acne that was treated with an over-the-counter medication.

Daddy Parker's physical therapy is a medical expense. However, Momma Parker probably can't deduct the amount paid for the procedure to whiten her teeth or for the liposuction treatment (i.e., it was for cosmetic purposes and not to treat a medical condition). Also, the Parkers cannot include the amounts paid for dancing and swimming lessons for Little Bebe Parker, even though they were recommend by the family doctor. Finally, Bobo's medication is not a medical expense because it was not a prescribed medication

With America's preoccupation with weight, whether or not an expense is for a true medical condition or to improve your general health, will depend on all the facts and circumstances. As a general rule of thumb, if you're trying to lose weight for health and vanity reasons, you can forget about deducting these as medical expenses. So, unless you're like Whitney and you "will never be fat" (as told by Whitney Houston in her 2003 Barbara Walters interview), you're going to have to treat all those weight-loss aides (i.e., diet foods and drinks that meet your basic nutritional needs) as non-deductible. Also, health club or gym dues, nutritional supplements, over-the-counter products, diet foods and exercise equipment are typically not deductible as medical expenses.

If you have a legitimate medical condition that requires weight loss, your related medical expenses may be deductible. Medical conditions that generally qualify include: obesity, type 2 diabetes, hypertension, hypercholesterolemia, heart disease, or other conditions where a doctor recommends weight loss for your medical condition. The following costs are also deductible: bariatric surgery, FDA-approved weight-loss drugs, physician and hospital-based programs, behavioral counseling, and dietitians and nutritionists. In addition, costs for popular weight-loss programs, like Weight Watchers™ and Jenny Craig™, may also be deductible, if recommended by your doctor. Only the costs of the programs themselves are deductible, and not the costs for food or other products.

### EXAMPLE 5.4

Aisha was morbidly overweight. From January 2004 to May 2004 alone, she spent $3,500 on many weight loss aides; including: diet books, diet food and drinks. Nothing seemed to work. In July 2004, she decided to go see a doctor about her condition. The doctor told her she was suffering from the disease of obesity and advised her that she might be a great candidate for gastric bypass surgery to help reduce her weight. In October 2004, she had the surgery. As part of her treatment, she also joined a gym, a weight reduction class, and purchased diet food and beverages. All of this cost her $15,000 and was paid for by Aisha. It was not covered or paid for by her insurance company.

The gastric bypass surgery is probably deductible because Aisha was diagnosed by her doctor as suffering from the disease of obesity. The fees paid for membership in the weight reduction class would also be deductible, but the membership dues for the gym would probably not be deductible. Also, the cost of diet books, diet foods or drinks would not be deductible medical expenses.

### Pointer 3: Meals and Lodging

In calculating your total medical expenses, include all meals and lodging at a hospital, or similar place, where you or your dependent received medical care. For nursing homes, this includes lodging and meals, and for medical care only. It does not include any cost of being in the home that are personal in nature. Practically speaking, if your main reason for being in the nursing home is not to get medical care, then it's personal.

### Pointer 4: Transportation Costs

In calculating your total medical expenses, include all your transportation costs associated with getting the medical treatment. Transportation includes costs spent on buses, taxis, trains, airplanes, ambulance services, parking fees and tolls. It also includes transportation expenses of a nurse or other caregiver who travels to give you medical treatment. Finally, if you use your own car for purposes of getting medical treatment, you can treat your actual out-of-pocket expenses (i.e., gas or oil,) as medical expenses. You can't include depreciation, insurance, general repairs or maintenance. But, you can take a standard mileage rate of 15 cents per mile for all the miles you use your car for medical expenses.

## 7.5% OF ADJUSTED GROSS INCOME

You're almost there. The third and last thing you must focus on is that your unreimbursed medical expenses must amount to greater than 7.5% of your adjusted gross income. Remember, adjusted gross income is calculated by adding up all of your income and deducting your Above the Rim

Deductions (e.g., IRA deduction, student loan interest, self employment tax, or alimony). Moreover, you only get to deduct the medical expenses that are above the 7.5% threshold. The first 7.5% of unreimbursed medical expenses are simply disallowed as deductions. For more on adjusted gross income, see Chapter 1: Tax Basics.

### EXAMPLE 5.5

Kathy's adjusted gross income for 2005 will be about $100,000. So far in 2005, Kathy had surgery that cost her $8,000 in out-of-pocket medical expenses (it was not reimbursed by her insurance company). She can deduct her medical expenses that are greater than 7.5% of her AGI; which are those greater than $7,500. In this case her eligible medical expense deduction is $500 ($8,000 - $7,500).

**Pointer 5: Bunch Your Medical Expenses**
One way to help meet the 7.5% threshold is to "bunch" two years of medical expenses into one year. Using the Example 5.5 above, since Kathy's medical expenses have surpassed 7.5% of her AGI, she might want to consider doing other medical procedures before December 31, 2005 that won't be reimbursed by her insurance company (e.g., Lasik eye surgery).

**Pointer 6: Self-Employed Health Expenses**
Some health expenses may actually be treated as business expenses, thereby avoiding the 7.5% threshold. The health expenses must be necessary for you to satisfactorily perform your job (i.e., taking arthritis medicine so you can work). Also, you may be able to deduct up to 100% of your health insurance policy for you, your spouse and dependents. Depending on the facts, you may be able to deduct the cost of the policy as an Above the Rim Deduction on Form 1040, line 29 (see Chapter 1: Tax Basics for more on this), or as a medical expense on *Schedule A, Itemized Deductions (Form 1040)*.

# Taxes

Believe it or not, certain taxes that you pay can be deductible as itemized deductions. The following type of taxes may qualify:

- State & local income taxes
- Real estate property taxes
- Personal property taxes
- Payments to mandatory state funds
- Foreign income taxes

*For The Love OF Money* focuses on the first three taxes. Please see the Instructions for *Schedule A, Itemized Deductions (Form 1040)* for more on payments to mandatory state funds and *IRS Publication 514, Foreign Tax Credits for Individuals* for foreign income taxes.

## STATE & LOCAL INCOME TAXES

You may be able to deduct your state and local taxes. This deduction includes state or local income taxes that are withheld from your paycheck (typically shown on Box 17 and 19 of your *Form W-2, Wage and Tax Statement*) and any estimated state or local income tax payments that you make. But if you receive a refund for state or local taxes in the year after you have taken an itemized deduction for paying them, you may have to treat that refund as income. Why? Because you got a tax benefit in year 1 when you deducted the taxes, but in year 2, you actually got some of that money back. So, to make sure your deduction is only for the amount of state and local taxes that you actually paid, you must include the refund in your income.

### EXAMPLE 5.6

Monique lives and works in California. In 2004, she paid state income tax of $3,750. Also in early 2004, she received a $500 state income tax refund from her 2003 state tax return. She expects to receive a state income tax refund in the amount of $750 for 2004, in early 2005. Monique can deduct the entire state income taxes of $3,750 on her 2004 tax return. She doesn't need to reduce the $3,750 by the $750 she expects to receive in 2005 as a state tax refund. She can deal with the refund on her 2005 tax return. But, the $500 refund for her 2003 state taxes that she received in 2004 must be reported on her 2004 tax return as income.

**Pointer 7: Estimated Tax Payments**
To increase your itemized deduction for taxes, you should consider paying your state or local income taxes early. For example, to include them on your 2005 tax return, you can pay your January 2006 estimated tax payments in late 2005.

**Pointer 8: States without Income Taxes**
You can now elect to deduct state and local general "sales taxes" that you pay, instead of state and local "income" taxes, as an itemized deduction on *Schedule A, Itemized Deductions (Form 1040)*. But you cannot deduct both state income taxes and state sales taxes under this new law. You must choose. For people in states that don't have a state income tax (such as, Florida, Texas or Tennessee), this means you can finally deduct state taxes (meaning sales taxes) as an itemized deduction. If you are deducting your sales taxes, you can either use your actual amount of sales taxes (you should have records to support this amount), or use a tax table provided by the IRS that is designed to come up with an amount that you probably paid. For more on this, see *IRS Publication 600, Optional State Sales Tax Tables*.

## REAL ESTATE PROPERTY TAXES

Real estate property taxes may also qualify as itemized deductions. These taxes are based on the value of any real property that you own (e.g., your home or vacant land), and they are generally charged by your state or local property tax assessor's office. If you're renting a home, you don't own it; so, you cannot take this deduction. This is the case, even if your landlord increases your rent to take into account a higher property tax that he has to pay. The landlord may be able to deduct the increased real estate property tax, but you cannot. Also, homeowner association charges are typically not deductible as real property taxes because they are not based on the value of your real property, and they are not paid to a state or local authority.

Real estate property taxes do not include assessments made by the property tax office for local benefits and improvements that increase the value of your home (such as, assessments for streets, sidewalks, water mains, sewer lines, public parking facilities or similar improvements). Although you can't deduct these amounts when you pay them, they do increase the value and the "basis" of your home (See Chapter 4: Capital Gains for more on how to calculate basis).

You may receive other assessments from the property tax office to cover things, like: trash and garbage pickup, or police and fire protection. These may or may not be deductible. As a general rule of thumb, if everyone in your community is charged for this service at a similar rate and the money collected is used for general purposes by the property assessor, you can deduct your payments. If, instead, you pay the property assessor a fee for a service (i.e., $10 for 20 bags of trash), a periodic fee for an ongoing residential service (i.e., $30 per month for trash collection), or a fixed fee for a single service (i.e., $25 to mow your lawn), you cannot deduct these costs as real property taxes.

When you're purchasing or selling a home, it is important to divide the real estate property taxes for the property between the buyer and seller. This may not be that straightforward, because real estate property taxes are often paid in advance. As a general rule, the seller is treated as paying the real estate property taxes up to, but not including, the date of sale. The buyer is treated as paying the taxes beginning with the date of sale. Both the buyer and seller are considered to have paid their own share of the taxes, even if one or the other actually paid the entire amount.

Make sure you know the status of the real property tax payments before you buy your house. Why? Because if the seller has past due property tax debts and you pay them, you may not get this tax deduction. The seller gets the deduction, but, you can add your payment to your basis in the home. Also the seller must increase the sales price of the home. Note: Having a higher sales price, and hence a higher gain, may not be a big deal if the seller gets to use the entire capital gains exclusion (e.g., none of the gain is taxed because it's less than $250,000 for an individual, or $500,000 for a married couple). See Chapter 4: Capital Gains for more on basis, sales price and the capital gains exclusion.

## EXAMPLE 5.7

Renee won the 2003 Compton Idol (like America Idol, but for sistas who can sing west coast style). The first thing she did with her winnings, after going to Disney, was to buy that big house in the Hills (Beverly, that is). She closed on the house on July 1, 2004, just in time for her July 4$^{th}$ video shoot to promote her new song "Ghetto Fabulous Palace."

The 2004 property taxes for Renee's Ghetto Fabulous Palace were $25,000 and had actually been paid on November 1, 2003 by the Seller. Renee owned the property for 183 days in 2004 (July 1–December 31$^{st}$). Thus, her portion of the real estate taxes that can be taken on her tax return for 2004 is $12,500 (183 days divided by 366 day in 2004—because 2004 is a leap year—multiplied by $25,000).

### Pointer 9: Prepay Property Taxes
Consider prepaying your real estate property taxes to the taxing authority so they may be taken in a year when you need larger itemized deductions to offset income.

**Pointer 10: Finding Your Annual Property Taxes**

Real estate property taxes are typically paid to your mortgage lender, and are included in the amount of your monthly mortgage payment. Your mortgage lender should include the total amount that you pay each year on *Form 1098, Mortgage Interest Statement*. If you don't receive the information on Form 1098, or you pay your real estate property taxes directly to the taxing authority, you may contact your local property assessor's office for this information.

**Pointer 11: Home Office Expense Deduction**

If you have a side business and you are claiming a home office expense deduction, remember, the business portion of your real estate property taxes must be taken on *Form 8829, Expenses for Business Use of Your Home* and not on *Schedule A, Itemized Deductions (Form 1040)*.

## PERSONAL PROPERTY TAXES

Personal property taxes are deductible if they are based on the value of your personal property and are charged on a yearly basis.

Take a look at some of the popular music videos and you will notice that cars are extremely important to our culture; not to mention how many songs focus on cars, like:

- "Little Red Corvette," (Prince, 1983)
- "You Remind Me Of Something" (his jeep), (R. Kelley, 1995)
- "Jeeps, Lex, Coup, Bimaz and the Benz," (Lost Boyz, 1995)
- "Freeway of Love (in a pink Cadillac)," (Aretha Franklin, 1983)

It's no wonder that the most common personal property tax is known, in many states, as the "car tax" or the "vehicle registration tax." This is a tax that you pay annually, typically based on the value of your car.; the more expensive the car, the higher the car tax. But in some states, it's also based on some other value (like the weight of your car). You can only deduct the car tax amount if it is based on the value of your car. If your state's car tax is based on weight, you cannot deduct the tax. If it's based on value and weight, you must pro rate the tax and only take the amount based on value.

## Interest Expenses

Interest is an amount you pay for the use of borrowed money. Everyone has paid "interest" at some point in their life. For example, remember the time you borrowed the Beat Street, Breakin' 1 and 2, or the Krush Groove VHS from your friend, and he would only lend it if you promised to return it in one week, along with a pack of Now & Later candy and your promise to teach him your smooth Ozone and Turbo breakin' moves. And then there was the time you borrowed your friend's car; you know the friend who always drove around on empty but made sure you brought the car back with a full tank of gas. In fact, if it weren't for "interest," the neighborhood loan shark would be out of business. Put simply, interest is a part of everyday life.

Only certain types of interest are deductible as itemized deductions (namely, home mortgage interest and investment interest). There is no deduction for personal interest (e.g., interest on personal car loans, or credit cards). Also, trade or business interest that you have from your side business is deductible, but not as an itemized deductions on *Schedule A, Itemized Deductions (Form 1040)*. Instead treat such expenses as deductions on *Schedule C, Profit or Loss from Business (Form 1040* for a sole proprietor, *Schedule K-1, US Return of Partnership Income (Form 1065)* for partnerships and LLCs, or *Schedule K-1, US Income Tax Return for an S Corporation (Form 1120S)* for S Corporations. Finally, interest you pay on your student loans may be deductible as above-the-line deductions for computing your adjusted gross income. For more on student loan interest, please see Chapter 1: Tax Basics.

## HOME MORTGAGE INTEREST

"A House Is Not A Home," (Luther Vandross, 1981); but if you own a house, you will most likely be able to take itemized deductions. Most folks are able to deduct 100% of the mortgage interest that they pay on the loans covering their homes. The loan may be for a primary residence or a second home. It also may be for a second mortgage, a line of credit or a home equity loan.

For most people, mortgage interest is not only their largest deduction, but it is also the reason why they can take itemized deductions. A taxpayer paying a full year of mortgage interest typically pays more than the standard deduction (i.e., married folks use $10,000 and single taxpayers use $5,000). This is particularly true during the early years of a typical mortgage loan, because you pay more interest up-front. But, as the monthly interest component of your mortgage payments decreases over the course of your loan, you may have less mortgage interest to deduct in later years.

Unlike most things in the tax laws, there's not much of a catch to this general deduction. First, you must simply be liable for repayment of the loan, and the collateral for the loan must be your home. So, if someone asks you to pay their "Bills, Bills, Bills" (Destiny's Child, 1999), and you are nice enough to pay their house note (i.e., they legally own the house and you don't), you will not be able to deduct the payment on your tax return. At best you have made a loan (i.e., you have a written promissory note as proof). Otherwise what you have done is called a "gift." For more on this, see Question 15 in Chapter 10.

Secondly, the loan must be for a home. The IRS defines a home as a house, condominium, cooperative, mobile home, boat, recreational vehicle, or any property that has sleeping, cooking and toilet facilities.

Finally, you can only deduct up to $1 million of mortgage interest for both your primary residence and one other residence. Also, you can only take a maximum of $100,000 of mortgage interest for any home equity loans. If you find yourself reaching these limits, you are definitely in "big baller, shoot caller" status and you will need to talk with a tax advisor. See the For The Love Of Money Signs You Need Tax Help in the Appendix. Below, get the lowdown on certain special situations that can impact your home mortgage interest deduction (such as, points, second home, vacation home and rental property).

### Pointer 12: Form 1098

You should receive *Form 1098, Mortgage Interest Statement* from your mortgage lender by the end of January. This statement will show your total mortgage interest paid during the year, and if you purchased a home, the points and any real estate property taxes paid (see the discussion below for more on points). Note: If you don't receive a Form 1098 (i.e., because you have loan from the previous owner of the home), you can still deduct the interest that you paid. Be sure to include the lender's name, address and Social Security number on line 11 of *Schedule A, Itemized Deductions (Form 1040)*.

### Pointer 13: Prepayments and Late Charges

You can deduct any prepayments that you make on your loan (including prepayment penalties). You might consider prepaying your next January's mortgage payment in December to get an extra month's interest deduction in the current year. For example, if $500 of your monthly mortgage payment is for interest, by paying your January 2006 payment by December 31, 2005, you will have an additional $500 of mortgage interest that you can deduct on your 2005 tax return. Also, you can generally deduct late fees too.

### Pointer 14: Home Office Expense Deduction

If you have a side business and you are claiming a home office expense deduction, remember, the business portion of your home mortgage interest must be taken on *Form 8829, Expenses for Business Use of Your Home* and not on *Schedule A, Itemized Deductions (Form 1040)*.

## POINTS

You can't even apply for a house loan without discussing how many points you want to pay. Points are the charges, or fees, you pay when you close on your house. Points may also be called discount points, loan discounts, loan origination or placement fees, or maximum loan charges. Points do not include any payments you make for the following: settlement fees, appraisal fees, credit reports, notary fees, recording fees for the mortgage note or deed of trust, mortgage insurance premiums or VA funding fees. These expenses are not deductible; but they may increase your basis in the home and thus decrease your potential capital gain when you sell it.

Why pay points? They allow you to get a lower interest rate on your home loan. Points are really nothing more than prepaid interest on debt secured by your home. They are generally deductible in full in the year you pay them (See *IRS Publication 530, Tax Information for First Time-Homeowner*), including the IRS nine-point test). If you can't itemize (i.e., because your standard deduction is greater than your total itemized expenses), all is not lost. You can choose to spread out the deduction for the points over the life of the loan. Finally, points you pay on loans secured by a second home cannot be fully deducted in the year paid. These points can only be deducted over the life of the loan.

### EXAMPLE 5.8

In 2004, Bubble-licious (real name Tatiana Jones), the latest teen pop star, has a great year. Her CD ("You Can't Pop My Bubble") went double platinum, she signed on as spokesperson for a national bubble gum company, and her TV pilot "Bubble Fun" just got picked up by a major network. Although Bubble (as her friends call her) appears young on her videos and plays a 15 year old on her show, she's actually 20 years old. She decided it was time to act like an adult and on December 1, 2004, she bought her first home. It was actually a condo in Santa Monica, because she loves the beach and she got it at a steal—$300,000 and a 15-year mortgage. Bubble had seen many child stars make bad financial decisions, so she decided she would educate herself. After all, she won't be able to play a teenager forever. She bought a copy of *For The Love Of Money* and learned that she could lower her interest rate and get a tax deduction by paying points on her loan. She decided to pay 3 points, for a total of $3,000. Assuming the IRS 9-point test is met, Bubble should be able to deduct the entire $3,000 on her 2004 return.

**EXAMPLE 5.9**

Pop-a-licious (real name Stephanie Winters), the arch rival to Bubble-licious in example 5.8, also did quite well in 2004. Popa (as she liked to be called) also had a successful CD ("Pop is better than Bubble") and is a spokesperson for several major soda companies. She is a little older than Bubble (Popa is 21) and had already purchased a home in Malibu a few years ago. For her 21$^{st}$ birthday, in 2004, she bought a second home, a $300,000 condo in New York (because a pop star must at least be bi-costal). Popa heard that Bubble paid points on her home. Not to be outdone, Popa bought *For The Love Of Money* to get the low down on points. Armed with this knowledge, Popa decided to only pay 1 point, or $1,000, on her 15-year loan. She got an interest rate that she could live with and remembered that, because this is her second home, she could not deduct the entire $1,000 on her 2004 tax return. Instead she can deduct 1/15 of the $1,000 or $66.67 a year for 15 years.

In addition, you may be able to deduct points that you don't actually pay. If the seller pays for the borrower's points, the borrower, and not the seller, is treated as having paid the points. This is often called "loan placement fees" and the seller typically pays this to help the buyer get the loan. The buyer gets to deduct these points as mortgage interest, but she also must reduce her basis, or cost in the house, by the amount of the deduction. The seller can deduct these points from the sales price of the house, however, when computing his capital gain or loss (See Chapter 4: Capital Gains for more on calculating basis and sales price.)

### EXAMPLE 5.10

Lil' Mo bought his first home in 2002 for $150,000. When he purchased the home, he was a little short on cash. The seller, his uncle, Big Mo, offered to pay the 2 points ($2,000) required by the mortgage lender, All In The Family Home Loan Bank, for his favorite nephew. In late January 2003, Lil' Mo received his first Form 1098 that showed points paid in the amount of $2,000. Assume Lil' Mo's itemized deduction is greater than his standard deduction. Lil' Mo will be able to deduct the points on his 2004 tax return, even though Big Mo actually paid the points. Lil' Mo must reduce his basis in the house by the $2,000 (i.e., it's $148,000 or $150,000 minus $2,000), and this new basis will be used to calculate any gain or loss when he sells the house.

### Pointer 15: Form 1098 and Points

If you purchased or refinanced your home in 2005, your mortgage interest statement, *Form 1098, Mortgage Interest Statement,* should show the amount of points you paid for the loan. If the points are not shown, contact your lender.

## REFINANCING & HOME EQUITY LOANS

"Refinance your home." "Get rid of that high interest." "Get money out of your home." All are common phrases from commercials you'll hear if you watch just 10 minutes of daytime TV. In the past few years, many homeowners have taken advantage of these home equity or home improvement loans. Some people have done this to reduce their monthly mortgage payment. Others have done so to take out cold hard cash (i.e., money, moohlah, dinero). The list of reasons why are endless; from the understandable (to pay off credit cards, consolidate debts, pay college tuition, make investments, or to make home improvements), to the financially-questionable (to fund new designer clothes, a new sports car, or a worldwind cruise).

You need to know that what you spend the money on will significantly determine if you can deduct as mortgage interest and points, and by how much. The good news is that, at least with respect to mortgage interest, you should generally be able to deduct all of the interest from a refinanced loan. The semi-bad news is that the amount of your interest deduction will probably decrease since, thanks to your refinancing, you are paying a lower interest rate. I call this semi-bad news because you may be increasing your cash flow situation, and you need to do this, even with a smaller tax deduction. Before refinancing, you should run the various scenarios with your tax advisor.

There's also good news for the points you pay in refinancing your loan using a "home improvement loan." You can generally fully deduct points paid on a loan to improve your main home, (that is if tests (1) through (6) under the IRS 9-Point Test are meet, See *IRS Publication 530, Tax Information for First Time-Homeowner*). Why? Because home improvements typically add value to your home, and include such things as new heating and air conditioning system, wiring upgrades, bathroom and kitchen modernizations. But home improvement does not include repairs which are done as upkeep to your home (such as repainting your home inside or outside, fixing broken windows or fixing faucet leaks.

The story is a bit different for points you pay to refinance your loan using a "home equity loan." Typically, with home equity loans, you can use the funds on anything (i.e., to consolidate debts, pay for college, etc.) except home improvements. The points that you pay must generally be spread out and deducted over the life of the loan.

Of course, many people will use the money for both reasons (i.e., home improvements and home equity). In these cases, you will have to pro-rate between the amount attributable to home improvements and the amount for other purposes.

## EXAMPLE 5.11

The facts are the same in Example 5.10. Two years after the purchase of his first and primary home, Lil' Mo's home has doubled in value. Lil' Mo decides that it is time to increase his real estate portfolio. In 2004, he refinanced his house with Familyless Bank to both reduce his mortgage payment and to take some of the equity out to purchase a second home in South Beach (Miami). To get a favorable interest rate on the new 10-year loan, Lil' Mo had to pay 5 points ($5,000).

Because Lil' Mo did not use the money to improve his primary home, he cannot deduct all the points on his 2004 tax return. Instead, he must deduct the 5 points ratably over the life of the loan (i.e., $500 a year or $5,000/10 years).

## EXAMPLE 5.12

Billy D. had credit card debt of $20,000, and an outstanding car loan of $5,000. In 2004, Billy D. refinanced his mortgage and took out $100,000 cash (equity). He used $25,000 to pay off his credit cards and car loan, and the remaining $65,000 to extensively remodel his house (e.g., he remodeled the kitchen and bathrooms, added a home theatre, and a pool). His new loan has a 15-year term. To get the loan, Billy D. paid 2 points ($2,000); that was for prepaid interest.

> In 2004, Billy D. can deduct 65% ($65,000/$100,000) of the points ($2,000). His deduction is thus $1,300. Billy D. will have to deduct the ratable part of the remaining $700 ($2,000 - $1,300) over the life of the loan (i.e., the next 14 tax returns).

Even though you don't get to deduct all of the points in the year you pay them, you still get to take a recurring deduction for the points paid on home equity loans. This deduction can turn what is, in essence, personal interest (such as credit card interest) and non-deductible interest, into deductible mortgage interest. As shown in example 5.12 above, Billy D. used some of the money to pay off credit cards and a car loan. This was interest that Billy D. was paying that wasn't deductible. Now that Billy D. took out the home equity loan, those amounts have been rolled into his new interest amount. He can deduct these, along with the points, over the life of the loan. This strategy can be a "win-win" situation, since it allows you to possibly refinance other debt that may be at a higher interest rate (such as credit card debt). It also allows you to receive a tax benefit, by deducting the interest on the loan; which, in effect, lets the government pick up part of the tab on the loan repayment. Finally, it allows you to remain in your current home which you may feel you would have to otherwise sell to cash out.

If you sell your house or refinance your mortgage again before you finished deducting these points (either from your original loan or a refinanced loan), all is still not lost. At the time of your sale or refinance, you can typically deduct, in full, the remaining points that you were patiently deducting over the life of your mortgage. There's one exception to this rule. If you are refinancing with the same bank or lender, you can't take this deduction. Instead you must re-spread the points out over the life of your new loan, and thus start to patiently deduct the points again over 20, 30, 40 years, etc.

### Pointer 16: Home Improvement Loans

These are loans used to make material improvements to your home (e.g., new roof, remodel bathroom, pave driveway as opposed to making a repair (e.g., repainting the inside or outside of the home). Remember, if the improvement materially adds to the value of your home, considerably prolongs its useful life, or adapts it to new uses, you must add the cost of any improvements to the basis of your home. Also, keep in mind that you can deduct up to $1,000,000 of points and interest from both your original loan and the home improvement loan.

### Pointer 17: Home Equity Loans

Home equity loans allow you to leverage the equity in your home (i.e., pull cash out of your home). Cashing out some of the gains from your main home can be a great tax strategy if you're using the proceeds to pay off other debt on which the interest is not deductible. Keep in mind that you can only deduct up to $100,000 of combined mortgage interest and points for home equity loans. You cannot deduct interest on the home equity loan where the loan itself, plus the original mortgage, are greater than the fair market value of the house. For more information, check out *IRS Publication 936, Home Mortgage Interest Deduction*.

## SECOND HOME

As more and more baby boomers are retiring, many have paid off their primary home mortgage and are buying second homes. Thank goodness the interest you pay on a loan for a second home, or in some cases a vacation home, is also deductible. But, this deduction is only good up to the "Second Time Around" (Shalamar, 1979). If you own, three, four or five homes, you will not get an itemized deduction for the interest you pay on them. If you find yourself in this situation, you may want to consider turning some of those homes into rental property. At the very least you should definitely get help from a tax advisor.

A second home can include anything from a traditional three-story house to a trailer home, or even a boat. Keep in mind, the IRS defines a home as a house, condominium, cottage, cabin, cooperative, mobile home, boat, recreational vehicle, a timeshare, or any property that has sleeping, cooking and toilet facilities.

A second home is also a home that you significantly use yourself; it's not a rental property. You must use the home for either more than 14 days in a given year, or for more than 10% of the total days that you rent the house to others at a fair rental price. Otherwise, your home will not qualify as a second home.

**Pointer 18: Vacation Homes and Time Shares**
Vacation homes can qualify as second homes. They meet all the requirements of a home which is essentially any property that has sleeping, cooking and toilet facilities. A time share can also be treated as a second home, if it meets all the same requirements as a home.

### RENTAL REAL ESTATE

Mortgage interest you pay for your rental real estate is not taken as an itemized deduction. Rental activities are treated as passive trade or business activities. You must report all of your income and deductions from this on *Schedule E, Supplemental Income and Loss (Form 1040)*. Note: A vacation home, or other home that doesn't qualify as a second home above, is treated like rental real estate. For more on handling your income and expenses from rental real estate, see Chapter 2: Side Business Part I.

### INVESTMENT INTEREST

Investment interest is an itemized deduction that's easy to miss. It's the interest you pay on money borrowed to acquire an investment (like stocks, bonds and annuities). This interest may be tax deductible as an itemized deduction, but the amount of the deduction is limited to your "net investment income." As these rules are complicated, please consult your tax advisor. Also, see *IRS Publication 550, Interest Income and Expenses* for further details.

## TRADE OR BUSINESS INTEREST

As discussed above in this Chapter, trade or business interest is interest that you incur in connection with your side business (i.e., as a sole proprietor, partnership, corporation, or limited liability company). This interest might be incurred, for example, on a bank loan used to purchase supplies and goods to expand your business, and is typically tax-deductible against your business income. However, this interest is not deductible as an itemized deduction on Schedule A. The form you use to take this deduction will depend on the business form for your side entity.

- *Schedule C, Profit or Loss from Business (Form 1040)*—Sole Proprietorship
- *Schedule K-1, US Return of Partnership Income (Form 1065)*— Partnerships and Limited Liability Company,
- *Schedule K-1, US Income Tax Return for an S Corporation (Form 1120S)*— S Corporation
- *Form 1120 US Corporate Income Tax Return*—For C Corporation

## STUDENT LOAN INTEREST

Interest you pay on your student loans (or for your spouse or dependents) may be eligible for a tax deduction. To qualify, your AGI (adjusted gross income) must be less than $65,000 for single folks or $135,000 for married taxpayers filing jointly. The student loan interest deduction can reduce the amount of your income subject to tax by up to $2,500. Because this deduction is taken as an adjustment to income ("Above the Rim Deduction"), it's available even to taxpayers who don't itemize. See *IRS Publication 970, Tax Benefits for Education* for further details, or contact your tax advisor. Also, see the discussion in Chapter 1: Tax Basics.

**PERSONAL INTEREST**

"All Falls Down," by Kanye West (2004), may very well be the anthem for personal interest and why you get no tax benefit from it. The song describes a woman who is so "self-conscious" and caught up in the material trappings of life that she was a sophomore in college for three years majoring in an area in which you can't even get a job (i.e., basket weaving), and not able to afford a car (so she names her daughter Alexis-get it, "a lexus"). He calls her a "single black female, addicted to retail."

Personal interest is not deductible. So, all the interest you pay on your credit cards, monthly car payment, or late fees on utility and cell phone bills, are simply not deductible. True, it's a big outlay for many people, but it's not the type of expense that the tax laws encourage. Instead, they focus on things like home ownership; which is one reason why mortgage interest expenses are an important deduction.

It may be nice to have the latest clothing and the newest car, but to have all this before you even have a house? Again, just listen to the lyrics of Kanye West in "All Falls Down," when he apparently talks about himself going to Jacobson's (a Midwest department store), and spending $25,000 before he even had a house. The bottom line is, if you want to be financially savvy and save as much as you can on taxes, you must seriously take a look at the amount of your personal interest, and work with your tax advisor to keep this in check.

### Pointer 19: Refinance Your Home

As stated earlier in this Chapter, there is no deduction for personal interest. But you can refinance your home with a home equity loan and use the proceeds to pay off car loans and credit card balances; thus, turning this non-deductible interest into deductible mortgage interest. While this may be a good idea, there is some risk. For instance, using your home's equity could turn a normal five-year car loan into a 15 or 30-year home loan. Also, if you default on your loan payments, instead of only losing your car, you could lose your home.

## REMIX

Here's the remix on what we learned in the Chapter:

1. Unreimbursed medical expenses that exceed 7.5% of your adjusted gross income for you, your spouse or any dependents are deductible as itemized deductions.

2. If you're close to the 7.5% threshold, consider accelerating some of your elective medical procedures (i.e., eye exams, new glasses, etc.) to "bunch" your medical expenses, and thereby surpass the 7.5% threshold.

3. Remember, you can deduct state & local income taxes, real estate property taxes, and personal property taxes.

4. If you are in a state that does not have a state income tax, you can now elect to deduct sales tax that you have paid to your state as an itemized deduction.

5. Consider prepaying your real estate property taxes for next year to increase the amount you can deduct in the current year.

6. Your biggest deduction will probably be for mortgage interest. This can include interest from a first mortgage, as second mortgage, a home equity loan, and home refinance loans on up to two homes.

7. Points paid to get a loan are not always deductible in full in the year paid.

8. When you refinance your home, you can still deduct the mortgage interest.

9. The points you pay on a refinanced loan will depend on how you use the loan proceeds. If you use the proceeds to make home improvements, those points are fully deductible. If instead, you use the proceeds for any other reason (such as to pay off credit cards or for debt consolidation) you may have to deduct those points over the life of the loan.

**Chapter 6**

# Itemized Deduction Part II
*Itemize Your Life—The Remix*

> *Shower me with your love*
> *Shower me with the love that I long for*
> *Shower me with your love*
> *Shower me with the love I've been waiting for*
>
> "Shower me with Your Love," Surface (1989)

---

The party's not over (aka, "Teddy's Jam," by Guy, 1988)! It's time to shower you with more special deductions. This next group of itemized deductions is the more benevolent, good Samaritan, helping-thy-neighbor and feel-good type of deductions. This is why I picked Surface's "Shower Me With Your Love" as the most appropriate song to get you in the mood. Get the 411 on:

- Charitable Contributions
- Casualty Theft and Losses
- Miscellaneous deductions

For you high rollers who make more than $72,975 if single or $145,950 for married folks filing jointly, the actual amount you can take as your total itemized deductions may be limited. So get the 411 on the itemized deduction phase out. Also, even the not-so-high-rollers may have some of their itemized deductions disallowed because of alternative minimum tax issues. For more on this later point, please see Chapter 7: Alternative Minimum Tax.

## Charitable Contributions

Whether you tithe, like LL Cool J proclaims in his smash 2003 hit Paradise ("10% goes to God first"), volunteer with your local soup kitchen, play in that annual charity golf tournament, or just make donations to your local non-profit, the charitable contribution deduction is a very important itemized deduction. Everyone knows that donating money or property to your favorite nonprofit can help reduce your tax bill; but, of course, there are several rules you need to know in figuring out the actual amount you can deduct. Get the 411 on:

- ➢ 501(c)(3) organizations
- ➢ Volunteer Expenses
- ➢ Property Donations
- ➢ Charitable Contributions
- ➢ Receipts
- ➢ Business Deductions

### 501(C)(3)

If you don't remember any terms, in this book, at least remember this one—501(c)(3). The organization you donate your money to must be a "501(c)(3)" organization for you to get a charitable contribution deduction; not a 501(3)(c), or a 501(c), or a 501 something else. As you've probably guessed, 501(c)(3) is the specific section of the tax code where it discusses the type of organizations to which you may donate money to receive the special charitable contribution.

Other names you may hear for 501(c)(3) organizations are charity, public charity or charitable organization. You see these organizations in every community across the U.S. What they have in common is that they are organized (i.e., created) and operated for charitable purposes.

The term, "non-profit or tax-exempt," does not mean that the organization is a 501(c)(3) organization. Non-profit means the organization is set-up under a specific state law or statute to do and focus on certain areas (such as, social, fraternal, charitable, or business association-type activities). Tax-exempt means the organization does not pay income taxes to the IRS or a state taxing authority—like your local chamber of commerce. But a 501(c)(3) organization is a nonprofit, tax-exempt organization that also allows you to deduct your donations (sometimes called dues) as charitable contributions. If the organization doesn't qualify under 501(c)(3), you can't take charitable contribution deductions for your payments or dues. See Pointer 3 below for tips on how to determine if the organization is a 501(c)(3) charity.

As an example, most fraternities and sororities are tax-exempt organizations (meaning they don't pay state or federal income taxes) as social clubs under 501(c)(7). They are organized and operate more for social purposes. This is why your membership fees and other contributions made to these social clubs are not deductible as charitable contributions. However, many of these organizations set up sister-organizations as charities that focus solely on charitable activities. In the case of fraternities and sororities, these sister organizations are typically set up to further educational purposes (like scholarships). The sister organization does not focus on non-educational activities, like social parties or building a fraternity house. Thus, any contributions you make to the sister organization can be deducted as charitable contributions.

## EXAMPLE 6.1

Alpha Una Alpha, is a sorority, formed to celebrate the bond and camaraderie between college women around the world. Over the years, AUA has developed numerous programs and its members have donated thousands of hours to community service. Members of AUA have supported all of these activities, through blood, sweat, tears and, of course, money. But as AUA is a social organization, its members cannot deduct their membership payments or other fees as charitable contributions.

Tiffany is the new energetic President of AUA's Los Angeles Chapter. She just finished reading *For The Love Of Money* and has a number of new ideas. Her Chapter holds an annual luncheon to raise scholarships for poor high school students. Tiffany wants to do much with this program. An educator by profession, she wants to establish a year-long education program whereby AUA members tutor elementary school kids, serve as mentors and big sisters to middle school and high school kids, conduct SAT Prep, sponsor a "Take a Sista to Work" day where high school students go to work with AUA members to learn about their professions, and help high school students find after-school jobs under her "Hook a Sista Up" program.

If Tiffany and her LA Chapter set up another organization (a sister organization) as an educational/charitable organization under 501(c)(3), all of the contributions made to that organization (including some of the costs related to the annual luncheon, now put on by the new organization) can qualify as charitable contribution deductions. This 501(c)(3) could take on many of the activities in the educational program; which in turn would allow the members to deduct donations they make to these programs (and even certain out-of-pocket costs, and mileage to travel to and from the educational programs).

### Pointer 1: Set up a Charity

There are many great resources on how to set up a charity. The IRS has a lot of information on charities on their website (see http://www.irs.gov). Also, see the Tax Exempt Toolkit program chaired by Shannon Nash (published by the American Bar Association Tax Section) for tips with starting and operating a nonprofit—http://www.abanet.org/tax/pubs/tetk.html.

### Pointer 2: Business Deduction

Although your contribution may not qualify as a charitable contribution, it may be a bona fide business deduction. Obviously, you must have a business in order to take this deduction (hobbies don't count). For more on various business deductions, see Chapter 3: Side Business Part II. Also, see the discussion below in this Chapter on the Business Deduction.

### Pointer 3: A True Charity

Ever wonder if your neighborhood charity is really a true 501(c)(3), or even a charity, for that matter? Does "Help Lil' Ray Go to School" sound a little suspect to you? Never fear, this time it's the IRS to the rescue. The IRS maintains a searchable list of all 501(c)(3)s on their website (http://www.irs.gov, see IRS *Publication 78, Cumulative List of Organizations*). Also, check out Guidestar's website for tax information on 501(c)(3)s; including, revenues and expenses, down to how much the executive director makes (http://www.guidestar.org).

#### VOLUNTEER EXPENSES

Do you volunteer with your local church, soup kitchen, or non-profit? In addition to serving your community and being a role model, your good deeds may also bring you some tax benefits. Your out-of-pocket expenses, in connection with your volunteer activities, including your mileage to and from charitable events and meetings, may be deductible.

#### OUT-OF-POCKET EXPENSES

Your out-of-pocket expenses incurred while performing services for a 501(c)(3) organization may qualify as deductible charitable contributions. Common out-of-pocket expenses will include travel, transportation, meals (only when you away from your home overnight) and lodging. Out-of-pocket expenses can also include many things as long as they are truly related to your service for the organization. For example, if you volunteer at a hospital, where they require you to wear a certain uniform (i.e., a candy striper uniform), the cost of the uniform should qualify as an out-of-pocket expense.

Costs related to the use of your personal car may also be deducted, either by using the actual out-of-pocket expenses (such as gas and oil), or the standard mileage deduction (calculated at 15 cents per mile). Costs for parking fees, and tools may also be deducted under either method. Other costs for your car (such as, general repair and maintenance, depreciation, registration fees or insurance), are not deductible. Finally, out-of-pocket expenses also don't include the value of your time or services.

### EXAMPLE 6.2

Uncle Bill was a high flying entertainment lawyer in Malibu. His nephew, Little Willy (aka, The Hot Prince of Pacific Palisades), was always busy getting in trouble. To straighten Little Willy out, Uncle Bill made him volunteer in a soup kitchen for the homeless—The Get Low Soup Kitchen. It didn't take long for the people at the soup kitchen to fall in love with Little Willy. He even formed a rap group with some of the homeless—called Homeless Homeboys. Uncle Bill was so impressed, that he decided to volunteer for the Get Low Soup Kitchen.

The Homeless Homeboys finished a demo tape and want to donate a significant portion of any proceeds from their music to the Get Low Soup Kitchen. The President of the Get Low Soup Kitchen, D.J. Salsa Sal, wants Uncle Bill to draft all of the contracts between the Get Low Soup Kitchen and the Homeless Homeboys now, before they blow up and forget where they came from. Uncle Bill was happy to do so and didn't even charge for his legal services. Assume Uncle Bill would usually charge a client $10,000 for similar agreements. Although Uncle Bill is donating something of value (namely his time) he cannot take a charitable contribution.

## MILEAGE

As mentioned above, the standard mileage rate in connection with volunteer activities is 15 cents per mile. This includes mileage to and from events in which you volunteer for a 501(c)(3) organization.

### EXAMPLE 6.3

Kathy Smith (known as, the "Sanctified Lady") is the type of person that you can count on for anything. She sings in her church choir, teaches Sunday school, serves meals to the homeless during the holidays, mentors young women—and, that's just on Sunday. She participates in at least one walk-a-thon per month. She also serves as a board member of three 501(c)(3)s, and is an officer for one of the organizations.

Kathy racked up 4,750 miles in 2005 going to various board meetings, church activities and charitable events. She should be able to include $712.5 (.15 x 4,750) of mileage expenses in calculating her total charitable contribution deduction.

To claim your out-of-pocket expenses and mileage expenses, you must keep good records to prove or substantiate your deduction. In fact, if any one expense is more than $250, you must get a written receipt, with specific IRS language, from the organization to take this deduction. Note: You don't have to include these receipts when you file your tax return, but you will be asked to provide them if you are audited. Also, you're generally required to keep these records for 3 years. For more on this, including the IRS specific language, see *IRS Publication 1771, Charitable Contributions—Substantiation and Disclosure Requirements.*

### Pointer 4: Keep Good Records

You should keep a file for your out-of-pocket receipts and expenses. Also, try to use one credit card for all of your out-of pocket volunteer expenses. If that credit card provides expense summaries, all your costs will be documented by the card statements. Finally, you will need to track your volunteer miles. Whether you use the low-tech way (i.e., a pen and paper) or the high-tech way (a computer spreadsheet), come up with a system.

## PROPERTY DONATIONS

You can also deduct your donations of non-cash items made to a 501(c)(3) organization; such as, clothes, appliances, household goods, toys, or furniture. You can only deduct the fair market value of the items, not what you originally paid for them.

With the dot.com craze, in recent years, organizations have seen an increase in donations of stock. Contributions of stock enjoy favored treatment in that your deduction is based on the fair market value of the stock and not your basis (i.e., the amount you paid for the stock). So, if the stock has gone up in value, you may be able to deduct the fair market value of the stock without recognizing any capital gains. (For more on capital gains, see Chapter 4: Capital Gains).

In recent years, car donations have also become very popular. But beware: The IRS was so concerned about people taking large charitable contributions for cars that were basically worthless (sort of like those in Fred Sanford's junk yard) that the tax laws were changed to force more accurate valuations of car donations. Generally, you can find this dollar amount in any of the popular used car guides. But beware. If you take the highest value listed in the guide, be prepared to support it. Also, if your car needs major repairs, it will be difficult to prove that it is worth the highest fair market value listed in the used car guide.

But starting on January 1, 2005, if you donate a car to a charity, and the value of the car is more than $500, your deduction depends on what happens to the car after the charity gets it. If the charity sells the car without making any improvements or changes to it (i.e., they don't "pimp your ride"), your deduction is what the charity gets for your car (i.e., the gross sales proceeds). If the car is altered or improved by the charity (i.e., they turn your "hooptie" into a "whooptie woo"), your deduction is the new fair market value of the car. Also, you must get a receipt or thank you letter from the charity, and attach it to your tax return. For more on car donations, see *IRS Publication 4302, A Charity's Guide to Car Donations* and *IRS Publication 4303, A Donor's Guide to Car Donations.*

### EXAMPLE 6.4

Twaun (no last name), owns a successful beauty shop "T's Beautiful, Big and Bold Hair Salon." He has always been very charitable with his time and his money: He mentors kids, tithes every Sunday at church, and even sends 10 cents a day to feed a starving child in a 3rd world country. But this year he wants to do more. He got a flyer in the mail from a local charity that stated in big bold letters "DONATE YOUR CAR NOW."

As luck would have it, Twaun still had his first car from college, a 1988 Ford Escort. (4 door, manual, hatchback, with AM/FM radio cassette). Although he doesn't drive the car much, since he became a successful business owner and upgraded to a Cadillac Escalade, he's proud to say that his Escort still runs and is in mint condition; it only has 90,000 miles on it. However, there is a small scratch on the passenger side door. Assuming he determines, using several blue book used car guides, that his car's fair market value is $1,000, on the low side, and $1,275, on the high side. Twaun should talk to his tax advisor to help determine the best amount for his deduction. Given that his car has some blemishes, the amount will probably be less than $1,275. Twaun will also need to figure out what the charity is going to do with the car before determining the final amount of his deduction.

### Pointer 5: Real Fair Market Value

The Salvation Army has a value guide for donated items at http://www.satruck.com/Index.asp. You may be surprised at how little your used items are worth. Keep in mind this is only one source for valuing your used items and many tax preparation software programs provide valuation guides that can result in much higher values. If you are giving away your $500 Burberry purse (because it is so last season), the fair market value is probably significantly higher than the $20 value listed on the Salvation Army's website. For truly expensive item, try searching eBay or a similar website. Print out a copy of your search and include that in your tax file as proof that your one-year old Burberry purse is worth more than $20.

### Pointer 6: Form 8283

Complete *Form 8283, Non-Cash Charitable Contributions*, for all non-cash donations over $500 and attach it your tax return. Fill out Section A of Form 8283 for non-cash contributions less than $5,000. For non-cash contributions over $5,000, fill out Section B of Form 8283 and don't forget to have the organization sign the form. You also may have to get a written appraisal for the value of the property being donated. If the organization sells, or otherwise disposes, of the property you donated within 2 years after the date of receipt of your contribution, the organization must then file *Form 8282, Donee Information Return* (within 125 days from the date of sale) and send a copy of this to you. Note: This rule does not apply to property contributions of stock.

### Pointer 7: Keep Good Records

You must keep good records to prove or substantiate your property donations. Most charities have pre-printed forms that can serve as good receipts. You should keep a file for all your property donations and keep copies of these records for at least 3 years.

## CALCULATING THE CHARITABLE CONTRIBUTION DEDUCTION

As with many tax calculations, figuring out your actual charitable contribution deduction is not that straightforward. There are many rules and exceptions that can impact the amount you can deduct including:

- Percentage Limitation (50%, 30%, 20%)
- Pledges
- Quid Pro Quo

### Pointer 8: Date the Contribution is made

Many folks wait until the very last minute, at the end of the year, to finish making their donations. If you make a donation on December 31$^{st}$, does it count for that year? It depends on how you make it. Donations made by check count on the date that the check is actually mailed. So, you may want to send the check using an express mail service or some other way that you can prove the date that you mailed it. Donations made by credit card are made on date you make the charge. But pay-by-phone donations are made on the date that your financial institution pays the amount. So you probably don't want to make donations using the pay-by-phone method on December 31$^{st}$.

## PERCENTAGE LIMITATIONS—50%, 30%, 20%

In most cases, the amount you can deduct for your contributions is limited to 50% of your adjusted gross income. But in some cases, your contribution can be limited by as much as 20% or 30% of your adjusted gross income.

Most of your donations to 501(c)(3) organizations will qualify for the 50% limitation. Donations to organizations like private foundations (i.e., a family foundation or a corporate foundation) or of capital gains property (i.e., stock) to a charity may be subject to the 30% limitation. Finally, contributions of capital gains property to certain organizations (again, like private foundations) may be subject to a 20% limitation. For most people, these limitations don't significantly impact the amount of their charitable contribution deduction. After all, how many people give away over 50% of their income? Not many.

What happens if you're so charitable that you give more than your limit? All is not lost. You can take any unused contributions and carry them forward to your tax return next year (for up to 5 years). If you are carrying forward any contributions, make sure you still enter them on your current year's tax return so the IRS knows what you are claiming as a deduction in subsequent years.

**PLEDGES**

Whether it's the walk-a-thon for autism or the star studded telethon to send a child to college (i.e., the United Negro College Fund), many people pledge contributions to organizations. You cannot deduct your pledge as a charitable contribution, because you have not paid anything. Even if you sign a written commitment obligating you to make the contribution, you still cannot take the deduction until you actually make good on your pledge and pay the organization.

**QUID PRO QUO**

We have all been to that annual charity benefit where you paid a couple hundred dollars to dine with friends, colleagues, and, of course, support a worthy cause. As you dine on filet mignon, shrimp, chocolate truffles and toast the night away, your actual charitable contribution is not the couple hundred dollars. Part of your "donation" went to pay for food and drinks.

The amount you can deduct on your tax return must reflect what truly went to the organization.

This is called "*Quid Pro Quo*" because for giving your donation, you got something in return from the organization. Thus, your donation was partly for charity and partly for the goods and services you received from the organization. In many instances, the thing you get in return from the organization is of little significant monetary value (called "*de minims*" or "tokens," in tax talk). Examples include T-shirts or pens with the organization's name or logo on it. The good news is, you don't have to go crazy trying to value these small benefits. The IRS allows you to ignore valuing these "token" benefits (i.e., coffee mugs or T-shirts with the organization's name or logo). Examples of tokens that may be ignored include:

➤ Tokens costing the organization less than $8.30 for 2005. These must be received in connection with a contribution of at least $41.50 for 2005.
➤ Tokens where the fair market value does not exceed the lesser of two (2) percent of the donation, or $83 for 2005.
➤ The organization's newsletters.
➤ Certain annual membership benefits (i.e., free or discounted admissions to the organization's events, discounts on purchases from the organization's gift shop, or free or discounted parking).

## EXAMPLE 6.5

Enchanting Jones, a former baseball star, started an organization (The Enchanting Jones Foundation) to help disadvantaged boys in Detroit. Every year the Foundation sponsors an Enchanting Winter Evening as its major fundraiser. The weekend starts with an all-star baseball game, followed by a baseball clinic for the kids, a golf tournament, and is capped off by a gala dinner at a 5-star hotel. The dinner features numerous stars and athletes, and performances by several top recording artists. The minimum donation to attend the gala is $250 per person. In addition to the 4-course dinner, guests received a gym bag with the organization's logo on the outside. Inside the gym bag were the following items: a T-shirt, water bottle, pen, and baseball (again with the organization's logo). The Foundation estimates that the cost of the meal is $100 per person. Also the costs per person (and the fair market value) for the other items are: $9.50 for the gym bag, $5 for the T-shirts, $2.50 for the baseball and $1.00 for the pens.

Pretty Ricky, a former player himself (although it is not clear of which sport), decides he wants to go to the 2004 gala dinner and pays $500 for himself and his lady friend. Pretty Ricky had a wonderful time at the event and even met a casting director who expressed interest in featuring Pretty Ricky in a new black exploitation film. Pretty Ricky couldn't believe his luck. He might get a new film role and a $500 charitable contribution deduction. But if Pretty Ricky had read *For The Love Of Money*, he would know that he must deduct the value of the benefits he received to arrive at his true charitable contribution deduction.

He can ignore any token benefits costing less than $8.20, or with a fair market value less than $10 (2% of 500). Thus, he does not have to deduct the gym bag because its fair market value is not more than $10. Also, he doesn't have to deduct the cost of the T-shirt, pen or baseball because they all cost the organization less than $8.20.

Pretty Ricky's charitable contribution is $300 ($500 - $200 for the cost of the dinner).

### Pointer 9: Valuations
The Organization should provide you with a receipt or thank you letter that shows your actual contribution, less the value of any *Quid Pro Quo* benefits.

If this doesn't happen, contact the organization and remind them of their responsibility to do so, or contact your tax advisor for assistance. See the discussion below under receipts for more on this.

## RECEIPTS

As mentioned above in this Chapter, you must keep receipts (called written acknowledgements, in tax talk) to evidence your donations and take charitable contribution deductions on your tax return. You don't have to attach these receipts to your tax return, but you do need to be able to produce them in case you get audited. If you cannot produce them, the IRS may disallow your deduction.

Specifically, you are required to have written receipts or thank you letters from the organization if:

- You make a *Quid Pro Quo* donation of more than $75
- You contribute money or property worth, on any given day, more than $250

There are a few things to watch out for with these rules. First, even if you make a *Quid Pro Quo* donation for $75 or less, you should still keep a receipt or thank you letter. It's good practice to keep the receipts, even if not absolutely required by the IRS. Keep in mind; you must still deduct any benefits you receive from the amount of your donation (unless you receive token benefits). For example, if you pay $50 to attend a fundraiser and dinner for your local charity and it cost the organization $27 for the meal, your charitable contribution is $23 ($50 - $27).

Next, you can contribute up to $249.99 to an organization without getting a receipt or thank you letter to prove your donation (assuming *Quid Pro Quo* benefits are not received that would trigger the *Quid Pro Quo* rule). Again, although you aren't required to do so, it's good to obtain these receipts. Keep in mind that the rule requiring a receipt to prove your donation looks at each individual day in the year. So, you can give $249.99

every day and take a charitable contribution deduction without getting a receipt to prove your donations.

Most organizations send you "thank you letters" that can serve as the written acknowledgment or receipt for your donation. The IRS doesn't require any particular form of receipt, so, you can receive a letter, post card, computer-generated form, etc. The IRS does require a receipt, with certain magical language, to serve as proof of your donation. Below are some examples of IRS-approved language that must be included somewhere in the thank you letter. For more on thank you letters, see *IRS Publication 1771, Charitable Contributions—Substantiation and Disclosure Requirements.*

**Pointer 10: Thank You Letter For $250 or more on a single day**
Thank you for your contribution of $500 to the Local Charity received on November 22, 2004. No goods or services were provided in exchange for your contribution.

**Pointer 11: Thank You Letter *Quid Pro Quo* Contribution more than $75**
Thank you for your contribution of $500 to the Local Charity received on November 22, 2004. In exchange for your contribution, we gave you a gospel CD worth an estimated fair market value of $75. Please Note: You may only treat as a tax deductible charitable contribution, the amount by which the total contribution exceeds the fair-market value of this benefit. Please contact your tax advisor to determine the amount of your charitable contribution deduction.

### BUSINESS DEDUCTION

Up to this point in this Chapter, I've been discussing the charitable contribution deduction which you may take for amounts that you donate to 501(c)(3)s. What about payments you make to other organizations, like: trade organizations, associations and social clubs? You may also be able to take a deduction for these payments, but this time as a business deduction. In fact, even some payments that you make to 501(c)(3)s may qualify as business deductions.

To get this deduction, you must have your own a business (i.e., a consultant, a store, internet services—basically any business that's not a hobby). It doesn't matter if you also have a "9 to 5" job; side businesses count, too. Note: If you don't have your own business, you may be able to deduct these fees and expenses as miscellaneous itemized deductions (i.e., unreimbursed employee expenses). For more on miscellaneous itemized deductions, see the discussion below in this Chapter.

There are several advantages to taking a business deduction over a charitable contribution deduction. First, there are no percentage limitations on the business deduction. You can deduct 100% of your payment regardless of your adjusted gross income. Also, the IRS does not require you to prove your deduction with any particular magic language for your business receipts. The organizations are required to include a statement that your contributions to them are not deductible for Federal income tax purposes as charitable contributions or they could face a penalty. Note: As with most receipts, you should generally keep your business expenses for three years.

If your payment can qualify as both a business deduction and a charitable contribution deduction, the IRS requires you to take the payment as a charitable contribution deduction. So, you cannot take a charitable contribution deduction for most of your donation and then take a business deduction for the remaining amount that was disallowed under the percentage limitation rules (i.e., 50% of adjusted gross income).

**Pointer 12: Business Deduction vs. Charitable Contribution**

A payment made without the expectation of financial return is, generally, a charitable contribution. With a business expense, you are typically expecting a return that bears some relationship to your business, but, it's often hard to tell the difference. For example, take the case of an artist who is in the business of selling her art work. This artist makes a donation to become a member of a 501(c)(3) with the purpose of furthering artistic and cultural activities. Did the artist make this donation with or without the expectation of financial return? This answer will depend on the circumstances of the artist and the 501(c)(3). Please contact your tax advisor to help make these determinations.

## Casualty Theft & Losses

Thank your "Lucky Star" (Madonna, 1983) and "Knock on Wood" (Amii Stewart, 1979) if you've never had to deal with a casualty, theft or loss of property. For many people, this is not the case and thankfully, the tax laws provide a deduction to help ease the pain. The casualty and theft loss deduction allows you to deduct the value of your losses on your tax return. Below, get the 411 on:

- Casualties
- Thefts
- Calculating the Loss
- Proving the Loss

### CASUALTIES

We celebrate and fear Mother Nature at the same time, as reflected through our music, with songs like:

- ➤ "Rain (down on me)" (SWV 1998)
- ➤ "The Rain" (Oran Juice Jones, 1986)
- ➤ "Candy Rain" (Soul 4 Real 1995)
- ➤ "Through The Rain" (Tonya Blount, 1994)
- ➤ "Wish It Would Rain" (Temptation, 1968)
- ➤ "Can You Stand The Rain" (New Edition, 1988)

- "Rain On Me" (Ashanti 2003)
- "House Quake" (Prince, 1988)
- "Stormy Weather" (Lena Horne, 1943)
- "Fire" (Ohio Players 1975)
- "Quiet Storm" (Smokey Robinson, 1975)
- "Can You Stop The Rain" (Peabo Bryson, 1991)
- "Here Comes The Rain Again" (Eurythmics, 1984)
- "Blame It On The Rain" (Milli Vanilli, 1989)

We've experienced tragic weather-related casualties from coast to coast, from back-to-back hurricanes in Florida, blizzards in the Northeast and mud slides in California. Although nothing can replace the pain and sorrow felt due to a casualty, through insurance and tax deductions, you may be able to recover some of your financial losses.

You can take a deduction for the loss in your property value suffered from a casualty. A casualty is a loss you suffer from a sudden event such as a natural disaster or accident. It does not include losses that are caused by you, or from progressive deterioration or weakening of your property over time (i.e., termite or moth damage). Examples of casualties include:

| Casualties | |
| --- | --- |
| Car accidents (those that aren't your fault) | Relocation of a home that is unsafe |
| Earthquakes | Shipwrecks |
| Fires (unless you set the fire, or paid an arsonist to set it) | Storms (i.e., Hurricanes and Tornados) |
| Floods | Terrorist Attacks |
| Government-ordered demolition | Vandalism |

### Pointer 13: Filing After April 15th

If you suffered a casualty loss in a Presidentially-declared disaster area, you may be able to postpone filing your tax return for up to one year. You also may be able to postpone filings of other returns, like employment taxes and contributions to IRAs. For more on this check the IRS website at http://www.irs.gov.

## THEFTS

It's hard to mistake this discussion. A theft is when someone takes your property with the intent to permanently deprive you of owning it. It is not when someone borrows your property and takes too long to return it. The IRS lists the following as examples of theft:

| Theft | |
|---|---|
| ➢ Blackmail | ➢ Kidnapping for ransom |
| ➢ Burglary | ➢ Larceny |
| ➢ Embezzlement | ➢ Robbery |
| ➢ Extortion | |

### PROVING AND CALCULATING THE LOSS

You must be able to prove your loss, to take a casualty and theft loss deduction. Exactly how you prove it will depend on the type of loss that you are claiming. For casualty losses you need the following:

- ✓ The type of Casualty
- ✓ Date of the Casualty
- ✓ Proof that you are the owner of the property that was damaged
- ✓ Any insurance or other reimbursements you expect to receive

Also, for thefts you must be able to prove the following:

✓ The property was stolen
✓ Date you discovered the property was stolen
✓ Proof that you are the owner of the stolen property
✓ Any insurance of other reimbursements you expect to receive

The amount you can deduct as a casualty or theft loss is determined by an equation that compares your basis, or the amount you paid for the property, with the decrease in fair market value as a result of the casualty, theft or loss. You then take whichever amount is smaller and subtract any insurance money, government payments or other reimbursements that you received, or expect to receive. Finally, you subtract $100 then reduce the amount by 10% of your adjusted gross income. The result is the amount of your deduction.

You can deduct a loss from a casualty in the year that it happened, or in the case of Presidential-declared disaster areas, in another year. For a theft loss, take the deduction in the year the theft is discovered.

**Pointer 14: Schedule A, line 19**
Report casualty and theft losses from your personal property on Schedule A, line 19. Also, you must complete *Form 4684, Casualties and Thefts* and attach this to your tax return. For casualty and theft losses from your investment property (i.e., stocks and bonds) report these as miscellaneous itemized deductions on line 27 of *Schedule A, Itemized Deductions (Form 1040)*.

# Miscellaneous Deductions

Miscellaneous deductions are a patch-quilt, hodge-podge, or potpourri of expenses; sort of like the latest Andre 2000 (from Outkast) outfit. In many ways, they are like a catch-all. You can deduct anything that produces, conserves or protects your income. Check with your tax advisor, because you could be missing out on this deduction. Below, get the lowdown on the following miscellaneous itemized deductions:

- Unreimbursed Employee business expenses
- Tax planning and preparation expenses
- Legal expenses
- Investment related expenses
- Gambling losses

Also remember you can only deduct your miscellaneous itemized deductions that are greater than 2% of your adjusted gross income. So, this Chapter will also give you the 411 on calculating your miscellaneous itemized deductions. For more on the other itemized deductions, see *IRS Publication 529, Miscellaneous Itemized Deductions.*

### EMPLOYEE BUSINESS EXPENSES

Has your employer refused to pay for expenses that are legitimately connected to your work? If so, you may be able to take a miscellaneous itemized deduction. You must have paid the expenses without being reimbursed. Also, you must be an employee and the expense must be of the kind that is common and accepted in your particular field or profession. Finally, if you could have been reimbursed for the expense, but you simply forgot or neglected to request reimbursement, you cannot use this deduction.

A partial list of some of the more common unreimbursed employee business expenses include:

- Business meals and entertainment
- Depreciation on computer equipment or cellular phone
- Subscriptions for magazines or online services
- Dues to professional societies or a chamber of commerce

- Travel (including transportation and lodging)
- Car expenses
- Educator expenses
- Tool and supplies
- Licenses and regulatory fees
- Occupational Taxes
- Education expenses
- Job hunting expenses
- Work uniforms

I will discuss the last three in further detail below. Please Note: Expenses that are personal in nature (i.e., bribes, kickbacks, penalties, fines, or parking tickets) can never be deducted.

**Pointer 15: Form 2106**

Report your unreimbursed employee business expenses on *Form 2106, Unreimbursed Employee Business Expenses*, then transfer the amount to Schedule A. Note: If you're claiming depreciation for computer equipment or a cellular phone, you must first compute it on *Form 4562, Depreciation and Amortization* and then transfer the amount to Form 2106.

### EDUCATION EXPENSES

You can deduct education expenses that you pay to maintain or improve the skills related to your field or profession, but this education must be required by your employer to keep your current position or job. You also can't use this deduction if the education qualifies you for a new field or profession. Examples of education expenses include: tuition, books, supplies, fees and transportation costs.

### Example 6.6

Sean and Benjamin were best friends and fraternity brothers in college. They both landed great positions with a large corporation in New York City. Sean got a job in the finance department, while Benjamin took a paralegal job in the legal department. They both made decent money, for recent college graduates. But after 2 years of working, they both knew they would need graduate degrees to advance in the company. Sean spoke to his boss and chose to pursue an MBA at the Wharton School at the University of Pennsylvania. He was told that with an MBA in finance, he could expect to keep his job and possibly move into a higher management position at the company. Benjamin also spoke to his boss and decided to go to the University of Virginia School of Law. He was told that when he graduated and passed the New York Bar exam, he would be promoted to an attorney position.

Assume both Sean and Benjamin paid for all the costs related to their graduate school (i.e., tuition, books, supplies and fees). Sean will probably be able to deduct his education expenses as miscellaneous itemized deductions. The MBA in finance will help him improve the skills related to his profession, and this degree is required by his employer to keep his job. But, Benjamin, will not be able to deduct his education costs. Even though his paralegal experiences are helpful, his educational expenses qualified him for a new profession as an attorney.

Note: You may not have to pay taxes for certain education expenses that your employer pays for you. For more on employer provided educational assistance, see Chapter 1: Tax Basics.

**JOB HUNTING EXPENSES**

Like Gwen Guthrie said, "You got to have a J-O-B." ("Ain't Nothing Going On But the Rent" Gwen Guthrie, 1986). Luckily you can deduct your job hunting expenses, if you are hunting for a job in your present occupation. It can't be your first job, and it won't work if you've been unemployed for years (i.e., you took many years off after you had your baby and you're looking to re-enter the work force). For recent college graduates, you may still be able to take this deduction if you had an internship or job in college and this new job is in the same profession. Common job hunting expenses include: employment and outplacement agency fees, resume preparation costs, paper, telephone calls, photographs, postage and unreimbursed travel expenses (i.e., airfare and meals). It does not include new clothes that you buy for interviews. Also, you can deduct your mileage in searching for a job (i.e., at 15 cents per mile). Keep in mind, you must be looking for a job in your present occupation. You may not be able to use this deduction if you're changing careers. When in doubt, contact your tax advisor for help in making this determination.

## WORK UNIFORM

Do you work and "Get The Job Done" (Big Daddy Kane, 1989)? If so, your work uniform may qualify as a miscellaneous itemized deduction. To be clear, I'm sure the type of work Big Daddy Kane was doing does not qualify for this deduction. If you are required to wear a certain outfit to work, you may be able to deduct the costs of the uniform and the upkeep (such as, dry cleaning and alterations). Examples of workers who may be able to deduct the costs of the work uniform include: delivery workers, health care workers, firefighters, police officers and other law enforcement officials, letter carriers, professional athletes, transportation workers, musicians and entertainers. Work outfits that can double for regular clothes don't count, even if you never wear them outside of work. Also, safety and protective clothing that you pay for and are required to do your job may be deductible. Examples include: safety glasses, hard hats, work gloves, and safety shoes and boots. Unfortunately, as proud as we are of our Armed Forces, active-duty military men and women generally cannot deduct the costs of their uniform. However, some reservists may be able to deduct the cost of their uniforms.

## TAX PLANNING AND PREPARATION EXPENSES

You can count all of the fees you pay to your tax advisor as miscellaneous itemized deductions. This includes costs for preparing your tax returns and also costs for getting tax advice (such as, from books, magazines, computer software and online services). Yes, even the cost of *For The Love Of Money* can count as tax planning and preparation. It also includes your transportation costs and meals in connection with getting tax advice.

### EXAMPLE 6.7

Wanda meets with her tax advisor twice a year to discuss her tax situation. Those meetings are held over dinner and Wanda always pays. This year she purchased *For The Love Of Money* and two magazines that had tax tip articles. Wanda should be able to treat her mileage to and from her tax advisor's office as a miscellaneous itemized deduction. She should also be able to include the full costs of the dinners. Finally, she can add the costs of *For The Love Of Money* and the magazines.

Note: You may be able to deduct tax advice and preparation fees related to your side business (i.e., sole proprietorship) or your rental real property, but these expenses are not itemized deductions. Take these expenses on *Schedule C, Profit or Loss from Business (Form 1040)* for your business and on *Schedule E, Supplemental Income and Loss (Form 1040)* for your rental real property.

**LEGAL EXPENSES**

Have you been wronged, maligned or injured? Thinking about hiring Johnnie Cochran's law firm? How about filing for divorce on Judge Mablean Ephriam, suing your neighbor on Judge Mathis or small claims cases on Judge Hatchett or Judge Joe Brown?) If you find yourself needing to hire a lawyer, you may be able to deduct your legal expenses (i.e., attorney fees and court fees).

What type of legal fees count? You may be able to deduct legal fees that are connected to doing or protecting your job or your business (including in criminal trials). But any legal fees you have in connection with a discrimination lawsuit may be deductible as an adjustment to income (i.e., Above the Rim Deduction) in calculating your adjusted gross income. For more on these expenses, see Chapter 1: Tax Basics. You may also be able to deduct legal expenses for tax advice and alimony in connection with a divorce (but not for custody law suits).

Note: You may be able to deduct legal expenses related to tax advice for your side business (i.e., sole proprietorship) or your rental real property, but these expenses are not itemized deductions. Take these expenses on *Schedule C, Profit or Loss from Business (Form 1040)* for your business and on *Schedule E, Supplemental Income and Loss (Form 1040* for your rental real property.

### INVESTMENT RELATED EXPENSES

You can take a miscellaneous itemized deduction for your investment related expenses. These include: investment fees, custodial fees, trust administration fees, and any other fees in connection with managing your money. Don't forget to also include amounts you pay for: investment-related books and magazines, software or online services that manage your money, transportation to and from your investment advisor's office, meals with your investment advisor where you discuss management of your money, and any investment related attorney or accountant fees. You may also be able to deduct investment interest, at least to decrease the amount of your "net investment income." For more on investment interest, see Chapter 5: Itemized Deductions Part I.

Your costs for attending investment seminars, conventions or shareholder's meetings, as well as commissions you pay your broker for buying and selling your investments, do not count for this deduction. Note: Broker commissions can be added to your basis in an investment, thus decreasing the amount of a capital gain (or increasing a capital loss) when you sell your investment. For more on capital gains, see Chapter 4: Capital Gains.

### GAMBLING LOSSES

Do you feel like you need to "Touch a 4 Leaf Clover" (Atlantic Starr 1983)? Is lady luck never on your side? Well, the tax law is, sort of. The good news is that you can deduct your gambling losses as itemized deductions and they are not subject to the 2% limit for itemized deductions (see more on this limit in the next section). The bad news is, you can only deduct them to the extent of your gambling gains.

This tax rule may seem a bit unfair, because you must pay Uncle Sam on the full value of your gambling wins for the year. But, if you happen to be unlucky (as most people are) and have gambling losses, you can only deduct them up to the amount of your gambling winnings. Note: These gambling losses do not reduce the amount of your gambling wins. You must still report gambling winnings on your tax return. For more on gambling income, see Chapter 1: Tax Basics.

Moreover, most gamblers don't know this, but the IRS requires you to keep a gambling diary of your winnings and losses. This diary should include:

- ➢ The date and type of your specific wager or wager activity.
- ➢ The name and address of the gambling establishment.
- ➢ The names of other persons present with you at the gambling establishment.
- ➢ The amount you won or lost.

Also, gambling includes wagers you place on virtually anything such as: Keno, slot machines, table games (i.e., twenty-one, black jack, craps, poker, baccarat, roulette, and wheel of fortune), bingo, racing and lotteries.

## EXAMPLE 6.8

Ricardo, known for being quite the ladies man, is a high-roller in Las Vegas; but, 2004 was not such a great year for him. In the beginning of the year, he scored big by hitting the jack pot at the Bellagio (he won $7,000). The next day, he won $15,000 on the nickel machines at the Palm Casino! By summer time, he advanced to black jack and won a total of $5,000 at the Mandalay Bay. Of course, along the way he suffered a few set backs; losing $16,000 shooting craps in August at the Luxor. He took a break and in December decided to go for the big bucks. This time, poker was his game of choice. Poor Ricardo should have stayed away from the Bellagio that night, because he lost a whopping $20,000.

He remembered hearing somewhere that he could deduct his gambling losses and rushed to see his tax advisor, hoping for some good news. Unfortunately, Ricardo's deduction is not as large as he thought. His total gambling winning for the year were $27,000 ($7,000 + $15,000 + 5,000). He must include this in his income.

Although his gambling losses totaled $36,000 ($16,000 + $20,000), he will not be able to deduct all of this. He must limit his gambling losses to the amount of his gambling gains or $27,000.

### Pointer 16: Form W2-G

Are you a "social gambler" and think the IRS will never find out about your gambling winnings or losses? Think again—the IRS is cracking down on people who don't report their gambling winnings. Gambling establishments are required to report your winning over $600 to the IRS (1,200 for winnings from bingo or slot machines, and $ 1,500 for winnings from Keno) on *Form W2-G, Certain Gambling Winnings*. Also, if you win more than $5,000, the gambling establishment is required to withhold taxes from your winnings (i.e., to the tune of 25% to 28%).

### THE 2% CALCULATION

As mentioned above, the total amount of your miscellaneous deductions must be more than 2% of your adjusted gross income before you can start deducting anything. For example, if your adjusted gross income is $60,000, then you must have at least $1,200 (2% of $60,000) in miscellaneous itemized expenses. Keep in mind, you can only deduct the amount that is over 2% (i.e., 98%) or in this case $1,200.

There is an exception for certain miscellaneous deduction. These expenses are not subject to the 2% limitation, meaning you can deduct them in full. They include: gambling losses (but only to the extent of gambling winnings), excess educator expenses, certain bond premiums, casualty and theft losses for investment property (i.e., stocks and bonds), certain federal estate tax deductions, impairment-related work expenses (i.e., expenses to help those who are physically or mentally handicapped with being able to work), certain repayments of money over $3,000 and un-recovered investments in certain annuities.

Pointer 17: Schedule A, line 27
Report all of your miscellaneous itemized deductions that are not subject to the 2% limit on *Schedule A, Itemized Deductions (Form 1040)*, line 27.

## Limitations on Itemized Deductions

Now that you got the lowdown on the major types of itemized deductions, there are two remaining limitations on the amount you can deduct as your total itemized deductions for the year. They include:

- Income phase-outs
- Alternative Minimum Tax (or AMT)

## PHASE-OUTS

You're almost there. After this last calculation, you will finally have the amount that you can take as your total itemized deductions. The total amount you can deduct for itemized expenses may be further reduced by a calculation called phase-outs. For certain high-roller, shoot-callers and big-ballers, if you make over $72,975, if single or $145,950 for married folks filing jointly, you may not get to take all of your itemized deductions. You must perform a phase-out calculation that reduces the total amount of your itemized deductions.

There are a couple of things to remember about this phase-out rule. The good news is that not all of your itemized deductions are phased-out. This means, you can still deduct them without making this last calculation. These deductions include:

➢ Medical and dental expenses
➢ Gambling losses
➢ Investment interest expenses
➢ Casualty and theft losses (for your personal and investment property)

At most, your total itemized deductions will be limited by 80%. To calculate this phase-out, take your total itemized deductions that are subject to phase-out and decrease them by 3% of the amount that your adjusted gross income is greater than $145,950 for married folks filing jointly or $72,975 for individuals. But, in no case will your itemized deductions be reduced by more than 80%.

Note: You apply this overall limit after you have computed the various limits that apply to certain specific itemized deductions (i.e., 7.5 % of adjusted gross income for medical expenses, 50% of adjusted gross income for certain charitable contributions, etc.) See Chapter 5: Itemized Deductions Part I and this Chapter for specific limitations that apply to various itemized deductions.

 **Pointer 18: Itemized Deductions Worksheet**
Thank goodness you don't need to memorize or study the phase-out calculation. Use the Itemized Deduction Worksheet found in the Instructions for *Schedule A, Itemized Deductions (Form 1040)*. Also, many of the popular tax preparation software programs will make this calculation with the push of a few keys.

### AMT

AMT, not to be confused with an ATM, stands for Alternative Minimum Tax; although, it's easy to see why the initials can be confused since both take your money. AMT is an extra income tax that some folks have to pay in addition to their regular income tax. If you are subject to AMT, you will not be able to take some of your itemized deductions. It sort of makes you feel like Florida Evans (aka, from "Good Times") when James died—"Damn, Damn, Damn."

It should come as no surprise that some of the largest itemized deductions are lost or significantly reduced, such as interest, medical expenses, taxes and miscellaneous itemized deductions. There is one deduction that is spared. For you truly saintly, giving, caring folks, you can still take your charitable contribution deductions. For more on the Alternative Minimum Tax, see Chapter 7: AMT.

### REMIX

Here's the remix on what we learned in this Chapter:

1. You can deduct your charitable contributions as itemized deductions. Keep in mind these are donations that you make to 501(c)(3) organizations. Amounts you give to trade associations, business leagues, social organizations and chambers of commerce are not deductible as charitable contributions, but they may be

deductible as business expenses (if you have your own business) or miscellaneous itemized deductions (if you are an employee and your employer does not reimburse you).

2. You may also be able to deduct your out-of-pocket volunteer expenses (i.e., travel, transportation, meals and mileage).

3. If you donate property (like clothes or furniture), don't forget your receipts.

4. You must get a receipt for donations over $250 on a single day and for *Quid Pro Quo* contributions over $75 (i.e., when you get something in return for your gift).

5. Be careful with car donations. You can only deduct the true value of the car. Don't just rely on a used car book value. You will have to take the extra step of knowing what the charity got when it sold your car.

6. You can deduct losses that you suffer from casualties or thefts.

7. Casualty losses are losses you suffer from a sudden event, such as a natural disaster or accident. They do not include losses that are caused by you (i.e., you cause the car accident).

8. A theft is when someone takes or steals your property for good. A theft is not when someone borrows your property or takes too long to return it.

9. Keep in mind, your casualty and theft losses must be more than 10% of your adjusted gross income (AGI), plus $100, before you will receive a tax benefit.

10. You can also deduct your miscellaneous itemized deductions. There are numerous deductions that qualify in this category (such as, unreimbursed employee business expenses, including education expenses, job hunting expenses and work uniforms), tax planning and preparation expenses, legal expenses, investment related expenses and gambling losses.

11. Keep in mind, many of your miscellaneous deductions are subject to the 2% limit. They must be greater than 2% of your adjusted gross income before you can take a deduct anything.
12. If you make more than $72,975, if single or $145,950 for married folks, you may not get to take all of your itemized deductions.

# Chapter 7

# Alternative Minimum Tax
*A.K.A.—A Messy Thang*

> *Don't Mess With Bill*
> *No, No, No, No*
> *Don't Mess With Bill*
>
> "Don't Mess With Bill," The Marvelettes (1965)

What is AMT? What does this have to do with me? Aren't businesses the only ones that have to deal with this? Sounds like a messy thang, can I skip this Chapter? This is just a brief list of questions people have asked regarding AMT, or the alternative minimum tax.

Yes, AMT is a major mess and shock for most people who go along all year only to find that this AMT thing pops up and all but destroys their ability to take many tax deductions. I chose the song, "Don't Mess With Bill" by the Marvelettes (1965) for this Chapter, but there are so many songs dealing with messes or messing with someone that may describe how you feel if you've been subject to the messy AMT. There are the oldie songs like, "Mess Around," by Ray Charles (circa 1952), "Papa Don't Take No Mess (Part 1)," by James Brown (circa 1974), and "A Fine Mess," Temptations (1986). Then, there's the sensual, and open to many interpretations, song, "Pretty Mess," that topped the charts in 1984 by Vanity. Last, but not least, there's the 2002 version of "Don't Mess With Bill," now called,

"Don't Mess With My Man," by Nivea. The bottom line is, you know all of these messy songs. Some of them you like and others you probably can't stand. Stay with these emotions, as they will help you in gaining a basic understanding of AMT.

Here's the basic premise: Most people calculate tax liability using the regular method described in Chapter 1: Tax Basics (See also page 1 and 2 of Form 1040 (the Regular Tax Method 1). But did you know that you are also required to calculate income tax liability under the alternative minimum tax (AMT) method (Method 2). This method disallows certain tax benefits (called tax preferences) allowed under Method 1. You are required to pay the higher of the two calculations. So AMT is a completely separate income tax calculation.

In this Chapter, further your quest to taking control of your taxes. Get the 411 on AMT and some of the common reasons why you might have to pay this separate tax. I want you to walk away with a basic understanding of a very messy and complicated area; without giving you a Ph.D. in AMT (yes, it rhymes). There are several good in-depth resources and books on AMT that can help you with this (or put you to sleep). As there are numerous facts, situations and calculations that go into figuring out the AMT, if you find yourself in an AMT situation, please contact your tax advisor.

## Overview of AMT

Introduced around 1978, the Alternative Minimum Tax was originally created to target high-income taxpayers who claimed large, itemized deductions that resulted in the payment of little or no taxes. The AMT was meant to stop the super wealthy from using tax loopholes by making them calculate their tax liability twice.

So far, this doesn't sound like a big deal since you're not super wealthy. Think again. It's been widely reported that since the 1970s, the number of people subject to AMT has drastically increased; from the couple of hundred in the 70s to some estimates as high as over fifteen million in 2005. This means the definition of "super wealthy" has now become more like "average." How did this happen? One explanation is the fact that many of the AMT exemption amounts haven't been indexed for inflation. The AMT exemption will depend on your filing status and for 2005 are as follows:

- $40,250 for single and head of household
- $58,000 for married filing jointly, and qualifying widow(er)s
- $29,000 for married filing separate

The problem is that the AMT exemption vanishes (or phases-out) depending on your income. For 2005 the phase-out looks like this:

| Filing Status | Phase-out Begin | Phase-out Ends |
|---|---|---|
| Single/Head of Household | $112,500 | $273,500 |
| Married Joint/Qualifying Widow(er) | $150,000 | $382,000 |
| Married Separately | $ 75,000 | $191,000 |

As the median household income increases over time, less and less folks will be able to use the AMT exemption. For example, with a single person making $275,000 for 2005, the AMT exemption is completely lost! This may seem like a lot of money, but it's certainly not enough bling bling to be living J. Lo style. Many professionals, like doctors, lawyers, engineers, and corporate executives, can make well above this. If the tax laws don't change, the problem is only going to get worse. As seen in an April 2, 2004, Treasury Department news release:

> "National Taxpayer Advocate Nina Olsen today released a report to Congress that identifies the Alternative Minimum Tax (AMT) and sole proprietor tax noncompliance as the top two problems faced by taxpayers...Although the AMT was originally enacted to prevent wealthy taxpayers from avoiding tax liability through the use of tax avoidance techniques, it now affects substantial numbers of middle-income taxpayers and will, absent a change of law, affect

more than 30 million taxpayers by 2010." *IR-2004-8, Jan. 14, 2004*

In fact, a Foxnews.com report estimates that by 2005, 65 percent of married couples with an adjusted gross income between $75,000 and $100,000, and with two or more children, will be affected by the AMT ("What's Your 'AMT.' Under the AMT?," Gail Buckner, CFP—May 30, 2004). This seems completely unfair. What can you do about it? Not much, short of writing your "congressman and ask him to pass a bill," (aka, "Rumors" style by the Timax Social Club, 1986).

Do you fall in that income bracket? If so, keep reading. If not, but you aspire to, you also might want to keep reading and take Loose End's advice—"Stay a Little While Child" (1986).

## AMT Situations

Technically, every taxpayer is required to calculate taxes using both methods (i.e., Regular Tax Method 1 or AMT Method 2). Many folks who prepare their own tax returns are not aware of the AMT calculation and simply do not calculate it. Some of you have escaped AMT without knowing it, since the AMT calculation provides the exemption amount.

So what are the AMT situations that you need to look out for? Check out the following list of AMT items and issues (called tax adjustments or tax preferences):

- Personal exemptions
- Standard deduction
- State and local taxes
- Interest on second mortgages
- Medical expenses
- Miscellaneous itemized deductions
- Incentive stock options
- Long-term capital gains
- Tax-exempt interest
- Tax shelters

If you have large amounts of any of the items and your AGI exceeds the AMT exemption, you are required to complete *Form 6251, Alternative Minimum Tax—Individuals* to determine whether you must pay any AMT. Although every situation is different, any of these items can cause you to have AMT. Also, a combination of these items can land you in AMT world too. The point is that you must be aware of these tax preferences and adjustments and work with your tax advisor during the year to ensure that you avoid or minimize any AMT. Below, get the lowdown on some of the more common AMT situations.

### Pointer 1: Hefty Itemized Deductions

AMT does not impact all taxpayers. But, if you have certain things, like a large amount of itemized deductions, you should consider doing an AMT calculation. Do this calculation in September of every year to give yourself enough time to do additional tax planning before the end of that year. Generally, taxpayers most vulnerable to AMT are: (1) those married couples with income levels over $105,000, and with two or more dependents, (2) single individuals with income levels greater than $140,000, with two or more dependents, and (3) people with large itemized deductions.

## PERSONAL EXEMPTIONS

Personal exemptions are those amounts you automatically get to deduct from your income, for yourself, your spouse, and your dependents ($3,200 per person for 2005). As personal exemptions reduce your income, having too many could reduce you below that magical minimum tax that you must pay. It's not that hard to claim a lot of personal exemptions. Have you ever gone to the payroll department at your job and asked them to change your tax exemptions so you can get more in your paycheck this week? There are only three people in your family, but you change the number on your Form W-4 to seven, and suddenly you're paycheck goes up by several hundred dollars. It might sound like a good idea at the time, but having too many personal exemptions can create an AMT issue.

How many are too many exemptions, obviously, depends on your personal situation. It would be rare for too many personal exemptions alone to cause you to have an AMT problem, but it's not impossible. Even if the number of personal exemptions doesn't create an AMT situation by itself, if you wind up having AMT because of other issues, you won't be able to take you personal exemptions. That's right. You lose all of your personal exemptions in calculating your AMT. For more on personal exemptions, see the discussion in Chapter 1: Tax Basics.

## ITEMIZED DEDUCTIONS

If the amount of your itemized deductions is too large, it may cause you to fall below that magic income tax amount and force you to pay the AMT. For most taxpayers, these large itemized deductions will come from the following sources: state and local income taxes or property taxes, mortgage interest from a home equity loan, medical expenses, or miscellaneous expenses (like unreimbursed employee expenses).

## STATE & LOCAL TAXES

For many, state and local income taxes, property taxes can be some of the highest deductions taken. The likelihood of falling into AMT is increased by those taxpayers living in high income and property tax states; such as California, New York, and Massachusetts. If you live in one of these states, you should check with your tax advisor on ways to minimize or avoid AMT. For more on taking itemized deductions for state and local income taxes and property taxes, please see Chapter 5: Itemized Deductions Part I.

## MORTGAGE INTEREST

Mortgage interest is another large itemized deduction for many taxpayers. Luckily, for AMT purposes, you can still deduct your mortgage interest from your primary home, or from a home improvement loan. What you can't deduct, for AMT purposes, is mortgage interest for general home equity loans or second mortgages; where you use the money for other purposes not related to your home purchase or improvements (such as, to consolidate credit card bills or purchase at new car). Make sure you tell your tax advisor how you used the proceeds of your home equity line. For more on taking itemized deductions for mortgage interest please see Chapter 5: Itemized Deductions Part I.

## EXAMPLE 7.1

Lynette is single with no children, thirty years old, and works for a big corporation. Her base compensation is $110,000 and she lives in Harlem. Ten years ago, she purchased a townhouse for $125,000. Due to the rapid increase in market value the townhouse is now, in 2004, worth $400,000. Lynette decided to take out a home equity line of $175,000. She used $125,000 of the equity line to purchase a Mercedes CLK430, take a month long safari to Africa, and as a down payment on a condo for her grandmother. Once she calculates more than $33,750 of adjustments and preferences, she is in AMT.

| | |
|---|---|
| Personal Exemptions (self) | $ 3,200 |
| State Taxes | 10,000 |
| Home equity line interest | 3,000 |
| Real Estate Taxes | 5,000 |
| Total Before Other Adjustment & Preferences | $21,200 |

Lynette has a little room before she reaches the $40,250 AMT exemption amount. But her salary, $110,000, is getting close to the AMT Exemption phase-out of $112,500. This means that her AMT Exemption amount could be lower than $40,250 and suddenly her $21,200 in adjustments and preferences may cause her to have AMT.

## MEDICAL EXPENSES

Medical expenses are a third category of expenses that could create an AMT situation, if they're large. Moreover, once you have AMT, any medical expenses you try to deduct will be reduced. Under the regular tax calculation (Method 1), medical and dental expenses are deductible for all amounts that exceed 7.5 percent of your adjusted gross income or AGI. However, when calculating AMT, all medical and dental expenses are deductible for amounts that exceed 10 percent of AGI (not 7.5 percent). For more on taking itemized deductions for medical expenses please see Chapter 5: Itemized Deductions Part I.

### EXAMPLE 7.2

Fatima had a really hard year. She was diagnosed with breast cancer and incurred $20,000 in medical expenses after insurance payouts. Fatima's AGI is $110,000. For her regular tax calculation, her medical expense deduction was $12,300 ($20,000 less 7.5% x $110,000). Under the AMT calculation, her medical expense would be $9,000 ($20,000 less 10% x $110,000).

## MISCELLANEOUS ITEMIZED DEDUCTIONS

A large amount of miscellaneous itemized deductions may also create an AMT situation. The likely culprits are unreimbursed employee expenses, tax preparation fees, or investment expenses. It's bad enough that you can only deduct these miscellaneous itemized expenses once they reach greater than 2% of your adjusted gross income. If they are too large and create an AMT issue, you won't be able to deduct them at all. As a rule of thumb, if you have large amounts in other tax adjustments and preferences, you should weigh the option of claiming miscellaneous itemized deduction. You don't want them to be too small, like Raj from "What's Happening," but you may not want them to be too large, like Rerun. For

## ISOs

During the "dot.com" boom, many people got stock options, in addition to salaries, as a form of compensation. Stock options grant the privilege and right to purchase your corporation's stock. These options come in many flavors and sizes, but one of the most common types given to employees was incentive stock options ("ISOs"). The ISO price is at a discount (think of it like an employee discount.). This means it is cheaper than what it would cost you to buy the stock on the stock market (i.e., NYSE or NASDAQ).

ISOs are not as popular as they were in the 90s, mainly due to the dot.com crash. In fact many employers are not giving any type of stock options; choosing to give cold hard cash or restricted stock instead.

Typically, the company grants you an ISO (at a grant price), but you have to work for the company for a number of years (i.e., four or five) before they actually become yours (the period of time is called vesting). You don't pay anything for this grant. Also, as the ISOs vest, you formally accept the ISOs by "exercising" them. This means the ISOs are now yours. You get a benefit when you sell them, and thanks to your employee discount, your gain is now larger. Moreover, you usually don't have to pay a tax on the ISO spread (the difference between the grant price of the ISO and the price at the time you exercise) when you exercise them; but thanks to AMT this may not be the case.

Exercising ISOs, may very well be the largest cause of AMT for most taxpayers. For AMT purposes, you do have to include the spread in your income when you exercise them.

### EXAMPLE 7.3

Big Vibrant Voices, Inc. (BVV) grants The Super Real Roxanne Shante (the stage name for its latest female 80s rapper, also known as "The SRR Shante") an ISO on February 10, 1998, to buy 3,000 shares of BVV Corporation stock at $20 per share ($20 is the fair market value on this day)—a total of $60,000. On September 1, 2002, when BVV stock's fair market value is $41 a share, The SRR Shante exercises her options. She now owns the stock. On November 3, 2004, The SRR Shante sells all her stock when it's worth $50 per share, or $150,000 (3,000 x $50).

For her regular tax calculation, nothing happens when she exercises her ISOs in 2002. In 2004 when she sells the ISOs, she has a long-term capital gain of $90,000 on the sale ($150,000 selling price less $60,000 purchase price).

For the AMT calculation, she has a gain in 2002 when she exercises the ISOs. This is calculated as the difference between the ISO price ($20 per share) and the fair market value on the day of exercise ($41 per share). This results in $63,000 ($123,000 - $60,000) that must be added as an AMT preference. Depending on her other AMT preferences and adjustments, this could result in an AMT.

There is a little relief for AMT caused from exercising an ISO. If you pay an AMT because of an ISO exercise, you may be able to claim an AMT credit in future years. You can get this credit by filing *Form 8801, Credit for Prior Year Minimum Tax—Individuals, Estates, & Trusts*, and you get this credit every year; even if you haven't sold the stock. The above example is only the tip of the iceburg on ISOs and AMT. So, if you have ISOs, you should talk with a tax advisor before exercising them.

**Pointer 2: File Form 6251 and Form 8801**

File *Form 6251, Alternative Minimum Tax—Individuals*, the year you exercise your ISO and every year thereafter until the AMT credit is gone. Also, file *Form 8801, Credit for Prior Year Minimum Tax—Individuals, Estates, & Trusts*, every year after you exercise the ISOs until the AMT credit is gone.

## LONG-TERM CAPITAL GAINS

In general, the preferential long term capital gains tax rate discussed in Chapter 4: Capital Gains, remains, even if you have AMT. But you may pay AMT, because you have a large long tem capital gain. Why? Because, although you get an AMT exemption (i.e., $40,250 for single taxpayers), if your income is high enough (say over $112,500 for a single taxpayer), this AMT exemption is phased-out; it's gone bye-bye. Keep in mind, to get to that $112,500, add together all of your income, including the amount of your long-term capital gains. For more on long-term capital gains, please see Chapter 4: Capital Gains.

### EXAMPLE 7.4

Kevin worked for the federal government in Washington DC for the past fifteen years, currently making an annual salary of $60,000. Normally, Kevin wouldn't have to worry about AMT; he is making a decent salary, but he is by no means rich or wealthy. However, you can't just look at how much someone makes. Things like long-term capital gains can create an AMT situation. For example: When Kevin first came to Washington, after graduating from the University of Virginia, he purchased his first townhouse for $125,000. As the Washington area real estate market soared, Kevin's put his townhouse on the market. Assume he recently sells it for $600,000 (a $475,000 long term capital gain). His AMT exemption will be completely phased-out! The good news is that

Kevin made a great investment. The fact that he may have to pay taxes is just a cost of this investment. Keep in mind, it is better to pay tax on some money, than to have no money at all.

## Calculating the AMT

Calculating your AMT can scare even the most diligent tax-return preparer. Think of it as a good "workout," like the feeling you get from your favorite work-out song like, "The New Work Out Plan," by Kanye West (2004) or "Work It," by Missy Elliott (2003). Keep in mind, the point of AMT is to ensure that you pay at least a minimum tax. This means you must add back some of those deductions and benefits you are trying to deduct, and add extra income from things like ISOs. Then, your tax is computed off this new AMT income, minus your AMT exemption. If the tax is higher than your regular tax calculation, the difference is your AMT. Here's an example of an AMT calculation.

### EXAMPLE 7.5

Evan is a widowed father of three. After his wife died in 2001, his financial affairs suffered tremendously; he almost lost the family home. Also, he did not file his state tax return from 2001–2004. In fact, his outstanding state tax debts grew to $40,000, after interest and penalties were included.

Evan vowed, in 2005, to get back on track and be a good example to his children. Evan makes excellent money at his 9 to 5, commanding a salary of $150,000 per year. In 2005, he paid off his debts, including the $40,000 he owed in state taxes.

Assume, using Method One, Evan computed his regular tax to be $21,647. But he recently purchased *For The Love Of Money* and knows he must also make sure that he doesn't have any AMT.

Assume he has the following on his *Form 6251, Alternative Minimum Tax—Individuals*:

| | |
|---|---:|
| Line 38 of Form 1040 (AGI) | $121,565 |
| Add back: | |
| —2.5% of Medical and Dental (10%-7.5%) | $ 3,750 |
| —Home mortgage interest | |
| (not used to buy, build or improve home) | $ 8,250 |
| —Taxes from *Schedule A* | 31,435 |
| AMT Income | $165,000 |

$165,000 is the base of his AMT tax calculation. But Evan's AGI of $121,565 is greater than $112,500 (the phase-out beginning amount for taxpayers filing as head of household status). Thus, his AMT exemption amount has to be decreased or phased-down. It started at $40,250, but assume it's now $32,125 after doing the phase-down calculations. This decreased amount is then subtracted from his AMT Income, arriving at $132,875 ($165,000 less $32,125).

Finally, applying the AMT Tax rate of 26%, results in an AMT Tax of $34,548 ($132,875 x .26). Because his AMT Tax of $34,548 is higher than his regular tax of $21,647, Evan has AMT equal to the difference, or $12,901.

## Tax Tips

Do you see the theme here, with all the AMT situations discussed above? In other Chapters, I talk about getting the most out of your itemized deductions or capital gains. Yet if these amounts are too high, the extra deduction, or in the case of long-term capital gain, the extra income at a preferential tax rate, might actually cause an AMT situation and cause you to pay more taxes. Here are a few tax planning tips that can help you in dealing with AMT. Of course, AMT totally depends on each taxpayer's specific situation, and you should always confer with your tax advisor concerning your specific facts and circumstances.

### TIMING

As you learned in Chapter 4 Capital Gains, timing is everything. There are many songs to help you think of time; from "Do You Know What Time It Is" (Kool Moe Dee, 1987), and "Time (Clock of Heart)," (Boy George and the Culture Club, 1982). The point is, there is a song about time for every taste. If you keep "time" in mind when you think of AMT, you're almost there on this tax tip.

The timing of the payment of your itemized deductions, can affect the calculation of AMT. Shifting the payment of state, local or real estate taxes can shift triggering an AMT situation. The same can be said for medical expense payments, exercising ISOs, or selling long-term capital assets. If your income is close to where the AMT exemption phase-out begins, it's worth the investigation to see if you can defer some income to the next year. Thanks to the section above, you now know the typical AMT situations; so, consider these when making financial decisions.

### EXAMPLE 7.6

It's November 2004, and Reggie is reflecting on his year. It was a year filled with ups and downs. On the up side, he has a beautiful, expensive home and owns a successful truck-hauling business. In past years, his tax planning included paying his 4$^{th}$ quarter estimated state taxes by December 31, so he could deduct them as itemized deductions for that year. He lives in California (a state with notoriously high state taxes). Thus, Reggie typically has large itemized deductions. In fact, his tax advisor ran an AMT forecasting calculation in September, 2004, and Reggie knew he was very close to having an AMT situation.

On the down side, in October, 2004, Reggie's mother slipped into a coma after having a bad case of the flu. She was very blessed and recovered from the coma and the flu. Since his mother qualifies as his dependent (she is retired and completely supported by Reggie; he covered all of her $52,000 in medical bills), Reggie plans to claim every cent possible of her medical bills on his 2004 tax return. Remember, for regular tax (method one), it would be the amount greater than 7.5% of his AGI, but for AMT purposes, it's the amount greater than 10% of his AGI.

Reggie could be in an AMT situation, thanks to the extra medical expenses. He could do a number of things, such as paying his 4th quarter estimated state taxes after the first of the New Year. This will decrease his itemized deductions, but may help him avoid AMT.

As a rule of thumb, you should start calculating and thinking of these possible scenarios in late September each year. By that time of the year, income and deduction projections for the last month can be determined; income tax projections can be generated for likely scenarios (i.e., pay taxes in December or January).

AMT continues to be highly debated in Congress (please pay attention to the AMT debate on your local television or newspaper). Generally, as you continue to increase your household income level, you will be getting closer and closer to the grasps of AMT.

## BE CHARITABLE

For all you faithful tithers, charitable persons and sponsors, be not dismayed. Charitable donations are one of the few itemized deductions that are treated the same for the regular tax (method one) and AMT (method two) purposes. That's right—you still can deduct all of your charitable contributions in calculating your AMT. So, make it a point to start, or continue, giving to your local church, theatre, Boys and Girls Club, or other charity. We all have things to be thankful for; but for those of you creeping close to AMT, you should know at least you are still BLESSED!

## REMIX

Here's the remix on what we learned in this Chapter:

1. There are two tax calculations that determine how much you pay in federal income taxes: Your regular income tax (method one) and the AMT (method two).

2. If you have large itemized deductions (i.e., from medical expenses, state taxes, miscellaneous itemized deductions, etc.) personal exemptions, exercised ISOs, or long-term capital gains, make sure to calculate your taxes due under both methods.

3. Mortgage interest, used for purposes OTHER THAN to acquire, improve or construct property, may create an AMT issue. In other words, tax deductions, for equity lines of credit used to consolidate debt or purchase a new car, are not allowed under AMT! Keep records of how proceeds of home equity lines-of-credit are used and provide them to your tax advisor—even if she doesn't ask.

4. Review your estimated tax position each September to see if AMT is creeping up.

5. Be charitable. It's good for the soul, it's good for the community and it's good for AMT, too.

# Investment, Education & Estate
*Planning For Your Future*

> *Sometimes the snow comes down in June*
> *Sometimes the sun goes 'round the moon*
> *Just when I thought a chance had passed*
> *You go and save the best for last*
>
> **"Save The Best For Last," Vanessa Williams (1992)**

---

Remember when your "nanna," "big mama," or "grandma" taught you the meaning of saving? You cleaned her house for two months straight just to be able to afford that new "watchamacallit" toy. You learned then that money doesn't grow on trees. In fact, you spend all of your life saving for something—saving for a vacation, saving for a new car, saving for your first house, saving to send your child to college and, of course, saving for retirement. This Chapter is all about saving, and it's no surprise that there are numerous songs to help get you in the saving mood. In addition to my top pick above, "Save The Best For Last," when I think of saving, I also think of "Saving All My Love For You", by Whitney Houston (1985) and "Save The Over Time (for me)," by Gladys Knight & the Pips (1983). Saving is a big part of our life and culture. Since you must save, get the 411 on how to use the tax laws to help you with your choosing investments for your retirement, and finding tax savings so you can afford your child's education. Also, check out the end of the Chapter for an overview of estate and gift taxes that you also need to know about for your retirement.

## Investment

Remember the chorus of the song "I Wanna Be Rich," by Calloway (1989); basically he wants to be rich (repeated over and over again). I'm not sure if he ever accomplished this lofty goal, but there are many ways to invest your money and become rich. However, take a lesson from this one-hit wonder, if you're looking for a get rich quick scheme or a way to double your money overnight, using the tax laws will probably not get you there. There are plenty of books out there on get rich quick schemes, but this is not one of those books.

If you can "be patient," you will accumulate wealth and get to those "Better Days" (Dianne Reeves, 1988). And you can thank Uncle Sam for several tax laws designed to help you get "Paid in Full," Erik B and Rakim style (1988).

Welcome to the land of Qualified Retirement Plans. These plans are everywhere; more common than a new Samuel L. Jackson movie. They are fairly easy to establish, and they provide tax benefits for your contributions and investment earnings. In fact, the benefits can be enormous; but as I said above, you've got to be patient.

With some of these plans, the money comes out of your paycheck before you've paid any taxes. While with others, you have to make contributions to the plan with after-tax dollars. No matter how the money gets in there, once you put it in, the money sits in the plan where it grows and accumulates gains that are tax-free. Then, you can take the money out when it's time for you to retire. For many of these plans, you pay a tax at this point; while for others, no tax is due since you made your contribution with after-tax dollars.

Thanks to years and years of not paying taxes on the money, you have a great nest egg. This "Beautiful," process (Snoop Dog, featuring Pharrell and Uncle Charlie, 2003) is called tax deferral. You may not remember the term, but hopefully you'll remember the next example that compares what happens if you don't get hip to this.

## EXAMPLE 8.1

The year was 1975 and Sheryl Len always wanted to be a star. She had a voice that made people say, "It's electric!" ("Electric Boogie" aka, the electric slide by Marcia Griffiths, 1989); but she couldn't get a break. One day her best friend, Evelyn "Merlot" King, talked her into auditioning for "The Bam Show," a show where contestants perform their talents in front of a live audience; but if they are bad, they got smacked upside the head as the audience yells "bam!"

Sheryl couldn't believe her luck. She won first place on the show and received a grand prize of $50,000. In fact, the show's producers said that she was the best contestant to ever be on The Bam Show.

Evelyn was quite the singer herself, but she was shy and decided not to compete on the show. She was an assistant at an up—and-coming record company and had no desire to perform like Sheryl. One late night, when she thought she was the only one in the office, she cranked up her boom box and began singing all of the songs "On the Radio," (Donna Summers, 1979). To her surprise, her boss, Tee Love, heard her singing and instantly knew he had found a star. Weeks later he convinced her to quit the 9 to 5 job and cut a demo tape. He also gave her a $50,000 advance.

Both women were sure that their success could be short-lived. Sheryl got the help of a tax advisor and was able to put her money in a tax deferred retirement plan (assume that a plan existed in 1975 that allowed her to put this much money away). Evelyn did not get any professional help; she put her money in a savings account.

Now it's 2005. Both women had successful singing careers in the late 70s/early 80s and still do limited performances. They both want to make sure that they will have sufficient money to retire comfortably. Assume the $50,000 that each of them invested 30 years ago grew at an 8% interest rate. Sheryl's $50,000 is now worth a little over $500,000, while Evelyn's is worth about $362,000. Why the difference? Sheryl made a tax deferred investment. This means she paid no taxes on the money over the 30-year period. Evelyn was paying taxes on the interest as her money grew over the same 30-year period.

These Qualified Retirement Plans are designed to provide you with cash flow during your retirement years. They use today's tax incentives to encourage and stimulate employees and employers to make contributions. The actual amount you can save in these plans on a yearly basis is subject to limitations. These plans come in many flavors and are typically set-up in various ways. In this Chapter get the 411 on:

➤ Employer-sponsored plans
➤ Self-employed plans
➤ Plans for everybody

As the name suggests, you must be an employee of a business to take advantage of the employer-sponsored plans. If you are self-employed, there are several tax advantageous plans "For You" (Kenny Lattimore, 1997), too. Finally, if you are not employed or are looking for ways to supplement your other retirement investments, you may consider IRA's (aka, plans for everybody). In fact, it's not uncommon for one person to have several of these plans (e.g., a 401(k) from the job, and a Keogh plan from a side business or an IRA).

Note: The above discussion and the rest of this Chapter focus on Qualified Retirement Plans; those that qualify for certain tax benefits in the tax laws. There is another popular retirement plan, known as the Deferred Compensation Plan, but it doesn't meet the requirements of a Qualified Retirement Plan. With a deferred compensation plan, you can elect to defer or postpone receiving your salary or bonuses. By doing so, you also defer paying income taxes until you actually receive your compensation. Some employers may want you to work for a number of years before your deferred compensation becomes vested; meaning the money is now yours and you can take it out of the plan or leave it in. Whatever the case, deciding how much to defer will involve a well-designed and complex financial retirement plan. Please consult with your tax advisor for more on this.

Also, note: The investment plans discussed in this Chapter are those that focus on saving money for your retirement and in some cases, the money can be used to purchase your first home. In addition, the next section focuses on savings and investments you can make to pay for your child's education. If you're looking for how to make investments and save taxes to pay for a vacation or new car, the tax laws won't help you much here. You're better off talking to a financial planner or tax advisor on how to best do this.

### Pointer 1: Before You Start Investing

As much as I want you to start saving, please do it wisely. As a general guide, you need about three months of expenses or six paychecks saved in a liquid account (like your bank savings account) BEFORE you even consider investing in a retirement plan (some advisors are now suggesting you need as much as six months of expenses in reserve). There are many tax advantages with these plans, but the penalties are high if you need to take the money out too soon. Please consult your tax advisor to set up a plan that's tailored to your needs.

## EMPLOYER-SPONSORED RETIREMENT PLANS

Employer-sponsored retirement plans are very common. The next time you look through the help wanted ads, take a look at how many companies list these plans under their employee benefit perks. Why do employers set any of these plans up? There are many answers to this, and here are some of them: First, the job market is very competitive for talented people. Offering great "benefits" is a way to attract the best employees. Also, employers can take tax deductions for the contributions that they make to these plans, and certain tax credits for setting them up in the first place. Finally, these plans are designed to help employees save for their future and not be so reliant on government benefits under social security); so, employers are just doing their part in helping with this higher goal. After all, the folks running the company are employees, too.

Common employer-sponsored plans can be broken up into two types: defined contribution plans and defined benefit plans. Defined contribution plans provide each person with a retirement account that is based on contributions made by the employer (or some by the employee). These are fairly easy to set-up; most investment banks offer these services. These plans "define" the amount of money that's goes in, but can't promise you a set amount of money by the time you retire.

On the flip side, a defined benefit plan allows the company to pay you a set amount during your retirement years; like the typical pension. It can define the benefit or the amount you will get "Somewhere Over the Rainbow," (take your pick as to which version you prefer, Judy Garland in the 1939 movie "Wizard of Oz," Patti LaBelle and the Blue Belles circa 1965, or Kimberly Locke's version in 2004 on American Idol). This is typically based off many factors, such as your compensation, age and years of service with the company. In other words you need an actuary to help with all of this.

Historically, defined benefit plans or pensions were popular employee benefits with bigger companies (i.e., like the car manufacturing companies).

Defined contribution plans were used by smaller companies, but thanks to such defined contribution plans as the 401(k) plan, this has all changed. Now, many companies, large and small, are using defined contribution plans; fewer are choosing to provide pensions, since these are harder to set up and administer. But some companies still use pensions because of the ability to possibly put more tax-deferred money away than with a defined contribution plan.

Get the 411 on the following defined contribution plans:

- 401(k) Plan
- Profit Sharing Plan
- Money Purchase Pension Plan
- Employee Stock Purchase Plan

Many employers offer combinations of these defined contribution plans. But, the most they will typically offer as contributions that you can make is 25% of your compensation (the maximum compensation that can be considered annually under this rule is $210,000 for 2005); or if you want to skip the math this translates into up to $42,000 for 2005 that you can contribute to these various plans. Finally, some of these plans have their own specific limits on how much you can contribute to them.

Note: Churches, government agencies and nonprofits all have similar retirement plans (sometimes called church plans, 457 plans or 403(b) plans). If you work for one of these entities, please contact your tax advisor for rules and restrictions particular to your employer. The principles discussed in this Chapter can still be generally applied to your situation.

## 401(K) PLAN

Perhaps the most common employer sponsored retirement vehicle is the 401(k); named, of course, after Section 401 and Paragraph k of the Internal Revenue Code. For close to twenty-five years now, employees have been able to shield away a part of their salary in these tax-deferred plans.

A 401(k) is a defined contribution plan that allows you to take pre-tax dollars from your salary and contribute them to an investment vehicle. These contributions are called deferred because you don't pay income taxes on them now. But, you will have an income tax when you take the money out. The contributions you make to a 401(k) simply don't count when you are trying to calculate your yearly taxable income. Also, you can have penalty taxes if you take the money out too early (i.e., before you reach 59½). Finally, you may be able to take a loan from the plan or take the money out due to certain hardship situations. All of these rules are discussed later in this Chapter.

Setting up the contributions is "Easy" (..like Sunday morning, Commodores, 1977). You can contribute 15% of your annual salary or a maximum of $14,000 to a 401(k). This is done by simply filling out some forms at your J-O-B instructing your employer to start taking your contributions off the top before you get your paycheck.

Many employers have "matching" programs where they contribute an amount equal to your contribution, or a percentage of your contribution, but your employer is not required to do this. However, when it happens, it's one of the best "2-for-1 deals" around. If you make a $1 contribution, it's like you made $2, because your employer puts in a matching contribution. Note: Some employers match less than 100%, so please check with your company's benefits department.

You will have several investment options for your 401(k) plan, including various mutual funds, and some companies allow you to also invest in their own stock. If you've learned anything from Enron, even if you love the company that you work for and they have been really good to you, be cautious about putting too much of your 401(k) money in your company's stock. Only investing in your company's stock could be disastrous; particularly if anything happens to your company (i.e., they go bankrupt). In addition to talking to your tax adviser, it's also a good idea to check with a financial planner in deciding where to invest the money in your plan.

Keep in mind that while 401(k) plans are employer-sponsored, the employer does not provide you with any advice or guidance regarding the investment of your 401(k) money. The employer has no risk or liability for the performance of your investments or the underlying investment vehicle choices. It's the employee's responsibility to be knowledgeable about the investment plan, its provisions, the investment options, and the performance of the investment choices and the stock market. For more on 401(k) plans, see *IRS Publication, 525, Taxable and Nontaxable Income* and *IRS Publication 560, Retirement Plans for Small Businesses (SEP, SIMPLE, and Qualified Plans)*.

### Pointer 2: Check Box 12 of Your W-2

Box 12 of Form W-2 should reflect the amount of your tax deferred earnings. It may have a letter "D" next to the amount, which means that this is the amount of 401(k) contributions that you made, but this amount is not included in your taxable wages reported in Box 1 of your Form W-2.

### Pointer 3: Finding Money to Contribute to a 401(k)

To find the "extra" money to contribute to a 401(k), work with your tax advisor to project your income taxes based on your salary reductions; which should result in tax savings. That savings should be the starting point for the amount you can contribute to your 401(k) each pay period. For more on this, see Chapter 10: FAQs #21.

## EMPLOYEE STOCK PURCHASE PLAN

An Employee Stock Purchase Plan (or ESPP) is another example of a defined contribution plan. ESPPs allow you to purchase your company's stock at a reduced price. Here's how it typically works.

Starting in January of year 1, the company sets a beginning purchase price for the ESPP. Again, this is typically discounted at some percent of what the stock is trading on that particular day (i.e., 15% below the stock's price on a certain defined date). You begin to set aside money to "purchase" your company's stock. This is done typically through a salary reduction in your paycheck (i.e., 5% of your salary is used to purchase company stock). You continue to purchase the stock throughout the year, but you don't actually own the stock until the beginning of year 2. At that time the company sets the ending discounted price for your ESPP stock (again, 15% below what the stock is trading on a date in year 2). The company then takes whichever price is smaller (i.e., the ESPP's beginning purchase price in year 1 or the ending purchase price in year 2). This becomes the price at which you finally purchase the company's stock.

Since the price is discounted, you will have a gain. You have two choices at this point; sell the stock and pay short-term capital gains taxes or hold on to the stock for over a year and get the more favorable long-term capital gains taxes rate. For more on capital gains tax rates, see Chapter 4: Capital Gains.

## PROFIT SHARING

A Profit Sharing Plan, also a type of defined contribution plan, is just what the name implies: a plan that allows you to share in your company's profits. They serve as an added bonus for employees and are typically based on some percentage of profit (e.g., 5% of the company's 2004 profit will go into the plan). This is only paid by the company. You don't make any contributions of your own money to the plan. Also, the amount that goes into the plan will often vary from year-to year since it is based on the company's performance.

What's your share of the profit-sharing plan? This, too, will vary from company to company, but it's typically based on a percentage of your salary. Also, employers often require that you stay with the company for a certain period of time (i.e., 5 years) before the money in the plan is yours (called vested). Thus, unlike a 401(k) plan where you have to wait until you are 59½, you can take the money out of a profit sharing plan anytime after you are vested, even if you leave the company.

Note: A stock bonus plan (called an Employee Stock Option Plan or ESOP) is a type of profit sharing plan where the company's stock is used to make the contributions. Also, many companies combine their Profit Sharing Plan with a 401(k). For more on profit sharing plans, see *IRS Publication 560, Retirement Plans for Small Businesses (SEP, SIMPLE, and Qualified Plans)*.

## MONEY PURCHASE PENSION PLAN

Under this final type of defined contribution plan, the employer makes contributions to an account for the employee; only this time it's a fixed amount (i.e., 10% of your base compensation, regardless of the company's performance). The employer will typically set a retirement age at which you can take out the money from a money purchase pension plan. For more on money purchase pension plans, see *IRS Publication 560, Retirement Plans for Small Businesses (SEP, SIMPLE, and Qualified Plans)*.

## SELF-EMPLOYED PLANS

Uncle Sam also gives several tax benefits for investment plans set up by self-employed businesses. Keep in mind that for many of these plans, you can make contributions on behalf of the employer (that's you) and the employee (that's you again). So you may be able to put away more tax deferred money in retirement accounts than your brethren employed by large corporations. The four common self-employed investment plans are:

➢ Individual or Solo 401(k)
➢ SEP IRA
➢ Simple IRA
➢ Keogh Plans (i.e., profit sharing plans or money purchase pension plans)

Generally, the maximum amount that can be contributed to any combination of these plans for a given year is 25% of your compensation, up to $42,000 for 2005. The maximum compensation that can be considered annually for these benefits is $210,000 for 2005. Note: There are a few exceptions, such as with the Solo 401(k) plan and SIMPLE IRA, discussed below.

### Pointer 4: Finding the Money

The challenge most self-employed business owners' face is having sufficient cash flow to fund a self-employed retirement plan and pay other business expenses, like income tax liabilities. Your business gets a deduction for your contribution to the self-employed retirement plan, but tax liabilities for income and self-employment taxes may still exist. Your tax advisor should compute the cash flow requirements of both scenarios, to help you determine how much you can actually afford to contribute to your self-employed business plan.

### Pointer 5: Part-Time Side Business

Even if your side business is part-time (because you also have a "9 to 5" job), you can still typically set-up these self-employed retirement plans (all except the SIMPLE IRA). This can be particularly helpful where your spouse doesn't have a "9 to 5" job, because some of these plans may also allow tax deferred contributions in a retirement plan for your spouse, too! There are some limitations, though, when combining plans, so please check with your tax advisor to see what combinations you may use.

### Pointer 6: Comparisons of Self-Employed Plans

Choosing the right plan, or combination of self-employed retirement plans, will depend on many factors; such as your cash flow, age and investment profile. You will need to consult a tax advisor to figure out the best mix for your situation. There are several on-line calculators that will let you compare how much you can contribute to some of these plans, such as:

- ✓ 401khelpcenter.com—
  http://www.pensiononline.com/poltools/netearn.asp

✓ Texas Pension Consultants—
http://www.texaspension.com/solo401ksupportservices.aspx#

**INDIVIDUAL 401(K) PLANS**

The individual 401(k) (or a Solo 401(k)) is a relatively new plan that allows self-employed business owners to establish employer-sponsored retirement plans for themselves. In general, only businesses without employees can use an individual 401(k). This can be used by any business that employs only the owner and his or her spouse including: sole proprietorships, limited liability companies, partnerships and corporations.

As with the 401(k) plans used with larger employers, the contributions you make to the solo 401(k) are not taxed; they are deferred until you withdraw the money for retirement. You can also make the contributions by making withdrawals from your paychecks before you calculate your taxes.

As an employee of your own business, you can contribute up to 15% of your annual salary up to a maximum of $14,000 for 2005. Also, as the employer, you can make matching contributions up to 25% of your compensation, but the maximum of both contributions cannot be more than $42,000 2005. Finally, you can contribute more to the solo 401(k) plan than any other self-employed retirement plan (i.e., IRAs, profit-sharing plans or money purchase pension plans).

**Pointer 7: Setting up the Plan**
You must set these plans up by December 31st of a given year. Also, these plans are becoming easier to set-up as many investment banks offer them. In addition to a set-up fee, you will have to pay annual fees of a couple hundred bucks. You will need to file *Form 5500, Annual Return/Report of Employee Benefits Plans* once the assets in the Solo 401(k) reach $100,000. Finally, there are several free 401(k) calculators that can help you determine the benefits of setting up a solo 401(k) plan.

## SEP IRA PLANS

The SEP IRA (Simplified Employee Plan) is another retirement plan used by self-employed business owners. Any business type can use these plans (i.e., sole proprietorship, partnership, limited liability company, corporation). It can also be used by businesses with employees or those without, and can cover your spouse. A SEP is very much like a traditional IRA, except you can contribute more money to it thanks to the employer matching contributions. See the discussion in the next section of this Chapter for more on Traditional IRAs. Typically, the company makes tax deferred contributions to the SEP IRA for each employee (including for the small business owner). The amount of the contribution can vary as long as it is not more than 25% of the compensation, up to $42,000 for 2005. Also, you aren't taxed until you take the money out for retirement.

Employees can also make their own contributions to the SEP IRA up to $4,000. Since the SEP IRA is really a Traditional IRA (it's just set-up by a small business), the employee cannot also make a contribution to another Traditional IRA that she has set up on her own (i.e., through her bank). If she does, she will not be eligible for certain tax benefits (i.e., the tax deduction for Traditional IRA contributions) and may have to pay penalty taxes.

As long as you set them up by the date your tax return is due (typically April 15$^{th}$, unless you file for extensions), you can recognize the tax benefits for the previous year (i.e., 2005 tax benefits, as long as the plan is set up by April 15, 2006).

What are the advantages of a SEP IRA? They are typically easier to set-up and have lower annual fees than other types of self-employed retirement plans. They can be set up by any business and can be great for folks who have a part-time side business (i.e., a freelance writer) in addition to what they save under a 401(k) at their full-time job. For more on SEP IRAs, see *IRS Publication 560, Retirement Plans for Small Businesses (SEP, SIMPLE, and Qualified Plans)*.

## SIMPLE IRA

For an investment with "simple" in the name, it must be easy. And actually, it is pretty "simple" to set up and maintain. The SIMPLE IRA (i.e., Simple means "Savings Incentive Matching Plan for Employees of Small Employers") is a retirement plan that allows the same tax benefits as with other self-employed retirement plans. It can also be used by businesses with employees, those without employees, and can even cover your spouse. But, you can't set up a SIMPLE IRA if you have another self-employed retirement plan (i.e., a SEP IRA, Keogh plan or Solo 401(k)).

You can make tax deferred contributions to the SIMPLE IRA, up to a maximum of $10,000 for 2005. Also, the company can make a matching contribution up to 3% of your compensation. The SIMPLE IRA should typically be established by October 1st of a given year in order for the employee and employer contributions to be eligible for tax benefits. You have until your tax return is due (i.e., typically April 15th, or the date it is due if you filed an extension) to put the money in the SIMPLE IRA.

What are the advantages of a SIMPLE IRA? They are typically easier to set-up and have lower annual fees than other types of self-employed retirement plans. They're typically set up by businesses with fewer than 100 employees and can be great for folks just starting their side business (i.e., a freelance writer). For more information, see *IRS Publication 560, Retirement Plans for Small Businesses (SEP, SIMPLE, and Qualified Plans)*.

## KEOGH PLAN

A Keogh Plan is just a profit-sharing plan, or a money purchase pension plan used by a self-employed business owners, such as sole proprietors and partnerships. For more on the specifics of each plan, see the discussion in the previous section of this Chapter. Generally, you can make tax deferred contributions, up to $42,000 for 2005 a year to a Keogh plan for each employee. As long as you set up the plan by December 31st, you have until your tax return is due (i.e., typically April 15th, or the date it is due if you filed an extension) to put the money in the Keogh Plan. You pay taxes on the amount you take out of the plan after your retirement age.

What are the advantages of a Keogh Plan? Folks typically used this profit-sharing type of plan to entice employees to stay with the company (i.e., you only get the money after it is vested). Also, since it is based on the company's profits, it gives employees incentives to work hard to increase profits. Finally, before the Solo 401(k) Keogh plans were the favored self-employed retirement plans because you could contribute the most money to these plans. But now with a Solo 401(k), if you are over 50 years of age, you can make certain "catch-up' contributions that will allow you to contribute a bit more than the amount you can contribute to a Keogh Plan (i.e., making the total possible amount you can contribute to a Solo 401(k) $46,000 for 2005). However, Keogh Plans can be somewhat complex to set-up and administer. For more on Keogh plans, see *IRS Publication 560, Retirement Plans for Small Businesses (SEP, SIMPLE, and Qualified Plans)*.

## PLANS FOR EVERYBODY

Just like the lyrics to the song, "Everybody, Everybody (Black Box, 1990)," almost anyone can set up an Individual Retirement Account or IRA. The good news is that you don't need much money to set these up and the tax benefits can be enormous. There are two types of IRAs: Traditional IRA and Roth IRA.

Your contributions to a Traditional IRA may be tax deductible, but you will pay taxes on the earnings when you take the money out. A Roth IRA has an opposite affect. You won't get a deduction for your contributions, but you don't pay taxes when you take the money out for your retirement. Also, an IRA (Traditional or Roth) can only be owned by one person. So, a couple must create a separate IRA for each person.

Which plan is better—The Traditional IRA or the Roth IRA? This question is sort of like asking which version of "Car Wash," do you prefer—the

1977 version by Rose Royce, or the 2004 version by Christina Aguilera, 2004? There is no right answer (then again). The answer will depend heavily on your personal facts. Some years it may be better for you to take the Traditional IRA deduction, while others the Roth IRA might be right. Know the rules, talk to your tax advisor and celebrate because it's all good since you are using these finance and tax skills to build your retirement nest egg. For more on IRAs, see *IRS Publication 590, Individual Retirement Arrangements (IRA)*.

## TRADITIONAL IRA

You can contribute up to a maximum of $4,000 for 2005 to a Traditional IRA. Also, if you qualify, you may be able to deduct your IRA contribution from your gross income (i.e., an Above the Rim Deduction). See Chapter 1: Tax Basics for more on this. But, you pay taxes on the amount you take out of the plan after retirement age (i.e., starting at 59½). If you participate in an employer-sponsored retirement plan (e.g., a 401(k)) you may not be able to take the deduction for your IRA contribution. For more on the Traditional IRA deduction, see Chapter 1: Tax Basics.

**Pointer 8: Reporting Your IRA Contribution**
Report your IRA deduction on line 25 of Form 1040. There are no additional forms or schedules that you need to complete to take this deduction.

## ROTH IRA

With a Roth IRA, you can also contribute up to a maximum of $4,000 annually, but the Roth IRA has the opposite tax treatment. Contributions to the Roth IRA receive no tax benefit. You make them with after-tax dollars, since you can't take a deduction for them on your tax return. When you take the money out at retirement age, you don't have to pay any taxes. This allows you to make money on an initial contribution without ever having to pay taxes. But you must keep the money in the Roth IRA at least for 5 years, or be subject to penalty taxes. Also, for certain big ballers and shoot-callers, you can't make a contribution to a ROTH IRA if your adjusted gross income is more than $160,000 for married couples filing jointly and $110,000 for single folks. For more on how to figure out your adjusted gross income, see Chapter 1: Tax Basics.

**Pointer 9: Roth Calculators**
Want to know the potential value of your Roth IRA? You can try using one of these calculators:
- Commerce Clearing House—
  http://www.finance.cch.com/sohoApplets/RothIRA.asp
- Financial Partners Credit Union—
  http://www.fpcu.org/calculators_ira.asp
- Dinkytown.net—http://www.dinkytown.net/java/RothTransfer.html

### RETIREMENT PLAN COMMON ISSUES

Now that you have the 411 on some of the common types of tax advantageous retirement plans, you may still have questions, like: When can I start taking the money out? What if I have an emergency and need the money right away? What type of penalties do I have to pay? Can I take a loan? How can I rollover the money from one plan to another plan that I think is better for me? Get the low down on several common issues that folks encounter with these plans, such as:

- Regular distributions
- Hardship distributions
- Early withdrawals
- Loans
- Rollovers

Note: If you are taking money out of your retirement plan before retirement age (i.e., 59½) for non hard-ship reasons, you should talk to your tax advisor first to see if there are other things that you can do. Remember, the entire point of putting money away in these plans was to save for your future and take advantage of certain tax breaks. By taking the money out early, you are undoing both of these goals and creating extra taxes.

## REGULAR DISTRIBUTIONS

You typically pay taxes on the amount you take out of the various retirement plans after retirement age (i.e., starting at 59½). You must take all of the money out by the time you reach 70 ½. If you don't do this or you take it out too early, you may have penalty taxes to the tune of 10%, and you also may have to pay taxes on the amount of your earnings in the retirement plan. See the discussion below on early withdrawals and *IRS Publication 575, Pension and Annuity Income*

## HARDSHIP DISTRIBUTIONS

I know that there are times when things are rough and you need a friend; we all need somebody to lean on ("Lean on Me," Bill Withers, 1972 or Club Nouveau, 1987). Believe it or not, the IRS might just be that friend. That's right. If you are taking money out of your retirement plan for certain emergencies or hardships, you might be able to do so without having to pay penalty taxes. What qualifies as a hardship? This will vary a bit for each type of retirement plan, and can't be used with SEP IRAs and SIMPLE IRAs, but it typically includes:

- ✓ Payments for medical expenses in excess of 7.5% of your adjusted gross income
- ✓ Purchasing your first home
- ✓ Payments for health insurance premiums for unemployed folks
- ✓ Paying tuition and related fees to send yourself, your spouse and/or your child to college
- ✓ Payments for expenses because you became disabled
- ✓ Paying off back taxes

If you plan to take the money out for an emergency, please check with your tax advisor to see if it qualifies as a hardship distribution. Also, see *IRS Publication 575, Pension and Annuity Income*.

### EARLY WITHDRAWALS

There are many reasons or emergencies that you may need to take money out of one of these retirement plans that don't qualify as hardships. In these cases, you can take the money out (after all, it is your retirement money), but you will probably have to pay penalty taxes. Most of these retirement plans are subject to a 10% penalty tax. In addition to the penalty tax, you may also have to pay a tax on those tax-free earnings that you enjoyed. For example, you put 3,000 in a Traditional IRA. Six years later you take the money out when it's now worth $4,200. In addition to paying a 10% penalty tax on the $1,200 ($4,200 - $3,000), you also have extra income to the tune of $1,200 on the earnings from that IRA.

The rules are a bit different with a Roth IRA. You don't owe any penalty taxes on the amount of your original contribution to the account. Why? Because you made your contribution using after-tax dollars and you haven't gotten any taxes benefits. But it's another story for your earnings in the account. These will be subject to a penalty tax and income tax if you take the money out of the account in the first five years.

If you plan to take the money out your retirement plans, please check with your tax advisor to understand the financial impact of doing so and to look for alternatives. Note: If you pass away before you turn 59½, the money can go to your heirs without any penalty taxes. For more on this, see *IRS Publication 575, Pension and Annuity Income*.

**Pointer 10: Form 5329,**
Pay your penalty taxes using *Form 5329, Additional Taxes on Qualified Plans (including IRAs) and Other Tax Favored Accounts* and attach it to your tax return.

### LOANS

Instead of taking the money out of your retirement plan and facing penalties, you may be able to take a loan from the plan. Most companies will let you borrow against your employer-sponsored 401(k) plan; but there are limits. You can typically only borrow up to $50,000. It's the same case for Solo 401(k) Plans. If your company won't let you borrow against their 401(k) plan and you have a side business (i.e., you're also a consultant or freelancer in addition to your "9 to 5" job), consider rolling over your company's 401(k) into a Solo 401(k) from your side business. Then, you can take a loan from your Solo 401(k).

You can't take a loan from your SEP IRA or SIMPLE IRA. Also, you can't take a loan from your Traditional IRA or Roth IRA. You can, however, take money out of your IRA account; and as long as you pay it back within 60 days, you won't have any taxes. Note: You can only use this 60-day exception once per year. Also, if you miss the 60-day window, you will then owe penalty taxes, and in the case of a Roth IRA, income taxes on any earnings.

If you can take a loan, it typically has to be paid back within 5 years and it must be a true loan—meaning you have to pay interest on the money that you borrow. Since you are borrowing from yourself, you are, in essence, paying interest to yourself. What happens if you don't pay the loan back? Even though it is your money, you got the benefit of a tax deferral, so you will have to pay a 10% penalty tax.

## ROLLOVER

A rollover is when you take the money from one type of retirement plan and put it into another type of retirement plan. They are pretty easy to do and just about any type of retirement plan can be rolled over into another type of retirement plan. For example, you can set up a Solo 40l(k) by rolling over funds from a SEP IRA, or another type of IRA.

Why do a rollover in the first place? The decision on whether or not to rollover will depend on your circumstances. Perhaps the most common type of rollover is from a Traditional IRA to a Roth IRA. Remember, with the Traditional IRA you are using pre-tax dollars to make money and then pay the tax years later. With the Roth IRA, you are using after-tax dollars to, again, make money, but pay no taxes later. If you take money from a Traditional IRA and roll it over into a Roth IRA, you will have to pay an initial tax. Why? Because Roth IRAs can only be set up with money that has been taxed. It may be worth it to pay this tax now to avoid having to pay a tax at your retirement. Please consult with your tax advisor to run the various scenarios to see which is best for you. Also, you might try these free on-line Roth conversion calculators:

➢ LeadFusion—http://www.leadfusion.com/products/tools.asp
➢ Mile High Accountancy (a product of CCH Tax & Accounting)—http://www.execusite.com/clmjr/tools.html

For more on IRAs, see *IRS Publication 590, Individual Retirement Arrangements (IRA)*.

## Education

Remember the slogans that used to be on T-shirts during the 90s? "Each One, Teach One" or "Don't Hate, Educate." Education is key for our young people to become and remain competitive in the workforce; but can you really afford to send your bundle of joy to college? It's no secret that college tuition fees are rising. At the same time, scholarships and grants are harder to come by. Although school loans can make higher education possible, this debt can result in significant financial hardships for parents and students while in school and after graduation.

Consider the following facts: According to the College Board, a non-profit organization, the average annual cost of attending college (i.e., for tuition, fees, room, and board) for 2004 was:

- $11,354 for a public college
- $27,516 for a private college

But, the lifetime benefits of a quality educational background and higher education can be significant. Using figures from The Employment Policy Foundation, the lifetime compensation for a person with four years of college is about $2.2 million. Toss in a master's degree and this figure grows to $2.3 million; with a doctorate, you're looking at almost $3 million. For someone with only a high school diploma, the estimated lifetime compensation is about $1.3 million; almost half that of the person with a college degree.

Like the slogan made popular by the United Negro College Fund, "A Mind is a Terrible Thing to Waste." Don't let your lack of good financial planning and savings keep your children from attending college. Get the 411 on some tax and financial savings plans and tax credits that can help you send your child to college without breaking the bank.

➢ 529 Plans
➢ Coverdell Education Savings Account
➢ US Savings Bonds
➢ UGMA (Uniform Gift to Minors Account)
➢ Education Tax Credits

Although this Chapter focuses on making investments and saving for your child's future, keep in mind there may be other tax break s that you can get now for your own educational expenses. If you paid for education expenses to help you in your current job, these expenses may qualify for a tax deduction. For more on this, see the discussion under miscellaneous itemized deductions in Chapter 6: Itemized Deductions Part II. Also, if you are still paying off your student loans, you may be able to take a tax deduction for the interest. Finally, you may be able to deduct certain higher education expenses you pay in 2005 under the tuition and fees deduction. For more on the student loan interest deduction and the tuition and fees deduction, see Chapter 1: Tax Basics.

## 529 PLANS

A 529 Plan (named after the tax code section number) is an investment vehicle that is used to cover qualified education expenses in connection with attending a college or university. These expenses include costs for: tuition, fees, books, supplies, equipment, and in many cases room and board. It may also be called a college savings plan or a prepaid tuition program (sometimes called the qualified tuition program or the guaranteed tuition program).

Many 529 Plans are actually operated by your state. The state sets up the plan with an investment management company. You and your neighbors open up an account with these state sponsored plans. The state then pools this money together and uses it to make investments on your behalf. In many ways this is like a mutual fund. This 529 Plan offers various investment options (depending on the particular state). Keep in mind, these are investments that still bear some risk. The amount of money that will eventually be available in the college savings plan will be affected by many factors (such as risk, rate of return, fees and expenses, restrictions, and amount and frequency of contributions).

But, in many cases, you don't have to open your 529 plan in your home state to get the tax advantages or only send your child to a college in your home state. However, some states give you state tax advantages (e.g., state tax deductions for contributions to that state's 529 Plan). So, "Shop Around," (Smokey Robinson and the Miracles, 1960) and see which plan best meets your investment objectives and state tax objectives. There are also some 529 Plans set up by private colleges and universities.

You own the 529 Plan and your child is the beneficiary of the plan. This means you, and not your child, control the plan and have access to the funds in the plan. Also, a 529 Plan may be set-up by anyone, whether or not they are your dependent and regardless of income. You can set one up for a god-child, or a grandparent may set one up for a grandchild. Anyone can contribute to the 529 Plan. This is a great way for family and relatives to all contribute to your child's education.

Although your contributions to the 529 Plan are not tax deductible, all of the earnings in the plan build tax-free, and remain tax free when you take the money out to pay for qualified educational expenses. Also you can contribute (cash only) a significant total amount to a 529 Plan (e.g., up to $250,000 for each beneficiary). But beware of gift taxes. Generally, you may have gift taxes if you contribute more than $11,000 ($22,000 for married individuals) per year to a beneficiary (i.e., your child). See the next section in this Chapter for more on gift taxes. Luckily there is an exception that allows you to make a big payment, up to $55,000 in one year (or $110,000, if it is a married couple making the contribution). The tax laws will treat it as if the amounts were contributed over a five-year period. Even if you don't have much money, the point is to start saving for your child's education in the most tax-advantageous way possible. Many 529 Plan contributions can start with as little as $50 a month.

Once the money is put into a 529 Plan, it must be used for educational expenses or be subject to a 10% penalty tax and an income tax on the earnings in the account. These penalty taxes don't apply if your child dies, becomes disabled, gets a scholarship or you transfer the account to another family member (but you may still have to pay income taxes). So, if your little bundle of joy wants to be a "College Dropout," (Kanye West, 2004) you can use the money to pay for educational expenses for your other children or even for yourself. As long as your transfer the account to another family member for their educational expenses, there will be no penalties.

**Pointer 11: 529 Plans and Financial Aid**
Some financial aid programs, grants and work study programs look at the parent's assets, which may include 529 plans. Right now the impact is probably small, because many financial aid programs only look at about 5.6% of the parent's total assets as being available to pay for education costs. This could change in the future, so you should investigate

the financial aid provision of several colleges your child may want to attend to determine how assets owned by the parents will impact qualification for financial aid.

**Pointer 12: More Resources on 529 Plans**
There are several books and internet websites on 529 Plans. Check out http://www.savingforcollege.com or http://www.collegesavings.org for a comprehensive list of state-sponsored and private college 529 Plans. Also, see *IRS Publication 970, Tax Benefits for Education*. Want to see how much you need to save now to send your child to a specific college or university? Check out, Salary.com's™ college tuition planner at http://swz.salary.com.

## COVERDELL EDUCATIONAL SAVINGS ACCOUNT

A Coverdell Educational Savings Account ("ESA," also called Education IRA) is a savings account you can set up to pay your child's education expenses (e.g., tuition, fees, books, supplies, equipment, transportation, internet access fees, room and board). Your child must be under 18 (or any age for a person with special needs or a disability, like autism) when you set up the ESA. You can contribute up to $2,000 per child to an ESA (or several ESAs) as long as you don't give more than $2,000.

Similar to a 529 Plan, contributions made to the ESA receive no tax benefit, but earnings grow tax-free until distributed to pay for educational expenses. You also have almost sixteen months to make a contribution to an ESA for a particular year. So, if you're putting your $2,000 in an ESA using the payment plan route, you can start in January and pay up all the way through April 15th of the next year (e.g., for a 2005 ESA, you have until April 15, 2006).

Anyone can set up an ESA. This is another great way for family and relatives to all contribute to your child's education. Also, like a 529 Plan, you can use an ESA to cover education costs for a college or university. The advantage of an ESA over a 529 Plan is that it can also be used to cover educational expenses for vocational, public, private or religious schools, from K-12th grade.

Of course, nothing in life is perfect and investment vehicles are no different. You can only set up an ESA if your adjusted gross income is less than $110,000 (or $220,000 for married couples filing jointly). For more on computing adjusted gross income, see the discussion under Chapter 1: Tax Basics. Also, you must use the money in the ESA for educational expenses and before the child turns 30, or face a 10% penalty tax. Note: There is no age limit for special needs children.

### Pointer 13: Big Ballers and Shoot Callers

If you can't use an ESA because you make too much money, consider giving the money to your child and then having the child set up the ESA. Why? Because any earnings in the ESA grow tax-free and, any distributions for education expenses are tax-free, too.

### Pointer 14: ESAs and Financial Aid

ESAs can also impact whether or not your child qualifies for financial aid and, in fact, are more likely to do so than a 529 plan. Why? Because typically up to 35% of a family's combined assets must be used to cover education costs before a student is eligible for many financial aid program. ESAs are owned by your child and will count as an asset for purposes of calculating the family's expected contribution to education. You should investigate the financial aid provision of several colleges your child may want to attend to determine how assets owned by the student will impact qualification for financial aid.

## U.S. SAVINGS BONDS

We are all familiar with savings bonds. You buy them at a discounted price and, many years later, their value grows (thanks to interest being earned) to the amount listed on the bond (known as the "face amount"). Generally, you must pay income taxes on the interest when the bonds are cashed in. But there is an exception for qualified U. S. Savings Bonds (called Education Savings Bonds) that are cashed to pay qualified education expenses for you, your spouse or dependent. Note: Qualified education expenses don't include room and board under these rules.

Although U.S. Savings Bonds are a relatively easy way to save for your child's education, keep in mind that as your income increases, the tax benefits decrease. In fact, married folks filing jointly with adjusted gross incomes equal to or higher than $121,850, and $76,200 for single taxpayers, aren't eligible for this tax break. Also, if your child decides not to go to college you could owe taxes.

## UNIFORM GIFTS TO MINORS ACCOUNT

A Uniform Gifts to Minors Act account (known as an UGMA, Uniform Transfers to Minors Act account or UTMA) is an account set up by you, for your child through a brokerage firm. You can control exactly what the account is invested in (e.g., stocks, bonds, mutual funds, etc.). However, the child is considered to be the "owner' of the account.

You can contribute up to $11,000 a year tax-free to the UGMA ($22,000 if you are married, and you and your spouse contribute). Anything over that amount may be subject to gift taxes. See the next section in this Chapter for more on gift taxes.

UGMA's are particularly good education savings vehicles where your income is so high (e.g., $220,000 for married folks) that you can't take advantage of an ESA. As long as the money is used for the benefit of the child, including education expenses, you should meet the requirements of an UGMA. But beware—your child owns the account and unlike with a 529 Plan your child can take the money of the UGMA at the age of 18 for any reason; even non-educational purposes. Note: Taking the money out of an UGMA before your child is 18 can be very difficult and you should consult a tax advisor to evaluate your options.

You don't get a tax deduction for your contribution to the UGMA, and unlike a 529 Plan or an ESA, you have to pay taxes on the earnings (i.e., interest and dividends) and any gains when you sell the stock. But, the first $800 of investment income (i.e., interest, dividends and gains) is tax-free and the next $800 is taxed, using your child's tax rate (which should be significantly lower than yours). Anything over $1,600 is taxed at the parent's tax rate.

When you sell the stock, you may owe taxes on the capital gain. Remember, the child owns the UGMA, so it seems like any gain would be calculated using your child's tax rate. Since your young child has no other income and will pay taxes at a lower tax bracket (i.e., 8% long-term capital gains tax rate) this may not sound like such a bad thing. The IRS has this one figured out. Thanks to the so-called "kiddie tax," your child's investment earnings (e.g., gains from selling stock) are taxed using the parent's tax rate. This kiddie tax (being taxed using the parent's tax rate) only applies when your child is under 14 years of age. For children 14 and over, the investment earnings are taxed at their own (often lower) tax rate. For more on UGMAs, see *IRS Publication 929, Tax Rules for Children and Dependents*

### Pointer 15: Fourteen and Over
Hold on to investments in the UGMA until your child is at least 14. You can avoid paying a capital gains tax at your higher tax rate and you can use your child's lower tax rate (e.g., 8%).

### Pointer 16: Transfer to a 529 Plan
You may want to transfer your UGMA account to a 529 Plan to take advantage of the tax-free treatment on the earnings and withdrawals for qualified education expenses. But remember, 529 plans can only accept cash; many UGMA's hold stock. You would have to sell this stock first and then contribute the cash to the 529 Plan. This sale will probably trigger taxes. Also, as your child was the "owner" of the UGMA, many states

require that this child be the beneficiary of the 529 Plan. This means you may not be able to use money from the 529 Plan you created with the UGMA money to pay for another child of family member's education; which you may need to do if the child that you originally set up the UGMA for decides to skip school and try the "rap thang." If this happens you may have to pay penalties to take the money out. Please consult a tax advisor about your best options for converting an UGMA to a 529 Plan.

### EDUCATION TAX CREDITS

Up to this point, I've been discussing tax-advantaged vehicles you can use to help pay for your child's future education expenses. There are two other tax credits you may be eligible for to help offset the cost of higher education.

➢ The Hope Credit
➢ The Lifetime Learning Credit

Keep in mind, tax credits reduce your taxes on a dollar-for-dollar basis. This means, for every dollar of tax you owe, a credit can decrease that tax by the same dollar. But a tax deduction only reduces your tax by a percentage. Assuming a 20% tax rate, for every dollar of tax, an itemized deduction will reduce the amount by 20 cents; so, you're left with a tax on 80 cents. Thus, tax credits are often more beneficial than some tax deductions because deductions only reduce the amount of your income subject to tax, while the credit reduces the actual tax. For more on deductions and other tax credits, see Chapter 1: Tax Basics.

There are a few restrictions on the amount you can take as education credits. First, these credits can only be used for tuition and related fees. They will not cover other expenses like room and board, or books. Second, if your adjusted gross income is greater than $53,000 for a single taxpayer and $107,000 for married taxpayers filing jointly, you cannot claim the credits at all. Also, you can not take the credit if you also take the tuition and fees tax deduction for the education expenses. For more on this deduction, see Chapter 1: Tax Basics.

Finally, while both credits cannot be taken for the same student in the same year, both credits can be taken on the same tax return; for instance, where both of your children are students and separately qualify for each credit. Also, you might not be able to take either credit if you are taking the tuition and fees deduction, which allows you to deduct up to $4,000 a year for certain education expenses. You should consult your tax advisor to see which education credit, or deduction, gives you the largest tax benefit. For more on the tuition and fees deduction, and where to report your tax credits on your tax return, see Chapter 1: Tax Basics. Also see *IRS Publication 970, Tax Benefits for Educations.*

### Pointer 17: Form 8863

Calculate your education credits on *Form 8863, Education Credits (Hope and Lifetime Learning Credits)*, then enter the amount of the credit on line 47 of Form 1040. You should also attach this form to your tax return

### Pointer 18: Form 1098-T

You should receive *Form 1099-T, (Tuition Payment Statement)* from any institution to which you pay tuition. Use this form to figure out your tuition expenses for the year. You do not need to attach this form to your tax return, but you should keep it for your tax files for at least three years.

## THE HOPE CREDIT

The Hope Credit provides a maximum tax credit of $1,500 for each eligible student. This means you can get multiple Hope Credits if you are paying for multiple children (or if you, or your spouse, also have education expenses).

Of course, there are a few rules you must know before taking the Hope Credit. First, this credit is only available for the first two years of education beyond high school for a student pursuing an undergraduate degree or other recognized credential. Also, the classes may be taken anywhere—even abroad. That's good news for the "Ethiopian queen from Philly taking classes abroad and studying film and photo flash record," who was so eloquently described by Black Thought in "You Got Me" (featuring Erykah Badu and Eve, 1999). In addition, the student must be enrolled at least half-time for one academic period during the year. Also, the student can not have a felony drug conviction for purposes of being eligible for the Hope Credit. Finally, to calculate the Hope Credit, you get 100% of the first $1,000 you pay for tuition expenses and 50% for the next $1,000 you pay in tuition expenses. This means the maximum Hope Credit you can take for each student is $1,500.

### THE LIFETIME LEARNING CREDIT

The Lifetime Learning Credit provides a maximum of $2,000 credit per tax return. So you can only get one Lifetime Learning Credit, even if you're paying educational expenses for multiple children. This credit covers all years of post-high school education and course work taken to acquire and improve job skills. There is no degree requirement and no time limit in eligibility. To calculate the Lifetime Learning Credit, take 20% of the tuition expenses that you pay (up to $10,000 in expenses).

# Estate

The saying, "Nothing in life is guaranteed but death and taxes," has never been truer, as this next section tackles estate and gift taxes. It's important to understand that throughout most of *For The Love Of Money*, I've been discussing taxes that you pay on the income that you earn on your gains from selling your assets. Estate and gift taxes are intended to make sure you pay more taxes on your assets at your death or on the value of certain gifts that you make during your lifetime.

Good tax planning can go a long way in minimizing the impact of these taxes. It's not just the rich and famous who have to worry about estate and gift taxes. Thanks to the internet boom, rising home prices and two-wage earner households, more and more of us are amassing resources that could create estate and gift taxes. As with most things, a bit of education can go a long way in helping to significantly reduce these taxes. Note: The discussion that follows focuses on the federal estate and gift tax. Many states have their own estate and gift taxes. Please check with your tax advisor for those rules.

### GIFT TAX

"I have to pay taxes when I give gifts?" Many people are very surprised to hear this; but yes, there is a gift tax on money and property that you give to another person. A gift is something you give to another person with no expectation that you will be repaid. It does not include payments you make for your obligations (such as paying for food, shelter, clothing and other necessities for your minor child). Typically, the person receiving the gift does not have to pay taxes on the value of the gift. Also, you don't get an income tax deduction for any gift taxes that you pay. But thanks to several broad exceptions, most people never actually pay this gift tax.

First, you can generally give an unlimited amount of money and property to your spouse or to a qualified charity without having to pay a gift tax. So, at least between spouses, you can give those "Diamonds and Pearls" (Prince, 1991) without worrying about gift taxes.

Also, you can give up to $11,000 a year ($22,000 if your spouse also makes the gift) to anybody without having to pay gift taxes. So, go ahead and splurge and buy your neighbor, friend, cousin or whomever a gift like those two pairs of "Air Force Ones," (Nelly, 2002). Unless you give more than $11,000 worth of these tennis shoes to one person in a year, you won't have any gift taxes.

Even if you give someone more than $11,000 in a particular year, you may not have to actually pay a gift tax. Why? Because there's a gift tax credit that applies first. With this credit, you can give up to $1 million over your lifetime in gifts before you have to actually pay taxes. But keep in mind, you will still need to file a gift tax return when you give more than $11,000 to a single person in a particular year, even if you don't have to pay gift taxes (use *Form 709, U.S. Gift (and Generation-Skipping Transfer) Tax Return*. Why? This is so the IRS can track how many gifts you have given over your lifetime and know when you have reached the $1 million mark.

The next good piece of news is that you can pay anyone's tuition and not have to worry about paying gift taxes (like for your kids, your grandkids or "your baby's mamas, mamas, mamas…"—"Ms Jackson," Outkast, 2000). Why? Because tuition paid directly to the school is excluded from the gift tax rules. The bad news is that any related educational expenses may be subject to gift taxes. So, you can pay the school for tuition, but if you also pay for someone else's room and board or a computer, this may be subject to gift tax. Also, you can still generally pay for these expenses for your child or dependent and not have to worry about gift taxes—just remember to file the gift tax return (*Form 709, U.S. Gift (and Generation-Skipping Transfer) Tax Return*).

Finally, you can pay for anyone's medical expenses without having gift taxes;, but you must pay directly to the medical hospital or establishment for these expenses. If you anticipate having a large estate (several million or more), making gifts during your lifetime can save you taxes. As this is a very complex area and will depend heavily on your facts and circumstances, please consult with your tax advisor to develop your own gift-giving plan.

## ESTATE TAX

The estate tax might apply to the value of your estate at the time of your death. This means the value of all your assets less your liabilities. As with everything in tax laws, there are numerous rules, restrictions and exceptions that apply to valuing your estate and the tax itself, such that not many people actually have to pay an estate tax.

First, assets typically include those that you "own" at the time of your death. This could mean your house, car, stock, and even life insurance death benefits; but there are certain exceptions, such as 529 Plans. Even though you own and control the money on this account, they are excluded for purposes of calculating your total assets.

Also, if the value of your estate is less than $1.5 million, you will not owe estate taxes. This is thanks to the estate tax credit. This $1.5 million may seem like a lot, but if you consider house prices, stock values and family owned businesses, some people may be closer to this threshold. Note: the estate tax credit increases to $2 million for 2006–2008 and then to $3.5 million for 2009.

Next, for married taxpayers, there is a marital deduction that takes all assets you leave to a spouse completely out, for purposes of calculating the estate tax.

Finally, there is another piece of good news. The estate tax has actually been repealed. The bad news is that unless you die in 2010, which is the only year the repeal is good for, the estate tax will still apply to you. It's one of those "Things That Make You Go Hmmm" (C+C Music Factory, 1991). This is one of those areas that is constantly being debated in Congress and will likely go through many changes over the next few years. As you are building your wealth and investment portfolio, make sure to ask your tax advisor about the impact of estate taxes.

## REMIX

Here's the remix on what we learned in this Chapter:

1. Investment planning should be done early in the year, rather than at tax-time. The sooner and more frequent contributions are made to a retirement plan the better. While making a contribution at April 15th may have some tax benefits, you have missed invest-

ment earnings that could have been earning from January of the previous year. Don't just think taxes; Think investment.

2. People working a "9 to 5" job have many tax-advantaged retirement options, including 401(k) plans, Employee Stock Purchase Plans, Profit-Sharing Plans and Money Purchase Pension Plans. You may also be able to defer a part of your salary or bonuses under a Deferred Compensation Plan.

3. If you have a side business (either full or part-time), you may also be able to set-up several self-employed retirement plans, like: Solo 401(k), SEP IRA, SIMPLE IRA or a Keogh Plan.

4. Uncle Sam also has several tax beneficial retirement plans that can be set up by anyone—whether you have a job, own a business, or just "got it like that". These are called IRAs (Traditional or Roth).

5. Too many workers and self-employed folks feel they cannot afford to put aside money from their wages to contribute to a 401(k) plan. I particularly find younger workers (e.g., those under 35), who feel they have plenty of time to begin retirement savings and may not take advantage of these tax advantageous investment vehicles. If you've learned anything from this book, you understand that the benefits from tax savings and interest compounding results in more money for things like your retirement. So, begin contributing early and contribute often.

6. Be in it for the long haul. Markets will fluctuate, the economy will go up and down, the Democrats will regain the White House, and P. Diddy will change his name once again. But keep your money invested; or all this great tax planning will go to waste thanks to penalty taxes. You can make penalty-free withdrawals for higher education (college and university, not private school for your K-12$^{th}$ grader).

7. Don't subject your child to college and graduate school loans. These loans often create significant debt for your child, even

before they have their first real job. Let's take it to another level and arm our kids with an education paid for by our good tax planning. Start contributing to an education plan, like a 529 Plan or a Coverdell Education Savings Account, or UGMA (Uniform Gift to Minors Account). Also, remember that you can use savings bonds to pay for education expenses and avoid paying taxes on your interest.

8. Contributions to 529 plans receive no tax benefit; but earnings buildup tax-free distributions and are tax free, if they do not exceed qualified education expenses. Which 529 plan to use is the question? The answer depends on many variables. Are you comfortable with investments and the inherent risks involved? What's the time-horizon? What is the amount to be contributed? Regardless of the decisions, start early—contribute early and regularly, and pay attention to contribution limits to avoid over-contributions.

9. Know the education tax credits. The Hope Credit is up to $1,500 for each eligible student, but it is only available for the first two years of education beyond high school for a student pursuing an undergraduate degree or other recognized credential. Lifetime Learning Credits is a maximum of $2,000 credit per tax return and available for all years of post-high school education and course work taken to acquire and improve job skill.

10. Gift taxes may apply to any gift of money or property that you give. But thanks to the $1 million credit, it's not likely that you will have to pay a tax for the majority of gifts that you will give. Don't forget, you still have to file a gift tax return, even if you pay no gift taxes.

11. There is also an estate tax on the value of your assets at your death. Again, because of many exclusions (e.g., it doesn't apply to assets worth less than $1.5 million) many people never have to pay this tax.

**Chapter 9**

# IRS Audits
*Your Guide to Responding & Dealing With IRS Audits*

> *Because I come stronger than the IRS*
> *Whenever you done got delinquent on your taxes*
>
> **"Let's Get Down," Tony Toni Tone, Featuring DJ Quick (1996)**

---

It's your worse nightmare—a letter in the mail from the IRS. Since your refund check has already been deposited directly into your bank account, you know it's not money. This could mean nothing but trouble. You're being audited and like the song says, the IRS is "bringing it on strong."

Most people believe that an IRS audit is like the kiss of death. You will surely owe a lot of money and it will take a vast amount of hours to comply with all of the auditor's requests. Moreover, the maze of IRS notices, letters, rules and regulations can frazzle even the most experienced tax advisor.

I've been asked by many people, time and time again, questions like "How do I avoid an audit?" "What do I do if I get audited.?" and even "My auditor is out to get me. What can I do?" With respect to this last question (which I hear very often), although it is certainly possible that an auditor could have a bias, some of my best buddies work for the IRS. By and large they are good folks just doing their job. If you truly believe you have an overzealous auditor (and the facts truly support this) you should raise your concerns with that auditor's supervisor or manager. If it only gets worse, you should contact the Taxpayer Advocate Service office that serves your area (see the IRS website for contact information http://www.irs.gov).

Another key to taking control of your taxes, is knowing how to respond to an IRS audit. The good news is that for the vast majority of IRS audits, the first rule is—there is no need to worry or panic. This Chapter will help you better understand the IRS audit process, and give you tips on how to respond to IRS Auditors; all in the hopes of making an IRS Audit less "taxing." Don't forget to also see the Ways To Avoid An Audit in the Appendix.

## Types of IRS Audits

Knowing the type of IRS audit is very important in developing your response. There are three basic types of IRS audits:

### THE CORRESPONDENCE AUDIT

The Correspondence Audit is the simplest and most common type of IRS audit. It is just what the name suggests—the IRS contacts you with a letter (i.e., correspondence) asking to resolve some basic information on your tax return. Examples may include questions regarding an incorrect social security number or an amount listed on your tax return (e.g., wages, dividend income, mortgage interest) that doesn't match the information that the IRS has in your file. Correspondence audits are typically for routine questions and most of these questions are requests for clarification of errors or discrepancies discovered by an IRS computer (Yes, the IRS has sophisticated computers that automatically match taxpayer records with their tax returns). These issues can typically be resolved relatively easily by sending the IRS documentation (e.g., verifying the correct social security number or correct amount, interest received from a bank account, or interest paid to a mortgage company).

This type of audit is started, initially, by the IRS sending you a nicely-worded letter asking for additional information on certain issues, and giving you 30 days to respond with documents to support your position.

**Pointer 1: Get an Extension**

Call the IRS on the number provided in the letter and request an extension of time to respond to the request. This will allow you more time to gather the appropriate records and develop an appropriate response. Typically, the IRS will grant you an automatic extension up to another 30 days on the first request. Be cordial when you call. Answer all questions, but do not "volunteer" any information on the issues listed in the letter. Your purpose for calling is to obtain an extension of time to respond appropriately and accurately. It's perfectly reasonable to explain the need for an extension (e.g., saying something like, "I have to meet with my tax advisor and my appointment isn't until after the IRS response date.")

## THE OFFICE AUDIT

The Office Audit (or office examination, as it is also called) requires that you go to an IRS office to meet with an IRS Auditor to discuss some questions about your tax return. This audit also begins with a letter from the IRS. The initial IRS letter will list the items that have discrepancies or other issues. It will also provide you with a date and time for the first meeting, the IRS office address, and contact information for the IRS Auditor who will conduct your interview. The Office Audit focuses on tax items that are more complex or can't be easily resolved through a Correspondence Audit. For example, where the Correspondence Audit might ask you to verify the total mortgage interest paid, the Office Audit may ask that you not only verify the total interest paid, the total number of properties, the ownership of each property, and how you use the properties (e.g., as rentals, primary homes or vacation homes).

This face-to-face meeting with an IRS Auditor can be very scary, but, there is no need to panic. Be certain you fully understand what is being questioned and then try to determine the IRS rationale for wanting to look into that item. As long as you approach it the right way, with all of your records and with help from your tax advisor, you should be able to "Breathe Again" (Toni Braxton, 1993).

### Pointer 2: Get Those Records

The first and most important step is to make sure you gather all of your relevant documents and records that can prove the position you took on your tax return. There are two schools of thought regarding how easy you should make it for the auditor to go through your records. Some tax advisors say if you make it really difficult, the auditor won't look at everything. Others say if you make it easy, the IRS Auditor can finish more quickly and not prolong the ordeal. I advocate the latter approach—make it easy. Organize your documents in a way that you can easily find what you are looking for, and so you will have all the records at your finger tips. If you can easily trace the issue through your records and the IRS Auditor can easily follow what you are providing, your face-to-face meeting will run more smoothly and you will be able to attend the Office Audit from a position of confidence and knowledge.

### Pointer 3: Talk to a Tax Advisor

The second and vital step is that you speak with a tax advisor. You will need to share the IRS notice and any relevant documents with this tax advisor. Also, ask the tax advisor to do a quick "pre-audit" by looking at your documents, statements, and your tax preparer's work papers (i.e., if you self-prepared your tax return using a software package like TurboTax™, the work papers are the schedules and other worksheets that you didn't send in with your tax return). Meeting with a tax advisor in advance of the Office Audit will give you a feel for any potential issues the IRS Auditor may ask, and give you time to prepare your response. For more information on picking a tax advisor, see Chapter 10: FAQ # 10.

## THE FIELD AUDIT

The Field Audit (often called the "Examination") is when an IRS Auditor comes to interview the taxpayer at the taxpayer's home, office or tax advisor's office. It's more common for an IRS Auditor to come out in the "field" and examine the tax returns of businesses (particularly small businesses or nonprofits) than to visit an individual. If you run a small business (e.g., a sole proprietorship) and report your net profit on Schedule C, you are considered a small business and you could be subject to an IRS Field Audit.

Field Audits can last for several months or even years. Also, with a Field Audit, the IRS Auditor is not required, on the initial contact (which may be by letter or telephone), to tell you the issues being audited. Even so, you should try to get more information. Explain to the IRS Auditor that you need to know exactly what tax issues the IRS wants documented so you can discuss them with your tax advisor. Remind the IRS Auditor that the more time it takes to get this basic information, the more you'll have to pay for your tax advisor's time (and the less money you will have to pay the IRS).

The same pointers listed above under the Office Audit section, regarding gathering records are equally as important, if not more crucial, with a Field Audit. You should also ask the IRS Auditor for the following:

- A copy of the IRS audit plan or list of items that the auditor plans to review.
- The projected time frame for the audit.
- His or her specific expertise. Is it in audits of similar businesses? With which specific group does the auditor work?

All of these responses may give you a hint as to what issues are being audited.

# IRS Audit Notices

After an audit (e.g., Correspondence Audit, Office Audit or Field Audit) is concluded, the IRS Auditor will make a determination as to the audit results. If the IRS Auditor proposes changes to your tax return and you don't agree to these changes, you will receive a letter. This letter will tell you what adjustments are being proposed and the additional taxes you will owe the IRS if the proposed changes become permanent.

This preliminary Notice of Audit Adjustment is known as the "30 Day Letter," because it allows 30 days for you to challenge the IRS findings. If you don't respond to the 30 Day Letter in a timely manner, the IRS can determine that you are in default and will then issue another letter, known as a Statutory Deficiency Notice (commonly referred to as a "90 Day Letter"). The 90 Day Letter begins the time period you have to register your challenge to the IRS adjustments in Tax Court. If you don't do this, you will no longer be able to pursue your challenge of the IRS adjustments. Also, after the 90 days, the IRS can begin an enforcement action—meaning they are looking to collect what you owe them and can seize your property and levy your wages.

**Pointer 4: Tax Settlements**
In general, the IRS Auditor in your examination (e.g., Correspondence Audit, Office Audit or Field Audit) does not have the power to "settle" your tax case. You may have heard that people have reached a settlement while still in an audit (e.g., before the 30 Day Letter). For example, let's say you agree that an adjustment should be made to the amount of income you claimed. You think the auditor's calculation method leads to too much income, but you would like to settle on a smaller amount. In this case, you should ask for a meeting with the IRS Auditor's supervisor or manager to discuss your position. If an agreement can be reached, you have, in essence, "settled" your tax case. If an agreement can't be reached, the IRS will issue the 30 Day Letter reflecting their adjustment. However, you can still have a settlement discussion with an IRS Appeals Officer (see the discussion

below under filing a protest letter). Keep in mind, this is different from asking for an IRS settlement where you can't pay the tax deficiency (e.g. you either agree with the adjustments or you waited so long that your tax case is now in collections). In that case, see the guidance below under Paying Your Tax Deficiency.

## THE 30 DAY LETTER

This is certainly not like a "4 Page Letter" (...sealed with a kiss, Aaliyah, 1996). The 30 Day Letter is straight and to the point. It includes the IRS Auditor's examination report that details the findings, calculations and the proposed adjustments. As the name suggests, you will have 30 days to respond using one of the following:

### Pay the Tax

If you agree with the IRS adjustments, simply sign the enclosed "Consent to Assessment and Collection" form and pay the additional tax liability within 30 days of the date of the letter. Even if you don't agree, you have the option of signing the consent form and paying the tax to stop the interest and penalties from racking-up. Folks do this particularly where they plan to sue the IRS for a refund in the Federal District Court or Claims Court (see later in this section for more on which courts hear tax disputes).

### Submit Additional Information

If you still contest the IRS Auditor's proposed adjustments and you have more information that may be helpful in supporting your position, by all means submit it. You will have fifteen days from the date of the 30 Day Letter to submit evidence to the IRS auditor and request that the auditor arrange an appointment with you to discuss the new information and any changes to the IRS adjustments.

### File a Protest Letter

If you've provided all of the information that you have and still contest the IRS Auditor's proposed adjustments, you can appeal the proposed adjustments to the IRS Appeals Office. This office is an internal quasi-court forum, which is separate from the IRS Examination office that conducted your audit. The IRS Appeals Office routinely hears disputes between taxpayers and IRS Auditors, and is required to review each case in an unbiased manner, based on the merits of the positions and the tax law.

The formal protest letter request should be made to the IRS District Director who issued your 30 Day Letter (see the contact information listed on your 30 Day letter). Your Protest Letter should briefly list the following:

1. A statement of the facts supporting your position;
2. A statement of law or other authority as to why your position is correct; and
3. An itemized schedule of the tax changes proposed by the auditor that you specifically disagree with.

After you file the Protest Letter, the IRS will respond to you within 30 days and set a date for a formal meeting. Typically, for small taxpayers, the IRS Appeals Office will try to meet and reach a final resolution of the matter within 90 days.

The IRS Appeals Officer has the authority to resolve or settle your tax case and can consider all aspects of your issue; even those that were outside of the scope or concern of the IRS Auditor. This is one of the advantages of filing this Protest Letter and also an excellent strategy when you believe you may have to litigate your position. Why? Because, you will be able to hear the IRS's positions and theories before you go to court. Also, if you lose your appeals case, this option will give you even more time to research and document your position. You should at least, talk to a tax advisor when preparing for an Appeals meeting. The following are tips for preparing and conducting an IRS Appeals Meeting:

> **Tips for an IRS Appeals Meeting:**
>
> - Organize your information so that you can quickly get to it. (Remember, if you provide new information, the IRS Appeals Officer may send the entire case back to the IRS Auditor.).
> - Be prepared to discuss and provide copies of any court cases or IRS opinions that support your position.
> - Any offer you make to settle your tax matter must be "reasonable."

### Do Nothing

This is not the time to "chill" ("You Gots To Chill," EPMD, 1987). Doing nothing is not a good option, but too many people follow this route. This is the way many people choose to deal with their bill collectors, and an IRS tax deficiency is no different (see the discussion about famous stars and athletes with IRS problems in the Introduction). Unfortunately, people forget that the vast power of the IRS to seize your property, freeze your bank accounts, and garnish your wages is unlike any other creditor you may have. If you find yourself in this position, all is not lost. Read on below about the 90 Day Letter and paying your tax delinquency.

## THE 90 DAY LETTER

The 90 Day Letter is a formal Notice of Deficiency stating that you have 90 days in which to file a petition in court to dispute the IRS assessment. If you miss this 90-day window, you cannot litigate your tax case. You must go straight to your options for paying the tax deficiency (see the discussion in the next section of this Chapter). There are three courts you can choose as the forum to litigate tax disputes.

### United States Tax Court

The Tax Court, as it is commonly called, is located in Washington DC. Cases are heard by a judge only (there are no juries), and the judge travels to hear cases in certain cities around the country. One of the biggest advantages of filing your tax claim in the Tax Court is that you don't have to pay the IRS tax assessment before you file your case—just a minor court filing fee. However, for most taxpayers the actual costs of litigating their tax cases far outweigh the actual tax deficiency claimed by the IRS. Practically speaking, most people opt to settle the case in the IRS Appeals level discussed above or engage in some sort of settlement or compromise discussed in the next section.

### Court of Federal Claims

United States Court of Federal Claims (or the Federal Claims Court) hears many types of cases, from contractual disputes and money claims based upon the United Sates Constitution to tax refund claims. There are 16 judges on the court, and as with the Tax Court, there are no jury trials. Also, like the Tax Court, the Federal Claims Court is located in Washington DC; and these judges will also travel to hear cases in certain cities around the country. Unlike with the Tax Court, you must pay the actual tax deficiency claimed by the IRS, first, before your case will be heard.

### United States District Court

The U.S. District Court has a separate court located in all fifty states. Unlike with the Tax Court and the Federal Claims Court, jury trials are available in U.S. District Court. This is one of the main reasons taxpayers choose to litigate their claims in District Court. However, as with the Federal Claims Court, you must first pay the actual tax deficiency claimed by the IRS first before your case will be heard.

# Paying Your Tax Delinquency

Once the audit is completed and the 90 Day Letter has expired, if you haven't responded or have lost your IRS appeals case (or court case), paying the IRS deficiency becomes a primary concern. The IRS transfers your case from the Audit function to the Collection function. The IRS Officer who will handle your case is not concerned with anything that happened or did not happen during the audit, appeals or in court. His job now is to collect the taxes owed and his authority ranges from granting an installment payment agreement, to seizing your property and garnishing your wages.

If you find yourself in this position, you should share the initial collection notice with your tax advisor and make immediate contact with IRS on the collection matter. Remember, the IRS has the power to take drastic actions to collect taxes, but normally does so only in instances where you're not cooperating. So, make that call. There may be different options regarding how you pay your tax liability and, in certain instances, the amount you actually pay. Keep reading for the 411 on some of your options to get right with the IRS.

### OFFER IN COMPROMISE

Most people know that this is a program where you can make an agreement to come clean on your tax debts. Under the IRS Offer in Compromise ("OIC") program, the IRS can agree to accept less than the full amount of the tax deficiency, interest and penalties as a full settlement of your tax liabilities. The IRS indicates that the objective of the OIC program is to accept a compromise when it is in the best interests of both the taxpayer and the government, and promotes voluntary compliance with all future tax payment and filing requirements. The real deal is that the IRS has historically accepted OIC's only when it had few other options for collecting the taxes. Don't get it twisted. The IRS is not in the business of accepting offers to pay only a portion of taxes due. While any taxpayer with a tax liability can submit an OIC, relatively few are accepted completely and even fewer can be considered "compromises" or "settlements".

To submit an OIC, you will need to complete *Form 656, Offer in Compromise*, along with either *Form 433-A or 433-B, Collection Information Statements*. You will include your basic financial information on these forms (e.g., your wages, rental income and other sources of income; your assets and other property that you own,; and your liabilities and monthly expenses. Note: Use Form 433-A if you are filing for an individual, Form 433-B if you are filing on behalf of a partnership, limited liability company or corporation, and both Form 433-A and Form 433-B if you are filing on behalf of a sole proprietorship.

In addition to completing the forms, there are a few things you'll need to know. It will cost you $150 to file your OIC with the IRS. For those true hardship cases, you can request a waiver of this fee, but be prepared to show the IRS some extreme situation as to why you can't afford the filing fee. I stress that only the extreme cases need ask for this waiver. If you drive a luxury car and wear the latest Sean John™ fashion, you can forget qualifying for this waiver. Also, you must be current on all your tax return filings. The IRS won't even talk to you about a compromise until they at least have copies of your tax returns. Also, if you run a business with employees, you must be current on all your payroll withholding deposits for the current quarter, and also on at least the two quarters prior to filing the OIC (i.e., at least the prior 6 months). For more on employment tax withholdings please see the discussion in Chapter 3: Side Business Part II.

As a practical matter, the IRS doesn't enter into OIC's unless it is highly likely that your earnings capacity and total assets would be significantly less than the tax deficiency. In other words, you must be truly broke or close to it to get an OIC. Just because you are behind a few months on your bills, does not make you a great candidate for an OIC.

Also, the IRS will not typically compromise for "pennies on the dollar." If you see ads for this or you meet a tax advisor offering to get this type of settlement for you, "BEWARE." For more on this, see the IRS Consumer alert issued on February 3, 2004 on their website at http://www.irs.gov. The IRS will go through your assets and liabilities and come up with an amount they think they can reasonably collect from you after taking into account what you need to pay your necessities. They come up with a standard amount for your necessities (such as your house, utilities, food, clothing, transportation, etc.) based on where you live and your family size.

If the IRS accepts your OIC, in words similar to those of the late ODB (a.k.a., Ol' Dirty Bastard) "you better have their money." (ODB, featuring Kellis, in "Got Your Money," 1999). It's time for you to pay up and here are your three choices:

➢ Cold, hard cash paid to the IRS within 90 days of your accepted offer;
➢ A short term payment plan over 24 months; or
➢ A longer payment plan (in limited circumstances)

If the IRS does not accept your OIC, you can submit a new OIC addressing some of the reasons why your first OIC was denied. You may also consider asking for an installment plan or significant hardship order. See the discussion below in this Chapter on those options.

**Pointer 5: OIC Frequently Asked Questions**
The IRS has a comprehensive list of frequently asked questions on the OIC program listed on their website. Start with this list before you begin completing any of the tax forms requesting an OIC. Also, contacting a tax advisor who has done numerous OICs is highly encouraged and could probably help you get a more favorable OIC. I reiterate that you need to make sure that this advisor is actually experienced in negotiating with the IRS. Also, make sure to ask the advisor how many OIC's she has negotiated and how much she has saved her clients.

**Pointer 6: OIC Warnings**
Keep in mind that until you have paid off your tax liability, you are still racking-up interest. Also, be careful. When you file Form 656, as may be required to extend the time the IRS is allowed to collect your taxes, this

can also extend the statutory period for an IRS enforcement action (e.g., to levy property or garnish your wages). While many people have taken advantage of the ability to submit and resubmit OIC's, they are surprised when the normal collection statute expires and they realize that the IRS would have had to close their case and no longer pursue the taxes. They unknowingly extended the limit every time they submitted an OIC.

## INSTALLMENT PAYMENT PLANS

Like the way many people pay their "Bills, Bills, Bills," (Destiny's Child 1999), you can pay your tax liability on a payment plan, too. The IRS encourages taxpayers to pay what they owe as quickly as possible. For those individuals or businesses not able to resolve a tax debt immediately, the IRS is willing to accept installment payments for the tax deficiency; but, be careful. The interest continues to rack-up on the unpaid tax balance until the amount is paid in full. So, even though an installment agreement may make paying the taxes easier, and it stops the IRS collection and enforcement efforts, you should pay the taxes in full as soon as possible.

To get an installment payment plan, you must first prove that you can't pay the entire amount in one lump sum, and this is why you need the payment plan. You will need to complete *Form 9465, Installment Agreement Request.* Practically speaking, if you owe the IRS less that $25,000, it will probably be easier for you to get an installment plan approved. If you owe more than $25,000, you may still qualify for an installment plan, but you must also complete *Form 433-F, Collection Information Statement.*

There are three ways to pay the IRS under your installment plan.

- ➢ Direct debit from your bank account;
- ➢ Payroll deduction from your employer; or
- ➢ Some other direct installment payment by you to the IRS.

Many people opting for a direct payment from their bank account or a payroll deduction from their wages. Keep in mind, as discussed with the OIC above, interest will keep racking-up with an installment payment plan until you pay your tax liability in full.

**Pointer 7: File Form 9465 with your Form 1040**
If you know when you file your return that you can not pay the taxes owed in full, complete *Form 9465, Installment Agreement Request*. Indicate how you wish to pay the taxes and submit Form 9465 with your tax return. The IRS will respond to the information on the installment request form. Keep in mind that although you will still owe the taxes and have to pay interest, you will get rid of the penalties for not filing a tax return.

**Pointer 8: Installment Plan Basics**
If you owe less than $25,000, the process for getting an installment plan is pretty simple. You can either, call the IRS at the number listed on your latest bill or notice. You will need to provide the notice number and your social security number. You can also go to the IRS website and fill in an on-line Form 9465. This form must then be printed out and mailed or faxed to the IRS.

**Pointer 9: Notice of Federal Tax Lien**
Even if you are paying your tax debt under an installment plan, the IRS may still file a Notice of Federal Tax Lien on your property. This is like the IRS's back-up plan. If you don't pay your tax liability in full under the installment plan, the IRS can still go after your property. Filing this lien can impact your credit rating. You should ask the IRS not to file this lien, or request to, at least, be notified in advance if a lien filing is contemplated. Many times it is often advisable to borrow the money from other sources than to have to deal with the effects of a tax lien. For more on federal tax liens, see the discussion in the next section of this Chapter, Dealing with Tax Lien, Levy and Offset.

## SIGNIFICANT HARDSHIP ORDERS

In situations where the IRS deficiency is so large that you will suffer a "significant financial hardship," you can request some relief by filing *Form 911, Application for Taxpayer Assistance Order*. What qualifies as significant? For some people, not being able to buy the latest FUBU™ jeans, Via Spiga™ pumps or Gucci™ watch might be significant. This is not what the IRS is looking for. Significant includes things like not being able to pay your utilities or your mortgage, because the IRS has seized your assets, or levied your wages or bank account.

To get a significant hardship, you must contact the Taxpayer Advocate Service. While they cannot reverse determinations made by the IRS, they may issue a Taxpayer Assistance Order to suspend, delay, stop, or speed up IRS actions to relieve your hardship. You should contact your local Taxpayer Advocate if, as a result of how your tax problem was handled by the IRS, any of the following circumstances apply:

- You are suffering, or are about to suffer, a significant hardship.
- You are facing an immediate threat of adverse action.
- You will incur significant costs (including fees for professional representation).
- You will suffer irreparable injury or long-term adverse impact.
- You have experienced a delay, in trying to resolve the issue, of more than 30 days.
- You have not received a response or resolution by the date promised.

You may gain quick access to the Taxpayer Advocate Service by calling or writing your local Taxpayer Advocate office; whose address and phone number can be accessed on the IRS website (http://www.irs.gov). Be sure to have a good grasp on your concerns and be ready to provide copies of any correspondence you have received from the IRS.

# Dealing with Tax Lien, Levy and Offset

When the dust settles after all the audits have been completed and notices have been sent, if you still owe the IRS money, you'd better pay up or face the wrath of the "Tax Man." Yes, the "Tax Man Cometh" and he is coming at you strong. If you fail to pay your tax liabilities, the IRS has the power to:

- File a Federal Tax Lien
- Levy your property including your wages
- Take any tax refunds (state, local or federal) due to you as an Offset.

### FEDERAL TAX LIEN

Filing a "Notice of Federal Tax Lien" is when all your serious IRS troubles begin. This lien "shouts out" to the world that you owe the IRS money. It's like any creditor's lien in that it establishes an interest in all your property, including property that you acquire after a lien is filed. It establishes priority to property as to other creditors in certain situations, such as bankruptcy proceedings or sales of real estate. Once a lien is filed, it may appear on your credit report and the IRS generally cannot issue a "Certificate of Release of Federal Tax Lien" until the taxes, penalties, interest, and recording fees are paid in full.

The IRS is not like any ordinary creditor. You may think "your mind is playing tricks on you" (in a Geto Boys style from their early 90s song, "Mind Playin' Tricks On Me"). Trust me, this is real. A federal tax lien will definitely hurt your credit rating, your ability to buy a house or a car, and even stop you from getting certain jobs.

### NOTICE OF LEVY

In addition to telling the world that you owe them money, the IRS can also come and take your property. The official document is called a Notice of Levy. It allows the IRS to take and sell your property like a portion of your wages, bank accounts, Social Security benefits, retirement income, car, boat, or real estate.

The IRS will usually levy your property only after these three requirements are met:

- You were assessed a tax and sent a Notice and Demand for Payment.
- You neglected or refused to pay the tax.
- You were sent a Final Notice of Intent to Levy and Notice of Your Right to A Hearing (levy notice) at least 30 days before the levy.

### Pointer 10: Garnishment of Wages

Until you pay your tax debt, the IRS may continue to take a portion of your wages. Remember, you still have to report all of your wages on your tax return even if the IRS is taking a portion of your wages out of every paycheck. So if your salary is $60,000, but the IRS is taking one-third of your money ($20,000), you use $60,000 in computing your income for the year. The $20,000 is for back taxes owed and has nothing to do with the taxes you may owe based on your current salary.

### Pointer 11: Levy on Bank Account

Does the IRS have your money on "lock-up" and they won't "let it out" (aka "Locked Up," Akon, 2004)? If the IRS levies your bank account, your bank must freeze your account up to the amount you owe the IRS, for 21 days. This means you will not be able to take any cash out, and any outstanding checks may bounce. After 21 days, the bank may actually take the money out of your bank account and send it to the IRS. In these cases, you should contact your tax advisor immediately. Get a copy of the levy notice from your bank along with the exact amount that is being held. Then you and your tax advisor should make arrangements with IRS so that the bank levy can be released.

**OFFSET OF A REFUND**

In this day of high speed computers and the internet, it should come as no surprise that government agencies talk to each other. Prior to sending your tax refund, the IRS checks its computer system to determine if you have an outstanding tax liability. If you owe the IRS money for past tax debts, but this year you are fortunate enough to be getting a tax refund, you can kiss that money goodbye. The states are in on this, too. Many states, like California, New York, Maryland and Virginia, have refund intercept agreements which allow the states to send your income tax refunds to the IRS to pay off your past tax debts and vice versa.

# REMIX

Here's the remix on what we learned in this Chapter:

1. It's an audit lottery, but instead of hoping your number gets picked, you're praying don't "Let Me Be The One," (Intro, 1993). Knowing the type of IRS audit you are in can help "ease the pain" ("How Can I Ease The Pain," Lisa Fischer, 1991).

2. The Correspondence Audit is for routine matters and can be handled quickly by providing adequate records. An Office Audit will be a face-to-face meeting with an IRS Auditor and will require more documents and correspondence. The Field Audit is the most extensive type of audit where the IRS Auditor will visit your office and the audit may last for one month or longer.

3. The 30 Day Letter (Notice of Audit Adjustment) is your time to stop things before they get out of hand. If you don't have the money to pay the taxes, ask for an installment agreement. If you believe the IRS is wrong, file a Protest Letter. The point is, do something. Don't just let the 30 days go by.

4. The 90 Day Letter (Notice of Deficiency) is your last chance to challenge the IRS (this time in court) before your tax liability will become a true and fixed debt, and your only other option is to pay the tax in full or a reduced amount (e.g., an Offer in Compromise).

5. Keep in mind, interest and penalties are accruing on your tax debt everyday until you pay the IRS in full. Everyone knows somebody who bought that shiny new car, financed 100% on credit, and by the time they got done paying all of the interest (and late fees) they could've had two cars. The same holds true when you don't pay your tax debt. Owing the IRS $1,000 today is like owing them $10,000 five years from now. But, if you pay attention to your IRS notices, respond to them, provide records and when all else fails, set up a payment plan, you can significantly decrease the pain. Doing nothing is simply not an option.

6. Use the OIC Quick Checklist:

    ✓ Fill out Form 656 and Forms 433-A (individuals) or 433-B (corporations and partnerships).

    ✓ Pay the $150 application fee or file for a waiver of the fee (Form 656-A, *Income Certification for Offer in Compromise Application Fee*).

    ✓ Make sure that all of your past tax returns have actually been filed.

    ✓ For businesses, make sure you have paid all of your employment tax returns, at least for the two quarters prior to filing the OIC, and that you are current on any deposits due for the quarter in which the OIC is submitted.

7. If you don't have the money to pay your tax liability, by all means ask the IRS for an installment payment plan. Be ready to provide financial data to prove that you can't pay the whole amount in one lump sum, and this is why you need the payment plan. Remember

you can ask for an installment plan when you file your tax return. Simply not filing your return is not an option.

8. If your tax debts get so out of hand that the IRS has placed a lien on your assets, frozen your bank account, or garnished your wages, you need to talk immediately to the IRS (and a tax advisor) to make arrangements (e.g., a payment plan) to get the lien or levy released.

# Chapter 10

# Frequently Asked Questions
*A Grand List of Your Best Tax Questions*

> *Could you love me in a Bentley?*
> *Could you love me on a bus?*
> *I'll ask 21 questions, and they all about us*
>
> "21 Questions," 50 Cent, Featuring Nate Dogg

This Chapter was inspired by all the questions asked by my husband, parents, grandparents, brothers, sisters, cousins, aunts, uncles, college friends, graduate school friends, sorority sisters, co-workers, church members, and yeah, play cousin Lil' Ray—after all everyone has a Lil' somebody in their family. Here's the list of the 21 best questions to help you take control of your taxes and build your net worth. Sorry Lil' Ray, I couldn't put your question in print.

## 1. The "What Had Happened Was..." Question

*I did not file taxes three years ago. What should I do? The IRS has not contacted me.*

Toni, Richmond, Virginia

It's YOUR responsibility to file your tax return every year. It's not the IRS's responsibility to remind you. In fact, for some reason, they don't normally send out their letter requesting an explanation for several years. Maybe this has something to do with the large amount of interest income and penalties the IRS charges each day that you are late.

If you're ready to come clean, the first thing you should do is contact the IRS directly and request a taxpayer transcript so you can see what information they already have about you. That information should be a good starting point for you to create a tax file and to start preparing a tax return. If you don't have copies of your W-2's (and the IRS doesn't either), call your employer (or former employer) and request duplicates. If you have problems reaching your employer, as one of your last resorts, you can call the Social Security Administration (generally, some records take up to 6 months to get pulled).

You will probably have to pay interest and penalties, so the sooner you get this tax return filed the better. Depending on your circumstances, you may be able to make payments on an installment plan or the IRS may forgive part of your tax debt. As always, you should talk to a tax advisor to help you review your specific options. Please Note: Once you call the IRS there is a high probability an agent might call you soon after and follow-up with you to make sure you file the return.

> For more on audit questions, see Chapter 9: IRS Audits

## 2. The "Moving On Up" Question

*I just purchased a new home. How many exemptions can I claim on my Form W-4 without owing taxes at the end of the year?*

*Kimberly, Bowie, Maryland*

Is this your year? Are you finally moving on up to the East Side, to a deluxe apartment in the sky? If this is the year you finally bought that new home; congratulations. Uncle Sam wants to say congratulations, too, with tax benefits for homeowners. Thanks to the home mortgage interest deduction, you will now have higher itemized deductions, which will cut down on your taxes and get you a greater tax refund.

But you want your money now, during the year, and I don't blame you. Remember, a tax refund feels great, but you basically gave the IRS an interest-free loan while they held your money all year. To get your money now, you should increase the number of exemptions claimed on your Form W-4 (see the tip box at the end of this question for more on Form W-4). This means less taxes will be withheld from your paycheck, resulting in more cash in your pocket. Just how many exemptions you should claim depends on your salary and other itemized deductions. The IRS has a W-4 withholding calculator on their website that can help you with figuring out the number of exemptions you may want to claim. Also, you might try the free W-4 or paycheck calculators on these websites:

- Tax Brain—http://www.taxbrain.com/taxcenter/w4calculator.asp
- paycheckcity.com—http://www.paycheckcity.com/w4/w4instruction.asp
- Commerce Clearing House—
- http://www.tax.cchgroup.com/taxcalcs/withholding/Default.asp

**Form W-4**
This is the form an employee will use to claim federal tax exemptions. It lets employers know how much federal taxes to calculate and withhold from your paycheck. States with a state income tax have a similar form. The higher your exemptions, the less the employer will withhold and the less you pay in federal income taxes. Go to the IRS's website at http://www.irs.gov to download a copy of this form. Also, see *IRS Publication 919, How Do I Adjust My Tax Withholding.*

> **For more on exemptions, see Chapter 1: Tax Basics**

## 3. The "Baby Boomer" Question

*As the eldest adult child, I take care of my elderly mother. She is 75 years old and lives with me. She receives social security, but it's not that much, so I really provide all of her cost of living expenses. Can I deduct her medical expenses?*

*Gerald, Washington, DC*

Assuming you provide more than half of her total support, she makes less than $3,200, and she's a U.S. citizen, your mother is treated as your dependent in the tax laws and you can deduct her medical expenses.

As your dependent, you can also claim much more than her medical expenses. You may also be entitled to other tax deductions and credits for her, such as personal exemptions, medical expenses, and dependent care credits. On top of that, if you're single, you may even be able to claim head of household filing status using your mother as your dependent. This will allow you to take higher tax deductions than you could as a single taxpayer. Keep in mind, much of this applies even if your mother does not physically live in your house (i.e., she stays in her own home or a nursing home).

> For more on your filing status and dependents, please see Chapter 1: Tax Basics

## 4. The "By The First Of The Month I'll Be Straight" Question

*I paid a tax preparer to complete my 2005 tax return. I have signed but not mailed it in yet because I can not pay the amount owed. Should I wait until I have the money to pay?*

*Kenneth, Philadelphia, PA*

Absolutely Not! Always try and file your tax return (or an extension) by April 15th. Notice: I'm saying "file;" meaning fill out the tax forms and mail or submit them electronically to the IRS. This is different from actually paying the tax. If you don't have the money to pay your tax liability, by all means at least avoid the interest and penalties you will rack up for not filing the tax return.

Keep in mind, the IRS will eventually find you; and by the time they do, the amount you owe will probably be mostly interest and penalties. This interest will add up every single day until you pay your tax liability.

If you owe less than $25,000, the IRS will probably allow you to set up an installment payment plan. The installment plan generally has a start-up fee of $150, regardless of the amount owed, and the interest rate may be higher than a credit card. The best thing to do is sign up for an installment plan at an amount that you are sure you can pay each month (even if it $100 a month), and then pay off your tax bill as soon as possible. Remember, the IRS is not like your other creditors. It is very difficult to get rid of an IRS debt (besides paying it); even in a bankruptcy.

Also, if you continue to owe the IRS money year after year, there is a chance they will cancel your installment plan and ask for the money you owe in one lump sum. So make sure that if you get on an installment plan for your 2005 taxes, that you make your tax payments in 2006, so that you won't need an installment plan for 2006 as well.

> For more on IRS audits and installment payments,
> see Chapter 9: IRS Audits

## 5. The "I Need My Money Now..." Question

*Should I e-file at one of these local tax preparation outlets and get an immediate refund?*

*Renee, Playa Del Rey, California*

 Examine the scenario carefully. Before you agree to a Rapid Refund™ or a tax refund "loan," from anyone, ask them to explain all of the extra fees and interest charges that they will deduct from your tax refund. To make it crystal clear, ask them to give you an example using an actual refund amount (e.g., a $100 refund means you will get $X from us today.) These companies charge very high interest rates and target those consumers who are more likely to spend cash before they have it. In many ways are similar to check cashing joints. In fact, according to a report issued by the Consumer Federation of America and National Consumer Law Center, these tax refund loan fees range from $30 to $90, depending on the amount of your refund; which equates to anywhere from a 67% to 774% interest rate. This is a high price to pay for a quick fix.

If you follow the tax planning talked about in *For The Love Of Money*, you should not need a tax refund loan. You have either been getting your money back all year (see the answer to FAQ# 2 above) or you realize that the IRS deposits your refund directly into your bank account.

Also, you can e-file without having to pay the high fees for a rapid refund. In fact in many cases, you get your refund within 7 to 10 business days, deposited directly in your back account. The IRS has been advocating the paperless filing process for the past couple of years and this is certainly the wave of the future. Keep in mind, if you e-file, make sure to get a paper copy of your tax return for your records.

Again, review the "Reasons" (Earth, Wind and Fire, 1975) you feel you "need" your money now; particularly when, if you can just wait a week or two, you can have ALL of your money.

---

**For more on e-filing, see Chapter 1: Tax Basics**

## 6. The "I'm A Consultant" Question

*I received a Form 1099-MISC. What do I do with it and do I send a copy with my tax return?*

Dawn, Miami, Florida

Have you ever met someone whose profession is consulting? You try as hard as you can to pin down exactly what they consult on, but, for some reason, you simply can't understand what going to Atlanta ten times a month has to do with consulting related to some sort of medicine.

All joking aside, hundreds of thousands of people today list consulting of some form (lawyers, doctors, IT, human resource, marketing, accounting, education, and the list goes on an on) as their primary business. Pick any profession and someone is making an honest living serving as a consultant in that field.

*Form 1099 MISC, Miscellaneous Income* is the form that reports how much a consultant receives from a particular engagement, project or client. You will get this form if you receive $600 or more for your services.

Regardless of your impression, as far as the IRS is concerned, you have a trade or business activity (a sole proprietorship) from which you earned non-employee compensation. You must include the amount listed on Form 1099 as compensation on your *Schedule C, Profit or Loss from Business (Form 1040)*. DO NOT attach Form 1099 to your tax return. Instead, just keep a copy of this form for your records.

In addition to knowing what a Form 1099 is, it's also important that you deduct all of the costs related to your consulting earnings. Some common expenses for a consultant might include a portion of what you pay for cellular phone, meals, office expenses, transportation, and internet charges. Of course, each industry is different, so be sure to check with your tax advisor.

Finally, your net profit (e.g., your Form 1099 revenues less your expenses) is taxed at 15.3% (self-employment tax). So, it's very important that if you receive income without tax withholdings, you pay the IRS (as well as your state tax authority) estimated taxes on a quarterly basis. Otherwise, you could be looking at tax penalties for underpayments. Work with your tax advisor to figure out an amount to set aside from each consulting check so you can make quarterly estimated payments. In my experience, consultants are far better off if they never consider this (e.g., the estimated tax payment) as their money and pay the IRS first.

> For more on tax issues related to consultants,
> See Chapter 3: Side Businesses: Part II

## 7. The "Help? Who Me?" Question

*I want to prepare my own tax return this year, what are some suggestions for me?*

Ted, Nashville, Tennesse

Many people prepare their own tax returns. With the technology age in full swing, there are some very good tax preparation software programs and websites available. If you don't have very many itemized deductions or capital gains/losses, most tax preparation software programs can do the job for you. Here are some of the self-preparation tax software programs you might start with:

- Intuit's Turbotax™
- TaxAct™
- WorldWideWeb Tax™
- IRS website (http://www.irs.gov). This website offers links to other on-line e-file websites that can be done at little or no cost.

If you have a complicated return, you should at least consult with a tax advisor. See Question 10 below, on tips for choosing a tax advisor.

> See the Appendix: Signs You Need Tax Help

## 8. The "Home Office" Question

> *I have an office outside my home (I'm an employee), but sometimes I work from home. Can I deduct my home office expenses since I work from home from time-to-time?*
>
> Tracey, Birmingham, Alabama

The answer depends on how much you work out of your home.

**Requirements to deduct home office expenses:**

- Exclusive use—the office area must be identifiable and separate. The area must not also be used for personal and/or entertainment.
- Regular use—must be consistently used, not just occasional or incidental.
- For a trade or business—business is conducted and managed at the home
- Either your principal place of business, place to meet and deal with clients, vendor, or a separate structure to the home.
- If you are an employee, for the convenience of your employer

In most cases, taxpayers qualify for the first three requirements. The fourth requirement can be more challenging, especially if you operate a "virtual office" and don't need clients to visit you in order for you to provide a service or sell your products.

If you are an employee and have a home office because it's convenient for you to work at home (either at night, on the weekends, when your child is sick, etc), this is not the same as having a home office for the convenience of your employer. Convenience depends on all the facts and circumstances. There are some things you can do that can help your case:

- ✓ Have a dedicated area or room in your house for your home office
- ✓ Make your home office the primary place where you conduct a substantial amount of business
- ✓ Conduct most of your client meetings at your home office
- ✓ Keep your business files at your home office
- ✓ Conduct most of your administrative business activities at your home office (e.g., bookkeeping, faxes, computer work, and other secretarial duties)

Also, please keep in mind that you cannot claim a home office if your employer compensates you for a portion of your rent or mortgage.

In this case, it looks like it will be difficult for you to claim a home office since you only use it from time-to-time and it is not your primary place to conduct business.

Use *Form 8829—Expense for Business Use of Your Home* to calculate the home office deduction. The home office expense calculated on this form is then transferred to *Schedule C, Profit or Loss from Business (Sole Proprietorship) (Form 1040)*. Also, see *IRS Publication 587, Business Use of Your Home*.

Home office deductions are still an area that could trigger an IRS audit. If you plan on taking a home office deduction, you should take pictures of your home office, including pictures with clients and vendors visiting your office. Also, make sure that all of your business cards, flyers and other information describing your business include your home address for the contact information. Finally, keep a notebook, calendar or use a computer spreadsheet to track visits to your house and the amount of time you spend in your office, and keep these files for your tax files. You don't need to attach them to your tax return. Be sure you get in the habit of doing them throughout the year, and by all means before you file your tax return. This will give more credibility to the fact that they are real documents and not done to fight an IRS audit.

> For more on the home office deduction,
> see Chapter 3: Side Business Part II

## 9. The "Mistakes" Question

*What are some of the common mistakes made on tax returns?*
Christy, Bowie, Maryland

Some of the most common errors on tax returns are:

- Mathematical errors
- Inaccurate social security numbers
- Not attaching schedules
- Missing statements, like Form 1099s, when completing your tax return

If you prepare your own tax return, make extra sure you double check your calculations. Even with the increasingly popularity of tax preparation software programs (see the tips regarding tax preparation software programs in FAQ# 7), transposed numbers or mistakes in adding up figures are still very common with folks who prepare their own tax returns. Each tax season, the IRS publishes common filing errors that taxpayers should try to avoid on their website. Before signing your tax return, review this list. This extra effort can go a long way, since these mistakes also are some of the common reasons tax returns are audited.

> See the Appendix: Ways To Avoid An Audit

## 10. The Beauty Contest

*What should I look for in a tax preparer?*

*Dee, Dallas, Texas*

Choosing a tax preparer can seem like a beauty contest—only the contestants are probably not that pretty. Check out this list of what you should consider when choosing your tax advisor:

- **Understand Billing Rates**

    Some tax advisors charge by the hour, schedule, or a standard rate. Whatever the case, they should clearly explain this to you upfront. Be wary of a tax advisor who simply can't give you a good estimate of his/her total fees, or has a fee structure based on a percentage of your tax refund amount.

- **Pick a Professional (e.g., CPA, Attorney or Enrolled Agent)**

    Your tax return should be prepared by a professional; such as a CPA, Attorney or Enrolled Agent. These individuals were required to go through significant training and rigorous qualification tests to gain entrance into their profession—not to mention the hours and hours of yearly continuing education they must obtain. You wouldn't take your sick child to the neighborhood "doc," a person who, while called a doc or doctor, has never even seen a medical school. Why would you trust your tax return with all of your financial information to someone who took a two-day training class?

- **Look for High Qualifications**

    Pick a tax advisor who prepares tax returns fairly regular. If you work in a special industry such a healthcare, entertainment, etc., find a tax advisor who has other clients in that field or seems to have the desire to research specific tax issues for your profession.

- **Explanation of your completed return**

  Although you might "just want to know how large your tax refund is," make sure you look for a tax advisor who will go over the return with you line by line, if necessary. This process normally does not take long, and you need to understand how the tax return flows and verify that the information is accurate. Even though the tax advisor normally signs off on the return, YOU are ultimately responsible for the accuracy and completeness.

- **Sophisticated Tax Software**

  In this internet age, be wary of a tax advisor who doesn't use sophisticated tax software programs to prepare your tax return. Keep in mind, silly mathematical errors are one of the top mistakes made by taxpayers and can often cause your tax return to be audited.

- **Enthusiasm and Presentation**

  Does the tax advisor appear to have genuine interest in doing taxes? Enthusiasm about his profession and his job will almost always translate into giving you good service. Also, the professional presentation of your tax return is a good indicator that you have a competent tax advisor.

## 11. The "Computer Love" Question

*I use my home computer at night to check work e-mail and sometimes on the weekend to draft documents. Can I deduct it as a work expense? How about the cost of the internet connection?*

Janice, New York, New York

We all love our home computers. Like Roger and the Zapp Band forecasted in their 1985 hit "Computer Love," we simply can't live without them. We use them to get our news, talk to friends, find entertainment and of course for work.

Depending on how you use your computer, you may be able to get a tax deduction. Now that's true computer love.

The cost of the home computer and internet connection may be deductible as an unreimbursed employee expense. You can take this as a miscellaneous itemized deduction whether you own your home or rent it. But keep in mind you can only deduct the amount that is for your business usage and the computer must be required by your employer. Personal usage (which you undoubtedly must have) does not count. This means you must come up with some sort of percentage or allocation of your business usage and it must be more than 50% to take advantage of this deduction.

Practically speaking, this calculation may or may not be worth it. Why? Because some miscellaneous itemized deductions may only be deducted once the amount reached is more than 2½% of your adjusted gross income. This means, for a person making $100,000, these costs must be more than $2,500 before you can deduct a penny. That's a lot of internet charges and a pretty expensive personal computer.

It may be worth it if you also have other large miscellaneous itemized deductions, such as: other unreimbursed employee expenses, tax preparation and planning fees (like the cost of *For The Love Of Money*), job hunting expenses, investment expenses, or certain legal fees.

Finally, you might want to consider opening your own side business, while keeping your "9 to 5" job. With a side business, you can deduct the cost of your equipment, such as your "Digital Display" (Ready For The World, 1985), without having to worry about beating a 2% limitation. But remember to back out any personal usage.

> For more on miscellaneous itemized deductions, see Chapter 6:
> Itemized Deductions Part II

## 12. The "Poor Broke Actor" Question

*What are some of the overlooked deductions for those individuals in the entertainment and/or real estate industries?*

*Any waitress or waiter in Los Angeles, California*

The entertainment and real estate industries commonly deal with income that is paid "All At Once" (Whitney Houston, 1985). This lump sum payment is reported on *Form 1099-MISC, Miscellaneous Income.*

However, due to things like commissions, the actual cash that goes to the artist or real estate broker is generally less than you might expect. For example, assume Sean, a starving actor, gets that big break; a small part in a movie, but the opportunity to work with several big marquee names. Sean's contract is for $50,000. It would take him almost two years waiting tables to make that type of cash; but not so fast. Sean will likely never see the entire $50,000. Why? Because out of the $50,000, he has to pay people, like his agent (10%), his manager (15%), and his business manager (5%). So far, out of a $50,000 movie part, Sean may only get $25,000 of actual cash.

A similar split happens for real estate brokers. Typically, they earn a sales commission based on the gross sales price of the property they sold. However, they still have to pay things, like referral and loan processor fees.

Since Form 1099 typically reports the gross amount (i.e., the total contract or full sales commission), it's very important that entertainers, athletes, real estate professional, etc, track their referral and/or commission expenses paid to others. Otherwise, they may be overpaying their taxes on money they didn't really receive.

Check out the 411 on some of the expenses that entertainers and real estate brokers should be on the look out for:

- union membership dues
- publications
- cable television
- auto washing and waxing
- auto insurance
- auto license plate fees
- driver license fees
- internet connection
- cell phone calls
- mileage

Remember, some of these expenses may be personal in nature, too. If that's the case, you can only take that amount that is attributable to your business usage. Do this by coming up with the percentage of your total expenses that can be based on business purposes. For example, you will undoubtedly drive your car for some personal miles (i.e., movies, vacations, visits to Nanna, etc.). You must back those miles out of your total miles. Also, take out miles that you use for other non-business purposes like, for medical expenses or for volunteering with charities. Although you can't take these miles as business expenses, they may be deductible as itemized deductions. What you have left is your business miles. When in doubt, make sure to consult with a tax advisor as to the deductibility of these expenses in your personal situation.

> For more on business deductions,
> see Chapter 3: Side Businesses Part II
> For more on itemized deductions
> see Chapter 5: Itemized Deductions Part I and
> Chapter 6: Itemized Deductions Part II

## 13. The "I Sold My House And I'm Rich" Question

*I have recently sold a house and made just over $200,000 in profit. I am concerned about the impact of the amount of taxes I will owe this year. Do I add the $200,000 to my earnings?*

*Michael, Atlanta, Ga.*

 The good news is that you may be able to exclude the entire $200,000 from your income thanks to the home sale exclusion of $250,000 for individuals or $500,000 for married folks filing jointly. To get this exclusion you must have:

- lived at the home as your primary residence for at least two years AND
- owned the home for at least two years

Even if you lived there less than two years, if you sold your house because of unforeseen circumstances (e.g., a new job, a divorce, death, etc.), you may be still be able to get the exclusion for all or a part of your gain. You will need to calculate a new exclusion amount by pro-rating the $250,000 or $500,000 for married folks filing jointly based on the percentage of time you actually lived in the house out of the two years.

The bad news is that if you truly fail the two requirements (and you didn't move due to unforeseen circumstance), your $200,000 gain may be taxable and you will need to report it on Schedule D, Capital Gains and Losses (Form 1040). Your gain will be taxed at a capital gains rate (e.g., around 15%). To minimize the impact of this gain, you should look to see any capital losses that you can use as an offset.

> For more on the home sale exclusion,
> see Chapter 4: Capital Gains

## 14. The "Nanny" Question

*What are the tax implications of in-home childcare when you are not utilizing a childcare agency or nanny service?*

*Jaqui, New Haven, Connecticut*

 When you hire a nanny to work in your home (even when hired through a childcare agency or a nanny service) you will, in most cases, be required to pay employment taxes. Did you know these rules may apply to anyone you hire to work for you. This includes a babysitter, housekeeper, yard worker, etc. If this person can be treated as your employee, you will probably have to pay employment taxes.

Many people try to argue that these folks are independent contractors and not employees. If you can "control" how the job is done, where the job is done, when the job is done or provide the means for doing the job, this person will be an employee. The fact that the person works part-time for you or you hired them using an employment agency is irrelevant. They can still be your employee. Keep in mind, this does not include someone who is provided to you by a business that you pay directly. For example, if you pay a cleaning service to come and clean your house twice a month and they send over the same cleaning woman, this woman is not your employee. Now let's say she quits her job with the cleaning service and you hire her directly to clean your house; she has now become your employee. This is the case, even if she cleans homes for other people, too. You make the payments directly to her and you control her job. Remember, when she was employed by the cleaning service, they controlled her job.

Are you panicking yet? There are a few exceptions to this. You don't have to worry about employment taxes if you pay the person less than $1,400 in a year. Take the case of the cleaning lady above. If she is only coming to your house twice a month you may not have to deal with these rules. This will depend on how much she charges you each time. If you find you're getting close to the $1,400 threshold, you may want to consider putting off some of her cleanings or have someone else clean your house until the new year starts. Although this may work in the case of someone who works for you periodically, a nanny tends to work many more days (i.e., every week day) and it's fairly easy to pass the $1,400 threshold.

Next, if you pay your teenage neighbor to baby-sit your children from time-to-time, you don't have to treat her as your employee and thus, you don't have any employment tax obligations. This exception will apply as long as she is younger than 18.

Finally, you typically don't have to worry about employment taxes where the person watching your child is your parent, spouse or your older child (this, of course, assumes that you pay these people something to watch your child in the first place).

If the person is your employee and none of the exceptions apply, you will need to understand your employment tax obligations. Nanny taxes are made up of Social Security tax, Medicare tax (both of which are called FICA for short), and federal unemployment tax (or FUTA for short). FICA taxes are calculated at 7.65% of wages, and both the employee and the employer have to each pay this same percentage. This means that if your nanny earns $4,000, you each pay $306. FUTA taxes work out to be about .8% of your employee's wages. It is calculated on the first $7,000 of wages; so, it totals about $56 ($7,000 x .08).

The employer must pay the FUTA taxes. There may also be state or local nanny taxes (i.e., state unemployment taxes). This leaves the largest amount of employment taxes—the FICA taxes. You can either withhold the nanny's portion from her paycheck or pay her share of the FICA taxes. Practically speaking, good nannies are hard to find. Thus, many people wind up paying these taxes on behalf of the nanny so the nanny can have more money in her take-home pay.

Before you start paying employment taxes, you will need to get an Employee Identification Number from the IRS. Use *FormSS-4, Employee Identification Number (EIN)* to do this. Also, at the end of February of each year, you will need to give your nanny or household employee a *Form W-2, Wage and Tax Statement* reporting her wages. Finally, you pay these employment taxes on *Schedule H, Household Employment Taxes (Form 1040)*, which is attached to your tax return; so, it is typically due on April 15th. There are many local payroll service companies that can help you do all of this. Make sure you do your homework and check out their reputation first. Of course your tax advisor can help you with this, too. Finally, many states have similar rules, so make sure to check these out.

What happens if you don't pay these employment taxes? If caught, you will certainly owe interest and penalties and the IRS will not be that lenient on making a deal with you. Also, if you ever plan to run for public office or get a prestigious government appointment, not paying your employment taxes can actually stop this from happening.

Calculate your nanny taxes on *Schedule H, Household Employment Taxes (Form 1040)*. You are required to get an employer identification number (EIN) if you are going to pay nanny taxes. It is this number, and not your social security number, that must be included on Schedule H. To get an EIN, file *Form SS-4, Application for Employer Identification Number*. Also, you should attach Schedule H to your tax return. Several websites have free nanny tax calculators including:

- Smartmoney.com—http://www.smartmoney.com/tax
- Home/Work Solutions Inc—http://www.4nannytaxes.com/calculator/taxcalc.cfm

> For more on the nanny tax, see Chapter 1: Tax Basics
> For more on employees and independent contractors,
> see Chapter 3: Side Business

## 15. The "It's Not My House, But I Pay For It" Question

*If I am not on the mortgage of my parent's home, can I deduct the real estate taxes and mortgage interest if I paid them?*

*Kathy, Los Angeles, California*

The "It's My House," question (aka, Diana Ross style, 1980) is becoming more and more common. I've heard of many cases where family members purchase homes for each other or co-sign on mortgages. The family members may have an "understanding" or "agreement." Be careful when you do this because everyone involved might wind up losing on of the biggest tax deductions.

Only the person who is <u>both</u> on the title and who makes the mortgage payments, can deduct the mortgage interest. It has to legally and financially be your house. So in your case, you cannot take the mortgage interest deductions since you don't own the home. It may surprise you to also learn that your parents don't get the mortgage interest deduction either. Why? They did not make the mortgage payments. Who gets the deduction? Unfortunately, no one does. On top of this, the payments you made for your parents may be considered as gifts and subject to the gift tax rules.

In addition to the mortgage interest, I will assume you will also be paying for the real estate property taxes. Generally the person listed on the title can deduct the real estate taxes. So even though you made the payments, since your parents are on the title, they can still deduct the real estate property taxes.

To summarize all of this, keep in mind that when non-married folks buy a house together (e.g., they are both listed on the title), they can split up the deduction for the real estate property taxes on their individual tax returns. They can do this even if only one of them is on the loan. But when it comes to the mortgage interest deduction, they can only deduct the amount that they personally pay for. So if you find yourself buying a home with a friend or relative, make sure you understand these rules from the beginning and always talk to your tax advisor to make sure you got it straight. It's better to have this all legally cleared up before either one of you has to ask "If I'm Not Your Lover" (…if I'm not your friend, then tell me what I am, Al B. Sure, 1988)?

> For more on mortgage interest deduction,
> See Chapter 5: Itemized Deductions
> For more on the gift tax rules,
> See Chapter 8: Investments, Education, Estate

## 16. The "Closing Statement" Question

*If I buy or refinance a home, what items on the escrow closing statement are deductible?*

*Stacey, Boston, Massachusetts*

Points, mortgage interest and real estate taxes paid at closing may be deductible as itemized deductions. These items are generally listed on your closing statement (or settlement statement) on a detailed page which includes the various costs that the seller pays and which ones the buyer pays.

You should ask your mortgage broker or lender to give you a schedule showing the interest and principal portion of your monthly payment each month during the term of the loan (i.e., $1,600 of your $2,000 monthly payment is for interest and $400 is for the principal). This information is useful at the end of the year to verify and confirm that the amount of interest you expected to pay equals what is shown on your *Form 1098, Mortgage Interest Statement* (i.e., the year-end statement that you should receive from your lender).

It's not uncommon for the Form 1098 and your lender's schedule to differ by a couple of hundred of dollars. If this happens, you should include the amount you actually paid when calculating your itemized deductions on *Schedule A, Itemized Deductions (Form 1040)*. Make sure to keep copies of your monthly mortgage statements, as well as cancelled checks, in your tax file. Since your figures will differ from what the mortgage bank reported to the IRS on Form 1098, if your tax return is selected for audit by the IRS (a chance as a Correspondence Audit since your numbers won't match in the IRS computer), you can explain the difference.

> For more on these deduction,
> see Chapter 5: Itemized Deductions, Part I
> For more on Correspondence Audits, see Chapter 9: IRS Audits

## 17. The "I Loaned Money to Myself" Question

*If I take a loan from my S Corporation, do I have to pay it back with interest?*

*Tim, Raleigh, North Carolina*

Absolutely! Yes, even though you own the company, you serve as CEO, CFO, COO, and you probably spend half of your time singing "I Talk To Myself," (Christopher Williams, 1989), please understand that the S Corporation is a separate entity from you. Using sound business practices, you must have a written promissory note from you to the S Corporation with the terms of your debtor/creditor relationship documented. You should include the following terms in the promissory note: the amount borrowed, repayment schedule, interest rate, and consequences of failure to pay.

Make sure the promissory note sets a fair market interest rate. The IRS releases applicable federal rates (AFR) as a gauge for interest rates. For the most recent AFR, go to IRS's website (http://www.irs.gov) and use Applicable Federal Rate as your key word search. Using a below market interest rate can be a red flag for the IRS.

If you fail to take these steps, your loan could be treated by the IRS as income to you (e.g., as salary), creating higher income taxes, and subjecting the money to payroll taxes; instead of a true loan where there is no income taxes.

Note: Although the question asks about an S Corporation, the answer applies to anytime you take a loan from your separate business (e.g., partnership, C Corporation or limited liability company).

> For more on side business issues,
> see Chapter 2: Side Business Part I

## 18. The "Rent to Riches" Question

*If you purchase a rental property with relatives, how do you account for the tax breaks/benefits? Do you create a "business"?*

Erika, San Francisco, California

Yes, renting out a home IS a business. You have numerous options as how to report that business—from using *Schedule E, Supplemental Income and Loss*, to creating a formal entity to own the property (such as a limited liability company or partnership) and using *Form 1065, US Partnership Return of Income*.

If you are purchasing the property with a relative or friend, you should consider setting up a formal entity, like a limited liability company, to detail your business arrangement and protect your personal assets from any liability that can arise in connection with your new rental business.

If you have a regular "9 to 5" job, having a rental property can also decrease your taxable income. You can now deduct things (like business meals, depreciation, transportation, or even write off a portion of your auto expenses), as long as they have legitimate business purposes.

> For more on side business issues,
> see Chapter 2: Side Business Part I

## 19. The "Mo' Rent" Question

*Many people are bullish on real estate investing. What is the maximum income level where I can no longer write off interest and property tax on my rental property?*

*Steve, Chicago, Illinois*

As a rental real estate owner, you can deduct many things (like mortgage interest, property taxes, transportation, internet, cell phone, and any other business expenses) you have in connection with running your business. Perhaps your biggest deduction will be from the depreciation of your rental property. Because depreciation is a tax deduction and not cash taken out of your pocket, it can result in lowering the taxable amount on a rental property to the point where you may actually have a rental loss.

Most folks can only take up to $25,000 in losses from rental real estate in a single year. Typically, the $25,000 limit must be reduced when your AGI is more than $100,000, and eventually completely eliminated as your AGI is more than $150,000.

You don't lose these losses forever. The losses that you can't deduct, because they are either over the $25,000 limit or you are phased-out because your income is too high, can be saved and used on your future tax returns, to reduce your rental income. This may come in handy the longer you own the rental real estate. Why? Because you will probably charge higher rents in later years, but your tax deductions for rental real estate may not increase as much. So, you can use these excess losses from the previous years to help balance your increase in income.

If you are a full time "playa" in the rental real estate business (i.e., you materially participate in the business by spending more than 750 hours a year on buying, selling, renting and managing rental real estate property), you may be able to take unlimited losses. This is very difficult for someone who is also working a "9 to 5" job. Check with your tax advisor for help with whether or not you can qualify as an active rental real estate professional.

Note: Unless you are a full time rental real estate playa, the IRS considers this to be a "passive" business activity. This typically means that your losses can only offset gains from passive income, and not from things like your active salary income from your "9 to 5" job. Luckily, there is an exception for rental real estate, as described above with the $25,000 loss rule. Also, since your activity is "passive" you don't have to pay self-employment taxes on your rental real estate activities.

For more on rental real estate, see *Publication 527, Residential Rental Property*. Also, see the discussion regarding rental real estate, Chapter 3, Side Business Part II, selling your rental real estate in Chapter 4, Capital Gains, and dividing the personal amount of interest and property tax expenses, Chapter 5, Itemized Deductions.

> For more on calculating rental real estate income or loss, see Chapter 1: Tax Basics and Chapter 3: Side Business, Part II

## 20. The "Innocent" Question

*If you are married filing separately, are you responsible for the IRS debts that your ex-spouse owes? Also, what about when you were married and filing jointly—do you still have to pay for the debt, even if you didn't know anything about the income that your spouse was hiding?*

*Denise, Detroit, Michigan*

The answer will depend on whether or not you are "Innocent" (Alexander O'Neal, featuring Cherrelle, 1985)? If the answer is yes, at least in the IRS's view of the word, you may not have to pay the tax debt.

The general rule is, if you sign a joint tax return with your spouse, you are both liable for the taxes owed. This is the case even if it's your spouse who was less than honest on the return, or somehow forgot to include that $1 million prize he received from being the winner of the latest reality show. The IRS is not going to get involved in that "he said, she said," dispute. If you make a false report on your tax return, the IRS is going to come after both of you for the tax liability. Many times, the spouse who caused the tax problems has skipped town or is suddenly broke when the tax man cometh; leaving the spouse who had nothing to do with it to clean up the mess.

There is some help. Under the "Innocent Spouse" rules, the IRS may "forgive" you for being naïve and only go after the spouse who made the false reports. You will need to show that when you signed this joint tax return, you didn't know, and had no reason to know, that your spouse was less than truthful on the tax return. For example, if you know that your spouse has a side consulting job where he makes a few thousand a year and you don't see this money reported on your tax return, you can't claim years later that you were innocent. You may not have agreed with what your spouse was doing or even thought it was that big of a deal since he didn't make that much money from it; but if you signed the joint tax return, it doesn't matter what your personal morals are on the issue.

If the IRS accepts your claim, you will not be responsible for the tax obligations, even though you signed a joint tax return. To see if you can use this rule, file *Form 8857, Request for Innocent Spouse Relief*. Also, check out *IRS Publication 971, Innocent Spouse Relief.*

You may also qualify for help under three other rules; Separate Tax Liability, Injured Spouse, and Equitable Relief.

Under the Separate Tax liability rules, the IRS treats you and your spouse as if you filed separate tax returns (using the married/filing separately filing status); even though you actually filed a joint tax return. They recalculate your taxes as two separate people and divide up all of the deductions, credits, etc. The result will be two tax returns and, of course, you will only be responsible for paying the taxes on your own tax return (and in many cases it will result in a refund to you). Folks tend to use this rule to help in situations where they can't get Innocent Spouse Relief, because they knew about the false statements on the tax return. With the Separate Tax Liability rules you can have knowledge of the discrepancies on the joint tax return, but you can only use the rule if you're legally separated, divorced, or live apart from your spouse for at least one year. To see if you can use this rule, file *Form 8857, Request for Innocent Spouse Relief*. Also, check out *IRS Publication 971, Innocent Spouse Relief*.

With the Injured Spouse rule, you are asking the IRS to give you your tax refund instead of using it to pay off your spouse's past due student loans, child support, alimony or prior federal and state tax debts. Here's how this rule typically helps:

> A couple files a joint tax return and expects a refund. One spouse has back taxes or child support payments. The spouse who had nothing to do with this keeps wondering what is taking the IRS so long to pay the tax refund. It turns out that they kept her refund check and used it to pay down her spouse's back taxes and child support. She's upset because she had nothing to do with these back taxes and child support in the first place. At the time this was all happening she was busy singing "Me Myself an I" (Beyonce, 2003) because she was one of the "Independent Women (Part I)" (Destiny's Child, 2000) with her own life and making her own decision; she's in "Control" (Janet Jackson, 1986). So why should her share of a joint tax return refund go to pay off his back taxes and child support? If she can prove all of this, she may get her share of the refund check back under the Injured Spouse rule. To see if you can use this rule, file *Form 8379, Injured Spouse Claim and Allocation*.

The above rules basically help you when you file a false tax return that causes you to underpay your taxes. What if you owe the money, but you just didn't pay it? Under Equitable Relief, the IRS can also forgive your debt if they determine that it would be "unfair' to collect taxes from you, the innocent spouse. Don't get your hopes up too high thinking this rule will help you, because very few people have stories compelling enough for the IRS to forgive you. To see if you can use this rule, file *Form 8857, Request for Innocent Spouse Relief*. Also, check out *IRS Publication 971, Innocent Spouse Relief*.

So far, I've been talking about what you can do for those tax returns where you filed jointly with your husband. When you file separately from your spouse, you are not responsible for his tax liabilities. After all, for many folks, that's the whole reason why they use this filing status. They know that their spouse is making false statements on the tax return and they don't want to have anything to do with it.

Practically speaking, if you still have a bank account with your husband, the IRS may come after that money to satisfy his tax debt. Although they are not technically coming after you for the taxes, it will certainly feel that way if they take the money out of your joint account. One way to protect yourself in this situation is to put your money into a new bank account that you own by yourself. I've heard of stories where the IRS still tries to come after that account, but if you can prove that they money is truly yours (i.e., it comes from your paycheck and it's not money that he is trying to hide from the IRS), you should be able to protect your money. Because of complicated stories like this one, if you're going through a separation or a divorce, please make sure to notify your tax advisor early so that you can protect your funds.

> **For more on dealing with the IRS,
> see Chapter 9: IRS Audit Issues**

## 21. The "401(k)" Question

*How much should I put in my 401(k)?*

*Linda, Houston, Texas.*

 As much as you can! Consider this: A 35 year-old, making $50,000 a year, decides to start investing in his company's 401(k). He puts in $5,000 a year and continues doing this every year until he's 65. By making annual tax-free contributions of $5,000 ($150,000 in total), his nest egg grows to about $625,000 (assuming an 8% interest rate). Not bad. Assume further that his company matches his 401(k) contributions by 50%. Now he's looking at about $937,000. And, if his employer matches 100% of his contributions, he is looking at about $1.25 million. "Curious" (Midnight Star, 1985)? Read on.

Folks under 40 often tell me that they have plenty of time to save for retirement, but right now they need to focus on getting their first-house, paying off school debts, saving to send their kids to college, and the list goes on. On the other side, folks over 40 may feel more pressure to start saving for their retirement, but also just can't seem to find the money to do this.

First of all, it's never too late to start saving. In the example above, I used a 35 year-old. Let's say the person was 45 years-old. The $5,000 annual contribution could still grow to about $247,000, $370,000 with 50% employer matching, or almost $500,000 with 100% employer matching. For my friends in their 50s, you can still save a little "Sumthin, Sumthin" (Maxwell, 1996). Using the same numbers if you start at 55 and only have 10 years to save, with a $5,000 annual contribution, you're looking at about $76,000, $115,000 with 50% employer matching, or $153,000 with 100% employer matching. The results may not be as dramatic with the younger folks, but every little bit helps.

Many folks come to me and profess a desire to want to save but can't find the money. You got to be in the game to win. If you aren't saving for your future, you might as well be sitting on the sidelines. Social security may not be around by the time you retire, and even if it is, the payments will certainly not let you retire to "Paradise" (LL Cool J, 2003). Here's a quick way to find that "extra" money to contribute to your 401(k):

- Calculate your taxes, based on your current income (e.g., using tax preparation software such as Turbotax™) to arrive at your current income taxes.
- Next, try to come up with a starting amount that you can afford to have taken out of your paycheck every month; such as $500.
- Reduce your current income by the amount of the total amount of the 401(k) contributions (i.e., at $500 a month, this would be $6,000 for the year) to arrive at your new income.
- Now calculate your taxes, based on your new income to get the amount of your new income taxes.
- The difference between your current income taxes and your new income taxes is your tax savings, thanks to the 401(k) contributions. Let's assume the difference is $1,000. This means that although you have to be able to currently live without the $6,000 to help pay your bills, you do get an extra $1,000 in tax savings. So you're really only temporarily without $5,000 (or about $417 a month). You get the money back when you retire after it has grown significantly.

You may have to run the numbers several times to come up with a figure that you can live with. You may also need to make some trade-offs; like instead of spending money for coffee 5 times a week you are down to twice a week, eating dinner at home more, and packing your lunch. You should do whatever you can to find the extra money and then perform this quick calculation. Keep in mind, every amount you can spare will be well worth it.

Want to see how much your own money can grow? There are several free 401(k) calculators on the internet such as:

- Bloomberg—http://www.bloomberg.com/analysis/calculators/401k.html
- Bankrate.com—http://www.bankrate.com/brm/calc/401k.asp
- DinkyTown.net—http://www.dinkytown.net/java/Retire401k.html
- Mile High Accountancy (a product of CCH Tax & Accounting)—http://www.execusite.com/clmjr/tools.html

Note: Although this question asked about 401(k)s, some of the principles apply to self-employed savings plans, like individual 401(k)s or IRAs. You should meet with your tax advisor once a year (preferably at the end of the previous year or at the beginning of a new year) to calculate the appropriate retirement plan for you, in light of your other savings goals.

> For more on 401(k)'s,
> see **Chapter 8: Investment, Education, Estate**

# THE NEXT TRACK

I hope you've enjoyed the various chapters on taking control of your taxes and building your net worth; all in the spirit of helping you save your, "Money, Money, Money, Money—Money" "For the Love Of Money" (O'Jays, 1973). I certainly had fun taking a trip back down memory lane and grooving to the funky beat. Tax and finance lessons don't have to be boring or confusing. Once you embrace these lessons, you're ready for the Next Track—building a solid financial base for you and your family, and teaching the next generation by way of example. Here are a few parting lessons to remember:

### 1. IT ALL STARTS WITH A LITTLE FORM

Working through the maze of Form 1040 is an inevitable requirement to reaching your tax and financial goals. Don't be "scured" ("Shake It Fast," Mystikal, 2000). Focus on your: filing status, personal exemptions, Above the Rim Deductions, itemized deductions and tax credits. Also, don't just look at the income from your "9 to 5." Remember, income from your side business and rental real estate can also be losses (at least in the early years). Finally, if you wind up owing and you can't pay your taxes, FILE the form on time and ask for an installment payment plan. There's no need to rack up interest and penalties unnecessarily. Instead, focus on doing tax planning for the next year so you won't be in this situation again.

### 2. START A SIDE BUSINESS

By now, you know that it will be hard for you to build your nest egg by relying only on your "9 to 5." There's no limit to the financial potential that may be gained from starting a side business. You'll be singing, "Ain't No Stoppin' Us Now," (McFadden and Whitehead, 1979). From doing freelance work (i.e., writing articles or grants, drafting business or marketing plans, giving speeches, etc.) to opening a day spa, follow your passion. With solid financial and tax planning, particularly in the early years, you can realize many tax benefits from your side business. Take these tax savings and plow them back into your business. Use them to fund retirement vehicles and education savings plans for your children.

### 3. BUILD WEALTH USING CAPITAL GAINS

Do you want true wealth? You still need to work hard at whatever you do, but use the money from your hard work to buy Capital Assets. The tax laws favor these assets and taxes them at a reduced rate. Whether it's stocks or rental property, focus on an investment strategy that takes advantage of the tax laws. Don't let these tax breaks keep "Passin Me By" (The Pharcyde, 1993).

### 4. SAVE TAXES WITH ITEMIZED DEDUCTIONS

These deductions are your major weapon in reducing your taxes—medical expenses, taxes, interest expenses, charitable contributions, casualty and theft losses, job expenses and other miscellaneous expenses. They each have many rules, exceptions and even more rules and exceptions. You don't need to have the memorized. Make sure that you devise a plan each year with your tax advisor as to the best deductions for you and then "get on it, dog-on-it!"

### 5. MO' MONEY MEANS MO' PROBLEMS LIKE AMT

AMT is a pure mess! After all your tax and financial planning, there's another tax that can creep up and ruin everything. So you need to get a tax check-up, at least "Just Once," (James Ingram 1980) a year, to make sure you're not getting to close to AMT—(i.e., because either your income is getting to high, you have too many deductions, you have ISOs, or all of the above). Remember, you want to pay your fair share of taxes and not a penny more. It's okay to use tax planning techniques to minimize the impact of AMT.

## 6. SAVE NOW FOR RETIREMENT AND EDUCATION

You have to find a way to save. There are so many tax-advantaged vehicles to help you fund retirement and send your kids to college that it's hard to know where to start. The good news is that you pretty much can't go wrong in picking a retirement vehicle. Whether it's a 401(k) or an IRA, the point is, you're saving. With a tailored retirement vehicle, you may decide, for example, that a Roth IRA and a 401(k) are the best vehicles for you and your spouse. The point is to come up with a plan, and like with the AMT, review it twice a year to make sure you're on track. Don't have the money? You would be surprised how tax benefits can help you "find" the money to make the contributions to these vehicles. The same goes for putting money away for your children's education. Many education vehicles allow you to contribute as little as $50 that will grow tax-free for your child's education. Again, set up a plan, plan, plan. Did I mention that you should set up a plan?

## 7. YOU CAN SURVIVE AN AUDIT

An audit is not the kiss of death. Like Gloria Gaynor said "I Will Survive" (1978). Remember to first, "Breathe" (Fabolous, 2004). If that isn't enough try to "Breathe, Stretch, Shake" (....let it go, Mace, 2004). And if you still need more, try to "Breathe Again," (Toni Braxton, 1993). Now that you're done with your relaxation routine, make sure you know the type of IRS audit so you can respond accordingly—Correspondence Audit, Office Audit, or Field Audit. If you owe money, work out a deal; which may be an offer and compromise, but will more likely be an installment payment plan. If you don't owe it, fight it; but make sure you got all your facts straight and the documents to support your case. You could be in for a long ride, but when you're right, by all means, "don't give up the fight"

("Get Up Stand Up," Bob Marley, 1973). Just make sure that you run your case by a tax advisor (a second opinion never hurts).

---

Don't forget to check out the Appendix for the Top 10 lists that apply to your situation. Whether you're a recent college graduate, trying to build your professional life, or in full cruise control and looking forward to retirement, there's a Top 10 list for you.

Can't get enough of this "Funky Stuff" (Kool & The Gang, 1973)? Look for future 411 Business & Money Guides focusing on:

- Business 411: Selecting the right type of business
- IPO 411: Ready for an IPO? Learn how to crawl before you walk
- Nonprofit 411: Run your own charity now!
- Fraternities and sororities 411—the biz side of social organizations
- Savings 411: You got to do more than a dime a day
- The blessed folks' 411: You ultimate savings and giving guide
- Franchise 411: Buying and running your business the smart way
- Retirement 411: Twist away with your ultimate tax and financial guide to retiring well

Got topics you want to see? Do you have tax or finance related questions? Let me know what you think. Visit my website at www.taxes411online.com—Holla!

# APPENDIX

 For The Love Of Money Lists

Check-out these For The Love Of Money Lists to help you get the 411:

- For Landlords
- For Single Parents
- For New Parents
- For Newlyweds
- For Lawyers
- For Freelancers
- For The College Grad
- For Doctors
- For New Homeowners
- For Stylists
- For Charities
- For The Self-Employed
- For Entertainers And Athletes
- For Good Stewards Of Blessings
- For New Money
- Reasons To Pay Your Taxes
- Check-Up List for Individuals
- Check-Up List for Side Businesses

- Ways To Avoid A Tax Audit
- Signs You Need Tax Help

# For The Love Of Money Top 10 For Landlords

☐ Congratulations on becoming a rental real estate owner! Having another source of income can be a "Sweet Thing" (Rufus, featuring Chaka Khan, 1975, or the remake version by Mary J. Blige, 1992). Make sure you report your activities on the right tax form. Use *Schedule E, Supplemental Income and Loss (Form 1040)* if you do this as a side business and attach the schedule to your tax return.

☐ If you own the property with your friends, families, co-workers, etc., in a partnership or limited liability company, use *Form 1065, US Partnership Return of Income* and make sure each member or partner is given a *Schedule K-1, US Return of Partnership Income (Form 1065)* which reports their share of the business profits and losses.

☐ Include all rental payments in your rental income, even if you receive it from a "Homie, Lover, Friend," (R. Kelly, 1993). What counts as rent? Pretty much everything your tenant pays you will count as rent and you have to report it in your income when you receive it. This includes the first and last month rental payments that you receive in advance. Don't include the security deposit if you plan to give that money back to the tenant at the end of the lease. Note: When you use the security deposit to cover the last month's rent, you should treat this as income at that time.

☐ Cash may rule everything around you, but rent doesn't just include the "C.R.E.A.M." (Wu-Tang Clan, 1994) you receive. It also includes the value of any services that your tenant provides for you in exchange for reduced or free rent (i.e., a handyman's services). You must also add in any of your expenses that the tenant pays on your behalf. So if the tenant pays to repair a broken furnace and you deduct this amount from her monthly rent, you still have to include the full amount of her rent in your income even though you didn't actually receive that amount in a cash payment. You can, however, deduct the cost of the furnace repair as a rental expense.

- [ ] Do you have "Work To Do," (Vanessa Williams, 1992) to get your rental property in tip top shape? If you plan on making some improvements to your rental property keep in mind that these expenses must be depreciated over what the IRS calls the useful life of the property (typically 27.5 years) rather than deducted in full in the year that you paid them. Think of an improvement as additions to a song like Snoop Dogg's "Let's Get Blown" (featuring Pharell, 2005) added to Slave's "Watching You" (1980). The beat and part of the chorus is pretty close but many of the lyrics are completely different. Whether the improvement is a better addition is up to the eyes of the beholder. An example of an improvement would be modernizing a kitchen or adding a swimming pool.

- [ ] Repairs can be deducted in full when you pay them. A repair helps maintain or replace something that was already working in good operating condition; like P. Diddy sampling of "I'm Coming Out, by Diana Ross (1980) in "Mo Money Mo Problems," (1997). A repair would be something like replacing a broken window or door.

- [ ] Your depreciation deduction will probably be your biggest expense. Remember, since residential real estate is made up of a building and land, to calculate your depreciation, you must deduct the cost of the land from your basis (i.e., what you paid for the property plus any improvements that you make). Next, take this amount and divide it by the property's useful life (which is typically 27.5 years).

- [ ] Unless you're "Working Day and Night," (Michael Jackson, 1979) or "Nite and Day," (Al B. Sure, 1988) only on your real estate activity, the IRS will probably not treat you as if materially participated in this business. This means that you are running a passive activity and you can typically only take up to $25,000 in losses from your rental real estate against your other income.

☐ Because you are running a passive activity, you probably won't have to pay self-employment taxes (to the tune of 15.3%) on your rental real estate income. But if you're spending most of your time as a landlord (i.e., over 750 hours in a year) you may be running a full-fledged active trade or business and self-employment taxes will probably apply to you.

☐ Keep good records to support your deductions. Besides depreciation, you can deduct anything that is reasonable and necessary to being a landlord. Don't forget to add expenses, like: advertising, cleaning, mortgage interest, property taxes, insurance, repairs, supplies, maintenance, utilities, landscaping and yard maintenance, pest control, travel, and professional and management fees; but make sure to back-out the personal portion of these costs. For example, if you live in one of the four-plex units that you rent, deduct 75% (3 out of 4) of the lawn bill because 25% is for your personal use.

# For The Love Of Money Top 10 For Single Parents

- [ ] You may be living the "Single Life" (Cameo, 1985), but you may be able to use the head of household filing status. You must provide more than half the costs of keeping a home for your child. Remember, your filing status can have a big impact on the amount of taxes you actually have to pay. Why? Because some of your tax deductions and credits are based on your filing status. Generally speaking, if you file as head of household, your taxes will be lower and your standard deduction will be higher than single status or married filing separately.

- [ ] Don't forget, you can claim a personal exemption for **each** child—to the tune of $3,200.

- [ ] Did you know you can get a tax credit just for having a child? That's right—there are tax credits just for having a kid. You may be able to deduct $1,000 for each child. The child must be younger than 17.

- [ ] Are you paying to send a child to college? If so, you may qualify for certain education credits. With the Hope Scholarship Credit you can take up to $1,500 credit for a child's tuition and related educational expenses. This credit can only be taken for the first two years of college—the freshman and sophomore year. But a $1,500 credit can be taken for each child that qualifies. You could instead choose the Lifetime Learning Credit, which could give you up to $2,000 in tax credits. With this credit you can deduct education costs for all years of post-high school education, and even course work taken to acquire and improve job skills.

- [ ] Do you bring home the bacon and fry it up in a pan? If yes, then you probably have daycare expenses. Don't forget, you may be able to deduct a child and dependent care tax credit, from $600 to $1,200, for some of your daycare expenses. To qualify, you must have daycare expenses for a child who is under 13 years of age (but there is no age limit for special needs children). Note: Practically speaking, if you participate in your company's flexible spending account for daycare expenses, you may not be able to take this credit.

- [ ] Invest in your child's future. There are several tax-advantaged education plans you can use to send your child to college (like 529 Plans or Coverdell Education Savings Accounts). The money you put in it grows tax-free and you pay no taxes when you take it out; as long as the money goes to pay for your child's education expenses. You can start some of these plans with as little as $50 a month. Remember, every little bit will help save your child from having large student loans.

- [ ] Are you going through a divorce? Make sure you talk to your tax advisor to help with how you and your ex-spouse will divide the tax benefits for your child. Typically, if you say nothing, zilch, nada on the issue, then the parent with whom the child lives will get the personal exemptions (called the custodial parent). But with a formal agreement, you can decide how to share the personal exemptions such as one parent gets it for the first three years, and then the other parent gets it for the next three years.

- [ ] Keep in mind, you don't have to pay taxes on child support payments, but you may have to include alimony payments in your income.

- [ ] Make sure you add up everyone's medical expenses. If these expenses are over 7.5% of your adjusted gross income, you qualify for this deduction. This basically means if you make $50,000, you must have medical expenses greater than $3,500 before you can deduct a penny. Medical expenses are much more than doctor's visits. Kids are a lot of work and before you know it you've spent thousands of dollars on doctor visits, braces, glasses, medicine, etc., for the entire family. All of these costs add up, but don't forget to also include prescription drugs, meals and lodging, mileage to and from doctor appointments (15 cents per mile) and other transportation costs.

☐ You've got your kids involved in all kinds of activities—from swimming at the "Y.M.C.A." (Village People, 1978) to singing in the youth choir at your church. You also help volunteer with all of these charities. Your out-of-pocket volunteer costs may count as charitable contribution deductions. Be sure to add up all of your travel for things, like: church conventions, meals (only when away from home overnight), lodging and any expenses you pay for (and don't get reimbursed for) on behalf of the charity. You can also deduct costs related to the use of your personal care for your volunteering activities, such as gas and oil, or the standard mileage deduction at 15 cents per mile. Costs for parking and tools may be deducted under either method.

# For The Love Of Money Top 10 For New Parents

- [ ] Congratulations on your new bundle of joy? May "God Bless The Child," (Billie Holiday, 1939). Make sure to get a social security number for your child so you can claim this little sweetie, who has you singing "You Light Up My Life," (Debby Boone, 1978), on your tax return.

- [ ] You can now claim a $3,200 personal exemption for your new beautiful child.

- [ ] Do you have "Work To Do" (Vanessa Williams, 1992)? If you plan on going back to work, you will probably have daycare expenses. You may be able to deduct a tax credit, from $600 to $1,200 for some of your daycare expenses. To qualify, you must have daycare expenses for a child who is under 13 years of age (there is no age limit for special needs children). Note: Practically speaking, if you participate in your company's flexible spending account for daycare expenses, you may not be able to take this credit.

- [ ] If you hire someone to watch your child as a nanny, you could have to pay the employment taxes (also called nanny taxes). This tax applies once you pay the nanny over $1,400 in a year.

- [ ] Are you a stay-at home mom? You may not miss many things about your J-O-B, but you did like the tax advantages of your 401(k). Well have no fear—the homemaker IRA is "Right Here," (SWV, 1992) to the rescue. You can contribute up to $4,000 to a Traditional IRA, take a tax deduction for this contribution, and the earnings grow tax free. You pay taxes when you take the money out after age 59½. Or, you can contribute the same amount to a Roth IRA, but, you don't get a tax deduction. Again, the earnings grow tax-free, but this time when you take the money out after 59½, you pay no taxes.

- ☐ Start saving for your child's education now. There are several tax-advantaged plans you can use (like 529 Plans or, Coverdell Education Savings Accounts). The money you put in grows tax-free, and you pay no taxes when you take it out; as long as the money goes to pay for your child's education expenses. You can start some of these plans with as little as $50 a month. Remember, every little bit will help save your child from having large student loans.

- ☐ You may be able to deduct the interest and points from a home improvement loan, where you use the proceeds for things like making additions to your house to help with your expanding family size.

- ☐ Having a baby can be expensive. You can deduct the medical expenses that you pay (after reimbursements from insurance) if they are over 7.5% of your adjusted gross income. This basically means, if you make $50,000, you must have medical expenses greater than $3,500 before you can deduct a penny. Medical expenses are much more than doctor visits. They include things, like: child birth classes, prescription drugs, meals and lodging, mileage to and from doctor's appointments (15 cents per mile), and other transportation costs.

- ☐ Is your child adopted? You may be able to claim up to $10,390 in adoption tax credits based on your adoption costs, such as adoption fees, court costs, attorney fees, and travel expenses.

- ☐ Want more money in your paycheck? Consult your tax advisor before, or right after, your child is born to see if you should change the amount of tax withholding from your paycheck.

# For The Love Of Money Top 10 For Newlyweds

☐ You finally tied the knot. You went from one to "Just The Two Of Us" (Bill Withers, 1981). Everyone is happy for you, even the IRS. You can file as a married couple for the entire year, even if you got married on December 31st.

☐ You are no longer a "wifey," and you probably can't wait to change your name to "MRS." But be sure that you change it legally with the Social Security Administration. The IRS will have a problem if the name on your tax return does not have a matching social security number on record with the Social Security Administration.

☐ You want all the money that you are entitled to, especially money that the IRS owes you. If you have moved as a result of marriage, report your change of address to the U.S. Postal Service and the IRS (Form 8822). If you are expecting a refund, it may not reach you if neither the IRS nor the post office has your new address.

☐ Marriage may have changed your tax bracket, so consult with a tax advisor to determine the appropriate form "For You" (Kenny Lattimore, 1997). You may now have sufficient deductions to use a Form 1040, as opposed to a Form 1040EZ.

☐ Consult with a tax advisor to determine the best filing status for you (e.g., married filing jointly or married filing separately).

☐ If you are a high-roller, big-baller or shoot-caller (i.e., you have assets over $250,000 between the two of you), talk with a tax advisor about estate planning. Now that 2 are 1, it's time you get your wills, trusts and estate in order.

☐ Make sure you get your investments in order. Getting married can impact things, like the amount you are able to deduct from making contributions to a traditional IRA.

☐ You have found your true love and soul mate. But like Al Green said, love will "make you do right and love will make you do wrong" ("Love and Happiness, 1972). So please, please, please discuss your pre-marriage tax situations. If your new "boo" owes the IRS money, you may now owe the IRS money, too! Yes, your vows predicted it. You married "for richer or for poorer." Just make sure you know how much "poorer" really is.

☐ Are you "Crazy In Love" (Beyonce, 2003)? Don't just rely on, "Everything is okay, sign here, you can trust me." When you sign your joint tax return, you are saying that you agree with the information being reported to the IRS. Signing a joint return may make you liable for any problems with that return (i.e., understatements of income); so review the return and ask questions if something is unclear.

☐ Were you shackin' up before you got married? Like Alicia Keys says, don't worry, "your secrets are safe with me" ("Diary," 2004). If you bought a house or other property together when you were two single folks, you may need to change the title on the assets to get the benefits of being married (i.e., the property automatically passing, upon death, to a surviving spouse). As local laws will differ on these points, please contact your tax advisor.

# For The Love Of Money Top 10 For Lawyers

Note: Most of the tips apply to solo practitioners or partners in law practices. A few tips apply to lawyers who are employees.

☐ Include the total amount of gross proceeds listed on Form 1099-MISC on your tax return. But, don't forget to deduct the amount that went to your client. Also, don't forget to deduct these business expenses: entertainment expenses (but only 50%), cell phone calls, mileage (at 40.5 cents per mile), subscriptions, magazines, professional dues, office expenses, continuing education expenses, and insurance premiums. Keep in mind, you may also be able to deduct the full cost of business assets up to $105,000 (i.e., you can skip depreciating them over numerous years).

☐ Do you work for a law firm? Like Gwen Guthrie said, "You got to have a J-O-B." ("Ain't Nothing Going On But The Rent," Gwen Guthrie, 1986). If you are an employee of a law firm, there are still many unreimbursed employee expenses you might be able to take as miscellaneous itemized deductions on Schedule A to Form 1040. These can include business meals and entertainment, depreciation on computers or cell phones, travel (including transportation and lodging), car expenses, job hunting expenses, subscriptions for magazines or on-line services, dues to professional organizations, state bar fees, and continuing legal education expenses. Remember, these miscellaneous itemized deductions are limited to 2% of your adjusted gross income. So, if your AGI is $10,000, you must spend more than $200 (2% of $1,000) before you can deduct one penny.

☐ Are you still singing, "Where the Party At?" (Jagged Edge, Featuring Nelly, 2001). Perhaps you should turn this curiosity into a money-making venture and throw parties on the side. This is another tip for those of you who are employees. Even if you have a full time legal job, you can still open a side business and use expenses from that business to offset your income. Note: Your business must eventually make money (i.e., after 3 years of losses, it may look like you're really running a hobby).

☐ Remember, you can deduct up to $2,500 of interest on your student loans; whether you have your own firm or work for a firm. However, the deduction phases out for taxpayers who are married filing jointly with AGI between $105,000 and $135,000 (between $50,000 and $65,000 for single filers).

☐ Know the difference between an employee and an independent contractor. Just because you are a solo practitioner, or a small firm, doesn't mean all your workers are independent contractors. Even the part-time receptionist, file clerk or paralegal, might still be an employee. For help on this, see *IRS Publication 1779, Employee Independent Contractor Brochure*.

☐ You may need to make estimated tax payments to the IRS every, "winter, spring, summer, fall," (aka, LeVert's 1990 song, "All Seasons"). The key to whether or not estimated taxes are required is knowing, by each quarterly period (April 15th, June 15th, September 15th and January 15th) if your net profit from operations will result in an income tax liability. If the answer is yes, then pay Uncle Sam in 4 installments; don't wait until you file a tax return. If the answer is no, taxes may still be due on your tax return, but you don't have to make an estimated tax payment for that quarter.

☐ Pay your employment taxes each and every month. Keep in mind, the quarterly estimated taxes you pay on operating net profits (see the tip above) are not the same as monthly employment tax deposits payments on wages and salaries for your employees. Remember, this money is not yours. It belongs to Uncle Sam and like Erik B and Rakim, he needs to be "Paid In Full" (1987). If not, the IRS has no problem coming after even your personal assets to get this money.

☐ Regardless of which income bracket you fall, if you have your own firm, you must pay self-employment taxes (at 15.3%, but you get a tax deduction for half) when you have more business income than business expenses Having a mortgage, giving to charity, etc., does nothing to remove this tax bill!

☐ Was Nas giving you this shout-out; "Owe me back like you owe your taxes" (Nas, featuring Ginuwine "You Owe Me" 1999)? You must pay all of your taxes. It's the right thing to do. It's the Christian thing, too. And, it's the law. For those who think you are sitting under the radar and the IRS does not know you exist, or that you have been working (because you haven't filed tax returns in year...)—THEY KNOW WHERE YOU ARE! Expect them to show up when your BIG settlement or case closes.

☐ I decided to "Save The Best For Last" (Vanessa Williams, 1992). Make contributions to a self-employed retirement plan (like, Individual 401(k), SEP IRA, SIMPLE IRA or Keogh plans). You may get a tax deduction, and also save for your future, as your earnings grow tax-free. For many of these, you can make contributions on behalf of your spouse, too. With a SEP IRA and Keogh plan, you can make contributions up to April 15, 2006 (or longer, if you filed an extension to your tax return), and have the contributions count as deductions on your 2005 tax return. If you are employed, try to max-out on your 401(k) contributions. You make contributions using pre-tax dollars and these contributions will grow tax-free.

# For The Love Of Money Top 10 For Freelancers

☐ After months and months of sending query letters, a magazine finally agreed to publish your article. You feel like "Mr. Big Stuff," (Heavy D. & the Boyz, 1987 or the original version by Jean Knight, 1971). Of course the article is a success and everyone loves it. At the beginning of the next year, the magazine sends you a *Form 1099-MISC, Miscellaneous Income*. This means you are being treated as an independent contractor (like someone who has her own side business). But don't attach Form 1099-MISC to your tax return. Include this income on *Schedule C, Profit or Loss from Business (Form 1040)*.

☐ Writing may be your passion and you know that the "Best Things In Life Are Free" (Janet Jackson, Luther Vandross, BBD and Ralph Tresvant, 1992); but be careful. Unless you start making some money from your freelancing, the IRS will look at you as running a hobby. Remember, if you have a hobby, you may not be able to deduct all of your expenses. Thus, you need to eventually start making money from selling your articles (i.e., after 3 years of no money or losses, it may look like you're really running a hobby).

☐ Your writer's haven is that place in your house that nobody can enter; where you have your computer, books, printer and everything you need to crank out your articles. This "home office" may also qualify for a tax deduction. You may be able to deduct the business portion of your home expenses for things, like: rent, leases, mortgage payments, insurance, utilities, general repairs, home owner association fees, trash removal, cleaning services, snow removal, grass and lawn maintenance. Make sure that this is truly your primary office and not a part-time place where you keep some business files and a computer. This office should be a separate room or place in your house that is only used for business purposes. As this is an area that the IRS tends to audit, meet with your tax advisor to make sure you can back-up your deduction.

- [ ] Social security may not be there to help you; and if it is, the benefits will probably be too small to meet your needs. Thank goodness that even if you have a full time J-O-B, you may also be able to save significant tax-free dollars in self-employed retirement plans. Look into setting up things like a Solo 401(k), SIMPLE IRA, SEP IRA or Keogh Plan. Your earnings in these accounts grow tax-free and they can be fairly easy to set up. Too busy piling money back in your side business to set this up? Think again. With proper tax planning, almost anyone can find tax savings that can be used to help fund your self-employed retirement plan.

- [ ] Report all of your freelance money. Remember the IRS knows you have this money, since a copy Form 1099-MISC is sent to them, too. An IRS computer will eventually match this to your social security number, and when it does they'll be "calling your name" and it certainly won't be "Gentle," (Frederick, 1985) since now you will owe interest and penalties. Expect them to show up about when you are about to sign the big royalty contract for your new novel.

- [ ] You can only deduct 50% of your business meals and entertainment. You will need to have good records to prove that this was truly a business expense. Thus you should get in the habit of writing things on the back of the meal receipt like, the names of everyone who was eating, how much you paid, a buzz word or brief description on what type of business you discussed.

- [ ] Don't forget, as a freelancer you are self-employed and will have to pay self-employment taxes (to the tune of 15.3%). Check with your tax advisor to see when your freelance income is high enough to start making estimated quarterly taxes payments to the IRS.

- [ ] Deduct your business miles at 40.5 cents per mile. These miles can add up. Even trips to mail your query letters can count.

☐ You couldn't even do your freelance job without your trusty "Digital Display," (Ready For The World, 1985). Don't forget to take all of the deductions associated with your computer, such as: the cost of your computer, computer software, internet charges, and website listing fees. Also, your other office technology may be deducted too such as: fax machines, printers, scanners, and personal desk assistants. Finally, don't forget the office supplies, like: computer paper, pens, pencils, notebooks, stamps, envelopes, etc. Make sure you back-out the personal portion of any of these expenses (i.e., if you also spend 25% of your time on the computer for personal purposes, then only 75% of the computer costs can be deducted as a business expense).

☐ Writer's workshops and conferences are great places to sharpen your writings skills. You can deduct your costs related to attending these conferences such as: the registration fee, travel to and from the conference, and lodging. Remember when it comes to meals, you can only deduct 50% of the cost.

# For The Love Of Money Top 10 For The College Grad

☐ Start saving NOW! If you can put away $250 a month in a tax-advantaged plan like a 401(k), your nest egg could grow to about $1 million by the time you're 65. If your employer matches your contributions, you could be looking at over $2 million. You have to start early, and you have to keep making your contributions. Before you know it, you'll be saying "I'm Rich!"

☐ If you're still singing, "Where The Party At," (Jagged Edge, featuring Nelly, 2001), perhaps you should turn this curiosity into a money-making venture and throw parties on the side. Even if you have a full time J-O-B, you can still open a side business and use expenses from that business to offset your income. The easiest and quickest way to form your business is as a sole proprietor you will need to file *Schedule C, Profit or Loss from Business (Form 1040)*. If you want more liability protection, you should consider setting up a formal business (e.g., a corporation, partnership or limited liability company). Note: Your business must eventually make money (i.e., after 3 years of losses, it may look like you're really running a hobby).

☐ Remember, you do have to pay taxes on all of your income. No full-time job yet? You're just freelancing? You should use the *Form 1099-MISC Miscellaneous Income* that you receive. Use this form to report your income on *Schedule C, Profit or Loss from Business (Form 1040)*. Remember to also include all expenses related to your consulting (or part-time) gig.

☐ You made it through four years of "Joy and Pain" (Maze, featuring Frankie Beverly, 1989), but now that you are a graduate, someone is surely now saying "You Owe Me" (Nas, featuring Ginuwine, 1999). It's time to start paying off your student loans. There is some good news. You may be able to deduct up to $2,500 of interest on your student loans. Note: The loan must be in your name, not your parents.

☐ Did you start a new job, too? If so, you may also be able to deduct your moving expenses, including mileage at 15 cents per mile. Moving expenses typically include: mileage, packing, storage and shipping costs, and costs for connecting and disconnecting utilities. Note: These moving expenses must pass several tests, including a 50-mile distance test.

☐ Are you still searching for a job? You may be able to deduct your job hunting expenses. To take this deduction you must have had some type of internship or job while you were in college, and now you are searching for a "9 to 5" job in that same profession (e.g., you interned with an accounting firm and now you are looking for permanent accounting job). Expenses that might count for this deduction include: employment and outplacement agency fees, resume preparation costs, paper, telephone calls, photographs, postage and unreimbursed travel expenses, and your mileage in searching for a job (i.e., at 15 cents per mile).

☐ Don't forget, you might have to include money you receive from scholarships, grants, student teaching or other services you provided in college as part of your income.

☐ Get in the habit of filing tax returns on time and making tax payments while you're young. You will save yourself years of having to say "No More Drama" (Mary J. Blige, 2001). Like President Bush said "You can run but you can't hide." The IRS always gets their man (or woman).

☐ Four years was not enough for you? Planning on going for a graduate degree? Well, "Here We Go Again" (Portrait, 1992). This time around you may be able to take a tax deduction for your graduate school costs. You can deduct education expenses that you pay to maintain or improve the skills related to your field or profession, but this education must be required by your employer to keep your current position or job. You also can't use this deduction if the education qualifies you for a new field or profession (i.e., to be a doctor or lawyer, but it may be okay for someone getting an MBA or Ph.D.).

☐ Each One, Teach One! Pass on your financial and tax knowledge to your younger friend, cousin, sorority sister, frat brother and anyone else you can mentor.

# For The Love Of Money Top 10 For Doctors

- [ ] Keep good accounting records. Use a separate bank account for all your business income and expenses, even if you work as a sole proprietor. Consider investing in accounting software (such as, Quickbooks® or Peachtree®). Separate accounts make it more cost effective when you have a bookkeeper or accountant handling your books.

- [ ] Include the total amount of gross proceeds listed on *Form 1099-MISC*. Also, don't forget to deduct these business expenses: entertainment expenses (but only 50%), cell phone calls, mileage (at 40.5 cents per mile), subscriptions, medical billings, magazines, professional dues, office expenses, continuing education expenses, and insurance premiums. Keep in mind, you may also be able to deduct the full cost of business assets up to $105,000 (i.e., you can skip depreciating them over numerous years).

- [ ] Whether you have your own practice or work as a partner, remember, you can deduct up to $2,500 of interest on your student loans. However, the deduction phases-out for taxpayers who are married filing jointly with an adjusted gross income between $105,000 and $135,000 and between $50,000 and $65,000 for single filers.

- [ ] Know the difference between an employee and an independent contractor. Just because you have your own practice or work in a small office, doesn't mean that all your workers are independent contractors. Even the part-time receptionist and file clerk might still be an employee. For help on this, see *IRS Publication 1779, Employee Independent Contractor Brochure*.

- [ ] You may need to make estimated tax payments to the IRS every "winter, spring, summer, fall," (aka, LeVert's 1990s song, "All Season"). The key to whether or not estimated taxes are required is knowing, by each quarterly period (April 15th, June 15th, September 15th and January 15th) if your net profit from operations will result in an income tax liability. If the answer is yes, then pay Uncle Sam in 4 installments; don't wait until you file a tax return. If the answer is no, taxes may still be due on your tax return, but you don't have to make an estimated tax payment for that quarter.

- [ ] Pay your employment taxes each and every month. Keep in mind, the quarterly estimated taxes you pay on operating net profits (see tip above) are not the same as monthly employment tax deposit payments on wages and salaries for your employees. Remember, this money is not yours. It belongs to Uncle Sam and like Erik B and Rakim, he needs to be "Paid in Full" (1987). If not, the IRS has no problem coming after even your personal assets to get this money.

- [ ] Regardless of your income bracket, if you have your own practice, you must pay self-employment taxes (at 15.3%, but you get a tax deduction for half) when your business income is greater than your business expenses. Having a mortgage, giving to charity, etc., does nothing to remove this tax bill!

- [ ] Was Nas giving you this shout—out: "Owe me back like you owe your taxes" (Nas, featuring Ginuwine, "You Owe Me," 1999)? You must pay all of your taxes. It's the right thing to do. It's the Christian thing to. And, it's the law. For those who think you are sitting under the radar and the IRS does not know you exist, or that you have been working (because you haven't filed tax returns in years…..)—THEY KNOW WHERE YOU ARE! Expect them to show up about two to three years after the balance was due, with interest.

- [ ] If you work for several hospitals, make sure to file state tax returns for each state. Often doctors that live close to the border of two states work at more than one hospital. You are required to file taxes in every state that you earn income. Consult your tax preparer or advisor if you fall into this category.

☐ I've decided to "Save the Best for Last" (Vanessa Williams, 1992). Make contributions to a self-employed retirement plan (like, Individual 401(k), SEP IRA, SIMPLE IRA or Keogh plans). You may get a tax deduction, and also save for your future, as your earnings grow tax-free. For many of these, you can make contributions on behalf of your spouse, too. With a SEP IRA, SIMPLE IRA and Keogh plan, you can make contributions up to April 15$^{th}$ (or longer, if you filed an extension to your tax return), and have the contributions count as deductions on your tax return.

# For The Love Of Money Top 10 For New Homeowners

☐ Welcome to the wonderful world of home ownership. You can't seem to stop singing "It's My House" (and yo vivo aqui, Diana Ross, 1979). The tax laws are happy for you, too! You can finally start deducting mortgage interest. For many people, this will be their largest deduction.

☐ The "points" paid to obtain the mortgage can also be taken as itemized deductions; but only as long as your down payment was greater than the points charged. If you got a mortgage with 100% financing, like Lil' Flip sings "Game Over." (2004), you won't get this deduction. Points can be very confusing, so check with a tax advisor.

☐ Don't forget to deduct your property taxes. This can also be a large itemized deduction; particularly if you live in high property tax states like California, New York or New Jersey. Note: Property tax assessments for things such as water mains, sewer lines, and other similar improvements are not deductible.

☐ Do you plan on working out of your home? You may be entitled to a home-office deduction as a miscellaneous itemized deduction. You may be able to deduct the business portion of your home expenses for things, like: rent, leases, mortgage payments, insurance, utilities, general repairs, home owner association fees, trash removal, cleaning services, snow removal, grass and lawn maintenance. Make sure that this is truly your primary office and not a part-time place where you keep some business files and a computer. This office should be a separate room or place in your house that is only used for business purposes. As this is an area that the IRS tends to audit, meet with your tax advisor to make sure you can back-up your deduction.

☐ Did you start a new job, too? If so, you may also be able to deduct your moving expenses, including mileage at 15 cents per mile. Note: These moving expenses must pass several tests, including a 50-mile distance test.

- [ ] Want more money in your paycheck? Consult your tax advisor before, or right after, you buy your house to see if you can change the amount of tax withholding from your paycheck.

- [ ] You must keep all paper work related to your home; from the original contract and settlement papers, to receipts from repairs and home improvements. If paperwork just "ain't your thang," give copies to your tax advisor. This paperwork will be required to calculate your tax deduction and to help you if you need to refinance, or when you sell the home.

- [ ] Planning on making any additions or repairs to your house right away? You won't be able to deduct these costs (unless you take out a home improvement loan). You will be able to add them to the basis, or the cost, of your house. This can reduce your gain when it's time to sell your home.

- [ ] I know you want your money, especially money that the IRS owes you. Don't forget to notify the U.S. Postal Service of your new address, so they can forward any tax refunds. The U.S. Postal Service will also pass your new address on to the IRS.

- [ ] When you sell your home, you pay no income taxes on gain as long as your gain is equal to, or less than, $250,000 for single folks and $500,000 for married folks filing jointly. You must meet certain rules (such as you must own your home for at least 2 years out of the last 5 years before you sell the house, unless you are selling because of a new job, health conditions or other unforeseen circumstances). Keep in mind, the old tax rules that required you to "roll over" your gain by purchasing a new home are gone "Bye, Bye, Bye," just like the group 'N Sync (2000).

# For The Love Of Money Top 10 For Stylists

☐ Do you run your own beauty shop or barbershop as a sole proprietorship? Report your income and expenses on *Schedule C, Profit or Loss from Business (Form 1040)*. Make sure you have a separate business checking account that is used only for business income and expenses.

☐ Does "Cash Rule Everything Around You? ("C.R.E.A.M.," Wu-Tang Clan, 1994)? As this is mostly a cash business, make sure you have receipts to support everything. If the IRS audits you and you don't have these receipts, they will come up with all sorts of methods to calculate your income. It should come as no surprise that their number will probably be higher than what you feel you actually really made. Consider using sale receipts for all transactions (yes, even cash) and include your tips. You may also use an appointment book with all the details, or computer software program.

☐ Is your shop at your "Home" (Stephanie Mills, 1989)? You may be eligible for the home office expense deduction. This includes deducting the business portion of your home expenses for things, like: rent, leases, mortgage payments, insurance, utilities, general repairs, home owner association fees, trash removal, cleaning services, snow removal, grass and lawn maintenance. Your shop should be in a separate room or place in your house that is only used for doing hair. As this is an area that the IRS tends to audit, meet with your tax advisor to make sure you can back-up your deduction.

☐ Know the difference between an employee and an independent contractor. Make sure you have written employment and contractor agreements for everyone. Be careful here. Just because you're a small shop and you don't have much money doesn't mean that all your workers are independent contractors. Even the part-time receptionist or the hair washer, may still be an employee. For more on employees and independent contractors, see *IRS Publication 1779, Employee*

*Independent Contractor Brochure* and tips on the IRS website (http://www.irs.gov) under Industries/Professions: Cosmetology.

☐ Did you receive a *Form 1099-MISC, Miscellaneous Income*? If so, you are being treated as an independent contractor (like someone who has her own side business). But don't attach *Form 1099-MISC* to your tax return. Include this income on *Schedule C, Profit or Loss from Business (Form 1040)*.

☐ Don't forget to also include all expenses related to your hair business (even if you are doing it part-time). Expenses like your travel, hair shows, workshops, supplies, cell phone may all be deductible.

☐ You may need to make tax payments to the IRS every, "winter, spring, summer and fall," (aka LeVert's 1990 hit "All Season"). The key to whether quarterly estimated taxes are required is knowing at each quarterly period (April 15th, June 15th, September 15th and January 15th) whether or not your net profit from operations will result in an income tax liability. If the answer is yes, then Uncle Sam wants you to pay him in 4 installments; no waiting until you file a tax return. If the answer is no, taxes will be due, but you don't have to make an estimated tax payment for that quarter.

☐ Pay your employment taxes each and every month. Keep in mind, the quarterly estimated taxes you pay on operating net profits (see tip above) are not the same as monthly employment tax deposits payments on wages and salaries for your employees. Remember, this money is not yours. It belongs to Uncle Sam, and like Erik B and Rakim, he needs to be "Paid in Full" (1987). If not, the IRS has no problem coming after even your personal assets to get this money.

☐ Do you sell hair products in your salon? If so, make sure to charge sales tax (if required by your state). Also, don't forget to pay these sales taxes over to the state (in most states this is on a quarterly basis).

☐ Ever have a client complain and threaten to sue you because she claims you made her look like Grace Jones when she wanted to look like Beyonce? What can you say? You're a great stylist, but even you can't work miracles. You may want to make sure you get general liability insurance. Don't forget to deduct the costs of your insurance premiums.

## For The Love Of Money Top 10 For Charities

☐ You've set up your charity (filed as a nonprofit corporation with your state, filed Form 1023, and received the acknowledgement letter from the IRS). You've also begun to collect donations, hold events and finally start carrying out your charitable mission. But hold up; "Wait A Minute," (Ray J., 2001). Did you file for tax-exempt status with your state, too? Many charities forget to do this last step and some wind up owing state income taxes.

☐ File your tax returns annually—*Form 990, Return of Organization Exempt from Tax*. Even if your nonprofit makes less than $25,000 a year, you still might want to file this form, because almost all grant-makers will want to see this before they give you any money.

☐ You must continue to be supported by the public to maintain your tax-exempt status (called the "public support test"). This typically means that at least 1/3rd of your money comes from individuals, the government, grant-makers or revenues from your events.

☐ You must send your donors receipts or "Thank You" letters (aka, Kirk Franklin and Mary Mary style, 2001) with IRS special "It Must be Magic" language (Teena Marie, 1984). See *IRS Publication 1771, Charitable Contributions—Substantiation and Disclosure Requirements* for the true 411 on what to include in this letter. You should send these letters out routinely after you receive a donation (i.e., within 30 days). For last minute gifts on Dec. 31st, send this out no later than January 31st of the following year.

☐ You must get a solicitation license before you start asking folks for money, and you need a license in each state that you solicit. So, if your nonprofit is in a tri-state area (like Maryland, DC and Virginia) you should probably have three solicitation licenses.

☐ Be careful with loans you make to your charity or loans you take from your charity. True enough, this is your nonprofit in the sense that you started it and put your hard work, blood, sweat and tears into it. But, once you turned your passion into a 501(c)(3) tax-exempt organization, it became the "public's organization," and taking out loans will look suspect to the IRS. You will definitely need to run this by a tax advisor.

☐ Know the difference between an employee and an independent contractor. Just because you're a small charity and you don't have much money doesn't mean that all your workers are independent contractors. See *IRS Publication 1779, Employee Independent Contractor Brochure,* for more on employees and independent contractors.

☐ Pay your employment taxes. Even though you are a tax-exempt organization and pay no income taxes, you still must pay employment taxes just like any other corporation.

☐ Train your board of directors on tax and financial matters. With all the corporate and tax scandals in the for-profit world (i.e., Enron) and the nonprofit world (i.e., United Way), it's no longer an excuse that the board didn't know. The IRS can come after board members personally for certain bad financial acts. Remember, this is the "public's money." Also, some states (like California with its new Nonprofit Integrity Act) are requiring nonprofit boards to take their fiduciary responsibilities to another level.

# For The Love Of Money Top 10 For The Self-Employed

- [ ] "Practice What You Preach," (Barry White, 1994). If you have a formal side business that is separate from you (like a corporation, partnership or limited liability company), you must act like you do. This means you have to follow the formalities, like: a separate business bank account, actual board meetings, minutes from those meetings, a stock ledger and stock certificates that have actually been issued, and formal resolutions to document the actions taken by your board. Failing to do the formalities may cause the IRS to disregard your business type and treat you like a sole proprietorship.

- [ ] Know the difference between an employee and an independent contractor. Just because you have your own practice or work in a small office, doesn't mean that all your workers are independent contractors. Even the part-time receptionist and file clerk might still be an employee. For help on this, see *IRS Publication 1779, Employee Independent Contractor Brochure*.

- [ ] You should pay yourself some amount of salary. What if you don't? If you take money out of this business account, the IRS may consider this to be a payroll expense and you could owe payroll taxes. This is the case, even if you call it a "loan" but yet you have no formal promissory note. Speak with a tax advisor about coming up with a reasonable amount for your salary, and structuring employee loans if you plan to pay the money back to your business.

- [ ] Do you have "Work To Do" (Vanessa Williams, 1992)? You are probably busy doing your passion, but make sure that you include some time in there for tax planning. You should be meeting with your tax advisor on a regular basis (at least twice a year) to ensure that you are making the right quarterly estimated tax payments and tracking the maximum amount of your deductions.

☐ While you're busy doing the "Work It" (Missy Elliot, 2002), don't forget to save for your future. Social security may not be there to help you, and if it is, the benefits will probably be too small to meet your needs. Look into setting up things, like: a Solo 401(k), SIMPLE IRA, SEP IRA or Keogh Plan. Your earnings in these accounts grow tax-free, and they can be fairly easy to set up. Too busy piling money back in your side business to set this up? Think again. With proper tax planning, almost anyone can find tax savings that can be used to help fund your self-employed retirement plan.

☐ Business transportation expenses, whether by your car, airplane, railway, or boat, really add-up. I don't care how you "Get Here" (Oleta Adams, 1990); make sure you only take the business portion of these expenses. Many times, there are personal elements associated with your travel (like personal miles on your car or personal time spent on a business trip or convention). You must back-out the personal portion of these costs. Also, remember that you can only deduct 50% of your associated entertainment expenses (i.e., the food at a business meeting).

☐ Do you run your side business out of your home? You may be eligible for the home office expense deduction. This includes deducting the business portion of your home expenses for things, like: rent, leases, mortgage payments, insurance, utilities, general repairs, home owner association fees, trash removal, cleaning services, snow removal, grass and lawn maintenance; but make sure that this is truly your primary office and not a part-time place where you keep some business files and a computer. This office should be a separate room or place in your house that is only used for business purposes. As this is an area that the IRS tends to audit meet with your tax advisor to make sure you can back-up your deduction.

☐ Regardless of your income bracket, self-employment tax is due when you have more income than your expenses. Having a mortgage, giving to charity, etc does not remove this bill!

- [ ] Do you always feel like "Somebody's Watching Me" (Rockwell featuring Michael Jackson, 1984)? For those who think they are sitting under the radar and the IRS does not know that you exist or that you have been working (because you haven't filed in years)—THEY KNOW WHERE YOU ARE! Expect them to show up when your BIG contract closes.

- [ ] Check for local and city tax permits and licenses necessary to operate your business. For example, many states and localities charge taxes on your business property. Make sure to research requirements. Thankfully, a lot of states have exemptions from these taxes for small businesses.

# For The Love Of Money Top 10 For Entertainers And Athletes

Are you dreaming of "Lights, Camera, Action"? Before you start to lead "The Glamorous Life" (Sheila E. 1984), make sure to get these tax tips in order.

- ☐ Track commission amounts paid to agents, accountants, and managers (all deductions), because gross income amounts are reported to IRS.

- ☐ Make sure to track out-of-state income. They require you to file returns if you work in their state, even if you don't live there!

- ☐ The IRS already believes that entertainers and athletes don't report all of their income and take excessive tax deductions. Protect yourself by keeping all supporting documents to back up your story.

- ☐ Try to use tax professionals that have experience working with other entertainers/athletes, or seem willing to perform the necessary research.

- ☐ If you have an EIN (Employer Identification Number), you HAVE to file quarterly payroll returns, even if you don't have any payroll expenses.

- ☐ If you own a side business (i.e., like a corporation) and you take money out of your business, the IRS might consider these withdrawals to be payroll expenses and you may owe payroll taxes. Speak with a tax advisor about structuring employee loans if you plan to pay the money back to your corporation within the same tax year.

- ☐ When thinking about how much bling, bling you want to get, REMEMBER that your actual cash flow is not your contract amount, but the contract amount less agent (10%), manager (15%), business manager (5%), and taxes (20%). Of course your personal percentages may differ, but you get the drift…think 50% is left.

- [ ] Meet with your accountant/financial advisor to calculate your quarterly tax estimates.

- [ ] Even if you are not incorporated, if you have a side business, make sure that you have a separate business checking account that is used only for business income and expenses.

- [ ] For those who think they are sitting under the radar and the IRS does not know that you exist or that you have been working (because you haven't filed in years), THEY KNOW WHERE YOU ARE! They read the trades and watch ESPN just like you! Expect them to show up when your BIG deal closes.

# For The Love Of Money Top 10 For Good Stewards of Blessings

☐ Max-out your charitable giving. Tithe and contribute to your local church, school and charity. Volunteer your gifts and skill set to others in your community. Remember, your out-of-pocket expenses can also count as charitable contributions, but let your motivation be your sharing. If not for (you fill in the blanks). II Corinthians 6:6-13 speaks of rewards of sowing into others with positive motives (heart attitude).

☐ Know just how much you spend and on what. This is called cash flow management, and good tax planning can help you here. You should have a good idea of your monthly obligations and how much they cost. Save a portion of your cash flow for emergencies. You should also pay your vendors in a timely fashion. Make sure your business practices mirror your character. Check out Romans 13:8 and Ephesians 6:9. Both scriptures speak about the way to treat creditors and people under your supervision.

☐ Lay proper foundation and plan all financial moves. Make sure all agreements are in writing, even if it's a personal loan from yourself to your company! Have a promissory note with real interest payments at fair market interest rate (like the Applicable Federal Rate or AFR). You may be able to take the interest payments that you make as tax deductions.

☐ Do you have a side business? Employ when your territory increases! Bless others as you get blessed, but remember to know the difference between an employee and an independent contractor. Just because you have your own practice or work in a small office, doesn't mean that all your workers are independent contractors. Even the part-time receptionist and file clerk might still be an employee. For help on this, see *IRS Publication 1779, Employee Independent Contractor Brochure.*

☐ Invest in your child's future. There are several tax-advantaged education plans you can use to send your child to college (like 529 Plans or

Coverdell Education Savings Accounts). The money you put in grows tax-free and you pay no taxes when you take it out, as long as the money goes to pay for your child's education expenses. You can start some of these plans with as little as $50 a month. Remember, every little bit will help save your child from having large student loans.

- [ ] Invest in continuous education for yourself, too. Take professional development courses to expand your skill set and territory of influence. You may be able to take a deduction for tuition and fees, or an itemized deduction for unreimbursed employee education expenses. You may also be eligible for education credits.

- [ ] Make sure you have a will, and that you start your estate tax planning. Your tax planning costs related to setting these up and keeping them going may be tax deductible. You can't take it with you, so plan on how your estate can help your family and church. Proverbs 13:22 states, "A good man leaves an inheritance for his children's children."

- [ ] File your tax returns and pay your taxes. Meet with your tax advisor to calculate your quarterly tax estimates. Romans 13:6-7 speaks specifically to paying your taxes as well.

- [ ] Don't cut corners. Start saving for your financial future by investing in tax-advantaged retirement plans like 401(k)s or IRAs. Putting $5,000 a year away for 20 years in one of these plans can give you over $300,000 (over $600,000, if your employer matches your contribution. Proverbs 13:11 states that the "Dishonest money dwindles away, but he who gathers money little by little makes it grow."

- [ ] Pass these principles and tips to your children and those younger than you. This will shape their future and make brighter jewels for you since children are your true wealth! Start teaching them by setting up their own accounts (like an UGMA). The first $800 in investment income is tax-free, too!

# For The Love Of Money Top 10 For New Money

- [ ] Do they say your "new money" and you have "no class"? ("This Is How We Do," The Game, featuring 50 cents, 2004)? Don't listen to what people say, "They Don't Know," (Jon B, 1997). You may be new money, but if you plan to keep it you will need to use tax planning as one of your weapons to do this. There is no reason to have bad credit or owe back taxes when you are making good money. If you don't have a tax advisor (someone doing more than just preparing your tax return), now is the time to get one.

- [ ] "Did You Ever Think" you would be this rich (R. Kelly, 1998)? Make sure your cash in is greater than your cash out. This sounds simple, but so many people make a nice salary, yet their cash flow is negative. Again, tax planning can help you with some of this.

- [ ] Was Nas giving you this shout-out: "Owe me back like you owe your taxes" (Nas, featuring Ginuwine, "You Owe Me," 1999)? Get in the habit of filing tax returns on time and making tax payments. For those who think you are sitting under the radar and the IRS does not know you exist, or that you have been working (because you haven't filed tax returns in years)—they know where you are. Expect them to show up about two to three years after your taxes were due, with interest. Like President Bush said, "You can run but you can't hide." The IRS always gets their man (or woman).

- [ ] You've worked hard to get where you are and probably didn't have time to think about retirement. But now it's time to start your "Next Episode" (Dr. Dre, featuring Snoop Dog, 1999). If you can put away $10,000 a year in a 401(k), in 30 years you'll have about $1.2 million. If your employer matches your contributions, you could be looking at over $2.5 million.

- [ ] Be charitable. There's a proverb that says you reap what you sow. Blessings passed on bring more blessings. If you think hard enough, someone or something assisted you to where you are in life. Whether it was a mother, grandmother, aunty or teacher, give to a local charity in their honor; maybe to your alumni association or local church. Giving is good for the soul and it reduces your taxes!

☐ It's like the song says, "Mo Money, Mo Problems," (Notorious B.I.G., featuring Kelly Price, Mase, Puff Daddy, 1997). Beware of this messy thing called the Alternative Minimum Tax (AMT). The more you make, the more you have to worry about this alternate way to calculate your taxes. This means that many of your hard earned tax deductions will be lost and you will owe more taxes than you thought. AMT particularly affects those with incomes from $150K to $500K. Speak with your tax advisor to get an assessment on how close you are to falling into AMT status.

☐ Before you start to "Spread My Wings" (Troop, 1989), make sure your will and estate plans are in order. Don't hold off on doing this. As an added bonus, you may be able to deduct your tax planning costs related to setting these up and maintaining them.

☐ You've got to "Keep Risin' To The Top," (Dougie Fresh, 1988). Making good money for your employer is great, but there is nothing better than working for yourself. Consider starting a side business. Even if you have a full time J-O-B, you can still open a side business and use expenses from that business to offset your income. The easiest and quickest way to form your business is as a sole proprietor (you will need to file *Schedule C, Profit or Loss from Business (Form 1040)*. If you want more liability protection, you should consider setting up a formal business (e.g., a corporation, partnership or limited liability company). Note: Your business must eventually make money (i.e., after 3 years of losses, it may look like you're really running a hobby).

☐ Pass it on! Teach your children about finances and taxes so they aren't "trying to make a dollar out of fifteen cents—a dime and a nickel" ("Get Around," 2 Pac, 1993). Set up tax-advantaged education plans you can use to send your child to college (like 529 Plans or Coverdell Education Savings Accounts). The money you put in grows tax-free and you pay no taxes when you take it out, as long as the money goes to pay for your child's education expenses.

☐ Watch out for phase-outs. Now that you are a high roller, big baller and shoot-caller, you may no longer be eligible for many tax deductions and credits that you've read about. Did you know that if you make over $72,975, if single or $145,950 if married filing jointly, your itemized deductions start getting phased-out and continue to do so up to an 80% reduction? So the list ends where it started. Get tax-planning help now so you can maximize your deductions and, where possible, avoid phase-outs.

## Reasons To Pay Your Taxes

- [ ] It's the law. Failure to pay taxes can result in fines and jail time.

- [ ] The interest and penalty for failing to pay your taxes on time can, sometimes, be far more than the amount of the tax itself.

- [ ] It will cost your more in the long term. Just ask countless stars and entertainers. The attorney or accountant fees that you will have to pay to resolve the problem, alone can be far more than amount you originally owed.

- [ ] A federal tax lien on your credit report will make it very difficult for you to get credit. Commercials may claim "Bad Credit, Tax Liens, No Problem." But beware. By the time you finish with the fees and interests on those credit cards, you could have paid off your tax debts and taken a vacation to the Bahamas twice.

- [ ] Some jobs require credit checks. Your tax delinquencies will certainly show up on your credit report.

- [ ] You don't want your employer to receive a Notice of Levy on your wages from the IRS. The last thing you want is for "what's his name" in payroll to know that you're having tax problems.

- [ ] You don't want to have to explain to your nosy neighbors why the IRS just took all your assets.

- [ ] The IRS has payment plans. So if you can't pay your taxes in full, at least try to work out a payment schedule.

- [ ] You can't buy a home easily if you haven't filed tax returns.

- [ ] Like Puffy said, pay taxes or die (or, wait a minute, was that vote or die?)

# Check-Up List for Individuals

Everyone thinks of April 15th as the tax day, but you should be thinking of taxes year round. Use this 411 checklist for some of the things to go over with your tax advisor.

- [ ] Look at your previous tax returns (i.e., the previous 2 years) to help you gather the same type of information that supports your income and deductions. Review itemized sheets to make sure you gather the same type of information.

- [ ] Collect all of your employee's Form W-2s and Form 1099-MISC's from business income.

- [ ] Gather all *Form 1098 Mortgage Interest Statements* and real estate tax vouchers. Bring a copy of your closing statement, as well.

- [ ] If you sold any stock, gather your information; including purchase and sales confirmations, and year-end summary statements from your brokerage company.

- [ ] If you've suffered casualty or theft losses, make sure to have receipts, police reports and other documents to support the amount of your losses.

- [ ] Gather social security information for all dependents. For those single mothers or fathers, verify with the other parent which of you is claiming the child.

- [ ] Invest in a tax-advantaged retirement plan (i.e., 401(k), Traditional IRA, Roth IRA, etc.) Keogh Plan, SEP IRA or SIMPLE IRA). Check to see if you should change your contributions to any existing plan or if you should rollover to a new plan.

- [ ] Add-up all of your unreimbursed employee expenses.

☐ Make sure to gather total amount of state taxes paid in the previous year. This includes any back taxes or balances paid in full with last year's tax return. Always keep a copy of all tax payments and voucher made. Also include vehicle registration tax if imposed by your state department of motor vehicle.

☐ Make sure to track all medical expenses paid, including (but not limited to):

| | | |
|---|---|---|
| Insurance premiums | Co-pays | Prescription Medicine |
| Medical devices | Eye exams | Glasses/Contact Lenses |
| Mileage | Office visits | Hospital/Clinic expenses |
| Dental cleanings | | |

☐ Gather your tithes or charitable contribution statements. Always keep Salvation Army and/or Goodwill contribution receipts. If possible, take pictures of items donated; especially if they are high retail and in superior condition.

# Check-up List for Side Businesses

Use this list every time you meet with your tax advisor.

☐ Verify you are following your business formalities.

- Board meetings
- Stock certificates
- Minutes of meetings
- Notice of meetings

☐ Discuss if it's time to change your business type.

- Business expansion or downsizing
- Liability Protection
- New or additional partners
- Less complexity and administration
- Get right with the IRS.

☐ Bring print-outs from your accounting records (cash flow statements, income statements, bank reconciliations, etc). You are required (by the IRS) to keep accounting books and records. Popular accounting software includes Quickbooks™ or PeachTree™. Make sure to update your books through the end of your tax year.

☐ Bring business records to back up what you claim; particularly the business usage of your assets, such as cell phones, computers, etc. It's not enough to just guess, and these records should be included in your tax file. For example, take your cell phone bills and highlight the calls that are for business purposes. This will make it easier to figure out your business usage percentage at the end of the year.

☐ Verify proper classification and treatment of employees versus contractors. In either case, make sure to issue Form 1099-MISCs and Form W-2s if applicable at year-end.

☐ Make sure you are current on all of your payroll tax returns, payments and filings. Review the returns, even if a payroll processing company prepares them. You are still liable for the accuracy of the returns!

☐ Keep a reminder calendar of state and local annual fees due for your business such as: statements of information, registration statements, business taxes and licenses.

☐ Verify that you are current on your quarterly estimated tax payments.

☐ Start a self-employed retirement plan (i.e., Solo 401(k) Keogh Plan, SEP IRA or SIMPLE IRA). Check to see if you should change your contributions to any existing plan or if you should rollover to a new plan.

☐ Bring proof that your home office is your primary office (such as, pictures of the office, a client log book that records when you met clients at your office, copies of business cards and stationery using the home office address, etc.). Also, bring receipts and copy of bills for expenses directly related to the home office, and those indirect expenses that benefit the entire house, like: rent, leases, mortgage payments, insurance, utilities, general repairs, home owner association fees, trash removal, cleaning services, snow removal, grass, and lawn maintenance.

☐ Review your tax planning schedule. Meet your tax advisor once each quarter (winter, spring, summer and fall). Here is a sample schedule you can use with your tax advisor:

- In February—Meet to go over tax return preparation
- In June—Discuss additional assets/expenses you need before year end
- In September—Review operational performance to identify year-end tax strategies
- In December—Complete the tax saving measures identified in the operational review.

- Quarterly—Project and pay estimated income taxes
- Monthly—Pay payroll tax deposits

☐ Track your business expenses and make sure you know where you stand on a frequent basis (i.e., monthly). Following are examples of some expenses to look for:

| | | |
|---|---|---|
| Advertising | Trade Publications | Dues |
| Legal Fees | Accounting Fees | Contractors |
| Business Entertainment | Equipment Repairs | Payroll |
| Business Travel | Local Transportation | Telephone |
| Seminars | Office Supplies | Insurance |
| Postage & Delivery | Business Gifts | Xeroxing |
| Internet | Research & Reference | Auto |
| Retirement Plans | Contributions | Furniture |
| Business Equipment | Computer | Office Utilities |
| Security | Bank Service Charges | |

## Ways To Avoid An Audit

Do you always feel like "Somebody's Watching Me"; even the IRS (Rockwell, featuring Michael Jackson, 1984)? For the record, an IRS audit is nothing to get worried about if you have accurate records and have performed all your filings properly. That being said, truth and perception may not always be consistent. Below are suggestions for preventive steps to lower the likelihood of you being audited.

- ☐ Make sure to report any and ALL income. Any income or expense that the IRS requires a third-party to verify by filing Forms 1099, 1098, 941, W-2, etc., are computer-matched during processing. You should double-check these figures before you file your tax return. It is good to keep copies of all checks received (cash receipts) to verify that your year-end statement is accurate.

- ☐ Review your tax return for simple mistakes before you file it, (like checking your total salary number against the amounts listed on Box 4 of your W-2's). Also, make sure all of your calculations, personal contact information and social security numbers are listed correctly on your return.

- ☐ The home office deduction has historically been one of those areas where it seems like the IRS is saying "No, No, No, No, No" while you're saying "Yes, Yes, Yes, Yes, Yes" (Destiny's Child, 1997). It is one of the red flags that may cause an audit. If you deduct the costs of your home office, the key is Documentation! Be able to prove that this is truly your primary office (i.e., it's a separate room in your house, the place where you meet clients, etc.) Also remember, indirect expenses (those that apply to the entire house) must be allocated, but you can deduct all of the direct expenses (those that apply only to the business space).

- ☐ Keep personal and business bank accounts separate; otherwise you'll be saying "How Will I Know," (Whitney Houston, 1985) which expenses to claim as business deductions and which ones are personal? Mixing use of accounts will generate more questions and may expand a simple question to a full-fledge search.

☐ Pay for all business expenses with a check or credit card, segregated for business. The IRS auditor is looking for a payment trail when reviewing your accounts. If the IRS auditor does not see routine expenses paid out of the account, it may lead her to ask "What's Going On" (Marvin Gaye, 1971)? Do you have cash transactions going on off the books?

☐ Carefully calculate and document the business usage of your automobile. Be careful not to take 100% of auto expenses (actual or mileage deduction) as business expenses. In most cases, you must have some amount allocated to personal use of the car, and maybe some commuting miles. Come up with a tracking system to help you do this every time you "Get Outta My Dream, Get Into My Car" (Billy Ocean, 1988).

☐ Do you have a side business? Deductions for contractors, commissions, and similar indications of independent contractor status should be supported by the Form 1099-MISC's you issued to these folks.

☐ Pay the IRS their money during the year. Those payroll taxes that you withhold belong to them. While you're at it, make sure your current on your own estimated quarterly tax payments. Even if you expect not to owe any taxes, it looks better to send the IRS something, like $100. Don't start "Falling" (the old school version by Melba Moore, 1986) or "Fallin" (the new school style by Alicia Keys, 2001) behind on this. Being delinquent on these taxes could cause a full blown audit of all your activities.

☐ Keep copies of checks or cash received, as well as any supporting documentation. This is especially important when depositing personal loans or gift deposits. You want to make sure you can explain cash deposits and identify those deposits that represent income and those that represent personal gifts and/loans since there may be a tendency to leave them off your books.

☐ The key is to make sure your cash flow in and out makes sense, given your annual salary, other investment activities and investments. Red flags come when you report minimal income and you look like you're living on "Top Of The World," (Brandy, featuring Mase, 1998) with your big house, fancy car and a bank account balance that has never been over $1,000!

## Signs You Need Tax Help

☐ You finally sold those stock options (after all, you learned your lesson from Enron).

☐ You purchased or sold a home.

☐ You start that new side biz (e.g., sole proprietorship, corporation, partnership, or limited liability company) and accounting is just not your "thang."

☐ You hit the PowerBall Jackpot (not only do you need a tax advisor, but you need to contact me—http://www.taxes411online.com).

☐ You have a lot of capital gains from stocks, selling a business interest or commercial real estate.

☐ You own rental real estate.

☐ You have income from several sources (e.g., as an employer, consulting, royalties, rental income, interests in businesses, stock and bonds).

☐ You're "internationally known" (unlike Rob Base of "It Takes Two" fame, 1988); meaning you earn money in the U.S. and another country.

☐ You're like a rolling stone—you have moved several times over the course of the year and you have a good feeling all of your year-end tax statements did not forward correctly.

☐ YOU WOULD RATHER [insert anything here] THAN READ TAX RETURN INSTRUCTIONS!!!!

# ABOUT THE AUTHOR

## Shannon King Nash, Esq., CPA

Shannon King Nash is a seasoned attorney and CPA who has practiced with a Fortune 500 corporation, several large law firms and a big six accounting firm. In addition to helping clients all over the United States, she recently completed an assignment in Switzerland. She is the owner of the Nash Group, a tax and non-profit consulting firm (http://www.nashgroup-usa.com). The firm specializes in non-profit consulting and tax planning services.

Besides *For The Love Of Money*, Shannon is also the author of *"Vault Guide to Tax Law Careers,"* (Vault Inc., 2004) and *"Helping the Non-profit Client,"* (Kleinrock Publishing, 2004). She serves as an adjunct professor at California Lutheran University, where she teaches Non-Profit Law.

She is the former Secretary of the American Bar Association ("ABA") Tax Section, a professional organization representing over 20,000 tax attorneys, and former Chair of the National Bar Association's Tax Law Section, the largest and oldest African-American bar association.

Shannon volunteers in her community and serves on the board of directors for several non-profits. She received her Bachelor's degree in accounting and her JD from the University of Virginia. Shannon lives in the greater Los Angeles area with her husband and their two children. In her spare time, Shannon likes to read, write non-fiction books and is an advocate for children with disabilities.

# CONTRIBUTIONS

**O'SUMBY KUTI**

O'Sumby Kuti, CPA, is a Contributing Author to this book, providing comments and support on Chapter 4: Capital Gains, Chapter 7: Alternative Minimum Tax, Chapter 10: FAQs, and several of the Top 10 lists. Sumby is a private wealth business manager who handles the personal and business affairs of high net worth individuals and entrepreneurs who specialize in the entertainment, music, sports, telecommunications, and real estate industries. The average personal net worth of accounts that she handles is in excess of $6M. Sumby is responsible for monitoring, tracking, and advising the day-to-day accounting needs of clients' personal, partnership and/or loan-out corporations.

Sumby serves her community and volunteers at her local churches, Faithful Central Bible Church and First Baptist of Glenarden, located in Inglewood, California and Glenarden, Maryland, respectively. Sumby received her Bachelor's and Master's degree from the University of Virginia. Sumby splits her time between Upper Marlboro, Maryland and Encino, California (north of Los Angeles). In her spare time, Ms. Kuti likes to read, view sports, travel, and advocate for young professionals to be financially sound and educated. Contact Sumby at oakmgmtgroup@sbcglobal.net.

**WAYNE A.S. HAMILTON**

Wayne A.S. Hamilton, Esq. contributed comments on Chapter 5: Itemized Deductions Part I, Chapter 6: Itemized Deductions Part II, Chapter 9: IRS Audits and many Top 10 lists. Wayne is a tax attorney who has practiced with the federal government, a Fortune 50 corporation, and a large privately-held corporation for the last thirteen years. He has participated on many panels regarding tax and business-related matters. As a member of the ABA, he has served as the co-chair of the Tax Section's Diversity Committee, as well as the Nominating Committee. In 2001, he received one of the ABA Tax Section's Nolan Fellow Awards, which is bestowed upon tax lawyers of achievement and promise.

Wayne is also actively involved in his community and volunteers his time with several charitable organizations. He is on the board of Friends of Children, a non-profit organization committed to meeting the needs of at-risk children. He is also currently Vice President of the 100 Black Men of Greater Fort Lauderdale, a non-profit organization whose goal is to improve the quality of life, and enhance the educational and economic opportunities for all African-Americans.

He received his J.D., cum laude, from North Carolina Central University, and his LL.M. (Taxation) from the University of Florida, College of Law. He earned his B.S. from Andrews University in Berrien Springs Michigan. Wayne and his wife have a daughter, and live in the Miami area. He would like to thank his wife Olga and his daughter Monica, who graciously gave him the time and freedom to work on this project.

**DONALD CARROLL MORAGNE**

Donald Carroll Moragne contributed comments on Chapter 2: Side Business Part I, Chapter 3: Side Business Part II, Chapter 8: Investments, Education and Estate and Chapter 9: IRS Audits. He is the Managing Principal of The Success Zone, a nationally-respected business development and financial management firm located in downtown Silver Spring, Maryland. The Success Zone serves a client base that is nationwide and in the Caribbean. The firm specializes in financial management for the entertainment industry and for tax-exempt organizations. He shares his extensive expertise in not-for-profit organizations across the nation—from formation, to obtaining IRS recognition of tax-exempt status, to operational and financial management, to training in finance and board development—by consulting and lecturing on not-for-profit management and tax exempt topics.

Adept in taxation, management and business development, Don is a skilled Management Consultant and Financial Consultant, with an aggregate of more than 30 years of business management experience. Don acquired his in-depth experience in corporate auditing, accounting, and management as an Internal Revenue Service Agent, and a corporate accountant and management consultant in the private industry.

Don is member of the Maryland Society of Accountants and the Alliance for Non-Profit Management. He is on the board of several for-profit and not-for-profit organizations nationwide.

# THE ULTIMATE RESOURCE GUIDE

For more resources see the following list. You can find these forms and publications on the IRS website at http://www.irs.gov.

**CHAPTER 1: TAX BASICS**

*Form 1098-E, Student Loan Interest Statement*

*Form 1098-T, (Tuition Payment Statement)*

*Form 1099-DIV, Dividend Income*

*Form 1099-G, Certain Government Payments*

*Form 1099-INT, Interest Income*

*Form 2120, Multiple Support Declaration*

*Form 2441, Child and Dependent Care Expenses*

*Form 3903 Moving Expenses*

*Form 4562, Depreciation and Amortization*

*Form 4868, Application for Automatic Extension of Time to File US Income Tax Return*

*Form 5329, Additional Taxes on Qualified Plans (including IRAs) and Other Tax Favored Accounts*

*Form 5498-SA, HSA, Archer MSA, or Medicare+Choice MSA*

*Form 8332, Release of Claim to Exemption for Child of Divorced or Separated*

*Form 8822, Change of Address*

*Form 8863, Education Credits (Hope and Lifetime Learning Credits)*

*Form 8880, Credit for Qualified Retirement Savings*

*Form 8889, Health Savings Accounts*

*Form SS-4, Application for Employer Identification Number*

*Form SS-5, Application for a Social Security Card*
*Form W-2, Wage and Tax Statement*
*Form W2-G, Certain Gambling Winnings*
*Schedule B, Interest and Dividend Income (1040)*
*Schedule C, Profit or Loss from Business (Form 1040)*
*Schedule D, Capital Gains and Losses (Form 1040)*
*Schedule E, Supplemental Income and Loss (Form 1040)*
*Schedule H, Household Employment Taxes (Form 1040)*
*Schedule SE, Self Employment Tax (Form 1040)*
*Schedule K-1, US Return of Partnership Income (Form 1065)*
*Schedule K-1, US Income Tax Return for an S Corporation (Form 1120S)*
*Publication 15, Employers Tax Guide*
*Publication 17, Your Federal Income Tax (Individuals)*
*Publication 501, Exemptions, Standard Deductions, and Filing Information*
*Publication 503, Child and Dependent Car Expenses*
*Publication 504, Divorced and Separated Individuals*
*Publication 521, Moving Expenses*
*Publication 527, Residential Rental Property*
*Publication 533, Self Employment Tax*
*Publication 535, Taxable and Nontaxable Income*
*Publication 544, Sales and Other Dispositions of Assets*
*Publication 550, Investment Income and Expenses*
*Publication 560, Retirement Plans For Small Businesses*
*Publication 555, Community Property*
*Publication 590, Individual Retirement Arrangement.*
*Publication 926, Household Employer's Tax Guide*
*Publication 919, How Do I Adjust My Tax Withholding*
*Publication 946, How to Depreciate Property*
*Publication 970, Tax Benefits for Education*
*Publication 971, Innocent Spouse Relief*

Publication 972, Child Tax Credit

Publication 969, Health Savings Accounts and Other Tax-Favored Health Plans

## CHAPTER 2: SIDE BUSINESS PART I

Form 1065, US Partnership Return of Income

Form 1099-DIV, Dividend Income

Form 1099 MISC, Miscellaneous Income

Form 1120 US Corporate Income Tax Return

Form 1120S, US Income Tax Return for an S Corporation

Form 2553, Election by a Small Business Corporation

Form SS-8, Determination of Worker Status for Purposes of Federal Employment Taxes and Income Tax Withholding

Form W-2, Wage and Tax Statement

Form W-4, Employee's Withholding Allowance Certificate

Schedule C, Profit or Loss from Business (Form 1040)

Schedule E, Supplemental Income and Loss (Form 1040)

Schedule SE, Self Employment Tax (Form 1040)

Schedule K-1, US Return of Partnership Income (Form 1065)

Schedule K-1, US Income Tax Return for an S Corporation (Form 1120S)

Publication 15, Circular E, Employer's Tax Guide

Publication 334, Tax Guide for Small Business

Publication 527, Residential Rental Property

Publication 533, Self Employment Tax

Publication 541, Partnerships

Publication 542, Corporations

Publication 535, Business Expenses

Publication 583, Starting a Business and Keeping Records

Publication 3402, Tax Issues for Limited Liability Companies

Publication 3998, Choosing a Retirement Solution for Your Small Business

**CHAPTER 3: SIDE BUSINESS PART II**

*Form 940, Employer's Annual Federal Unemployment Tax Return,*
*Form 941, Employer's Quarterly Federal Tax Return*
*Form 1040-ES*
*Form 1065, US Partnership Return of Income—*
*Form 1099 MISC, Miscellaneous Income*
*Form 1120 US Corporate Income Tax Return*
*Form 2210, Underpayment of Estimated Tax by Individuals, Estates and Trusts,*
*Form 4562, Depreciation and Amortization*
*Form 8109, Federal Tax Deposit Coupon*
*Form 8582, Passive Activity Loss Limitations*
*Form I-9, Employment Eligibility Verification*
*FormSS-4, Employee Identification Number (EIN)*
*Form SS-8, Determination of Employee Work Status for Purposes of Federal Employment Taxes and Income Tax Withholding*
*Form W-2, Wage and Tax Statement*
*Form W-4, Employee's Withholding Allowance Certificate*
*Schedule A, Itemized Deductions (Form 1040)*
*Schedule C, Profit or Loss from Business (Form 1040)*
*Schedule E, Supplemental Income and Loss (Form 1040)*
*Schedule SE, Self Employment Tax (Form 1040)*
*Schedule K-1, Partner's Share of Income, Credits, Deductions, etc, (to Form 1065)*
*Publication 15, Circular E, Employer's Tax Guide*
*Publication 15-B, Employer's Tax Guide*
*Publication 334, Tax Guide for Small Business*
*Publication 463, Travel, Entertainment, Gift and Car Expense*
*Publication 505, Tax Withholding and Estimated Tax*
*Publication 527, Residential Rental Property*
*Publication 533, Self Employment Tax*
*Publication 535, Business Expenses*

*Publication 550, Investment Income and Expenses*

*Publication 583, Starting a Business and Keeping Records*

*Publication 587, Business Use of your Home (Including Use By Daycare Providers)*

*Publication 946, How to Depreciate Property*

*Publication 966, Electronic Choices for Paying All Your Federal Business Taxes*

*Publication 969, Health Savings Accounts and Other Tax-Favored Health Plans*

*Publication 1779, Employee Independent Contractor Brochure*

*Publication 3998, Choosing a Retirement Solution for Your Small Business*

## CHAPTER 4: CAPITAL GAINS

*Form 1099-B, Sales Price for Stock and Bonds*

*Form 1099-S, Proceeds From Real Estate Transactions*

*Form 4797, Sale of Business Property*

*Form 8824 Instructions, Like-Kind Exchanges*

*Schedule D, Capital Gains and Losses (Form 1040)*

*Publication 523, Selling Your Home*

*Publication 527, Residential Rental Property*

*Publication 544, Sales and Other Dispositions of Assets*

*Publication 550, Investment Income and Expenses (Including Capital Gains and Losses)*

*Publication 551, Basis of Assets*

*Publication 587, Business Use of Your Home*

## CHAPTER 5: ITEMIZED DEDUCTIONS PART I

*Form 1098, Mortgage Interest Statement*

*Form 1099-S, Proceeds from Real Estate Transactions*

*Form 8829, Expenses for Business Use of Your Home*

*Schedule A, Itemized Deductions (Form 1040)*

*Schedule C, Profit or Loss from Business (Form 1040)*

*Schedule E, Supplemental Income and Loss (Form 1040)*
*Schedule K-1, US Return of Partnership Income (Form 1065)*
*Schedule K-1, US Income Tax Return for an S Corporation (Form 1120S)*
*Publication 502, Medical and Dental Expenses*
*Publication 504, Divorced and Separated Individuals*
*Publication 505, Investment Income and Expenses*
*Publication 523, Selling Your Home*
*Publication 525, Taxable and Nontaxable Income*
*Publication 530, Tax Information for First Time-Homeowners*
*Publication 550, Interest Income and Expenses*
*Publication 587, Business Use of Your Home*
*Publication 600, Optional State Sales Tax Table*
*Publication 936, Home Mortgage Interest Deduction*
*Publication 970, Tax Benefits for Education*

## CHAPTER 6: ITEMIZED DEDUCTIONS PART II

*Form W-2G, Certain Gambling Winnings*
*Form 2106, Employee Business Expenses*
*Form 3903, Moving Expenses*
*Form 4562, Depreciation and Amortization*
*Form 4684, Casualties and Thefts*
*Form 8282, Donee Information Return*
*Form 8283, Noncash Charitable Contributions*
*Schedule A, Itemized Deductions (Form 1040)*
*Schedule C, Profit or Loss from Business (Form 1040)*
*Schedule E, Supplemental Income and Loss (Form 1040*
*Publication 17, Taxes, Interest Expense, Job Expenses and Miscellaneous Deductions*
*Publication 78, Cumulative List of Organizations*
*Publication 525, Taxable and Nontaxable Income*

Publication 526, Charitable Contributions

Publication 529, Miscellaneous Deductions

Publication 547, Casualties, Disasters and Thefts (Business and Non-Business)

Publication 561, Determining The Value of Donated Property

Publication 584, Casualty Disaster, and Theft Loss Workbook (Personal-use Property)

Publication 584B, Business Casualty Disaster and Theft Loss Workbook

Publication 970, Tax Benefits for Education

Publication 1771, Charitable Contributions—Substantiation and Disclosure Requirements

Publication 4302, A Charity's Guide to Car Donations

Publication 4303, A Donor's Guide to Car Donations

## CHAPTER 7: ALTERNATIVE MINIMUM TAX

Form 6251, Alternative Minimum Tax—Individuals

Form 8801, Credit for Prior Year Minimum Tax—Individuals, Estates, & Trusts

Publication 525, Taxable and Nontaxable Income

Tax Topic 556, Alternative Minimum Tax

## CHAPTER 8: INVESTMENTS, EDUCATION, ESTATE

Form 709, U.S. Gift (and Generation-Skipping Transfer) Tax Return

Form 5305-SEP, Simplified Employee Pension—Individual Retirement Accounts Agreement

Form 5305-SIMPLE, Savings Incentive Match Plan For Employees of Small Employers

Form 5329, Additional Taxes on Qualified Plans (including IRAs) and Other Tax Favored Accounts

Form 5500, Annual Return/Report of Employee Benefits Plans

Form 8863, Education Credits

Publication, 525, Taxable and Nontaxable Income

*Publication 560, Retirement Plans for Small Businesses (SEP, SIMPLE, and Qualified Plans)*

*Publication 575, Pension and Annuity Income*

*Publication 590, Individual Retirement Arrangements (IRA)*

*Publication 929, Tax Rules for Children and Dependents*

*Publication 950, Introduction to Estate and Gift Taxes*

*Publication 970, Tax Benefits for Education*

*Publication 1577, Applying for Educational Financial Aid*

**CHAPTER 9: IRA AUDITS**

*Form 433-A, Collection Information Statement for Individuals*

*Form 433-B, Collection Information Statement for Business*

*Form 433-F, Collection Information Statement.*

*Form 656, Offer in Compromise*

*Form 656-A, Income Certification for Offer in Compromise Application Fee*

*Form 911, Application for Taxpayer Assistance Order*

*Form 1041, US Income Tax Return for Estate and Trusts*

*Form 9465, Installment Agreement Request*

*Publication 5, Appeals Rights and Preparation of Protests for Unagreed Cases*

*Publication 556, Examination of Returns, Appeals Rights, and Claims for Refunds*

*Publication 908, Bankruptcy Tax Guide*

# INDEX

**401(k),** 15, 29, 117, 240, 243-253, 257, 272, 325-328, 331, 341, 347, 349, 351, 356, 365, 370-371, 375, 378

**529 Plans,** 259-262, 265, 271, 273, 339, 342, 369, 373

## A

**Adjusted gross income,** 2, 18-19, 22, 28, 37, 50-51, 86, 99, 123, 126, 128, 159, 165-166, 172, 183, 185, 197, 203, 207-208, 213, 216-217, 219-220, 224, 228, 254-255, 263, 266, 310, 339, 342, 345, 354

**Adoption credit,** 41, 43

**Alimony,** 14, 18, 28, 37, 50, 166, 213, 324, 339

**Alternative Minimum Tax,** ix, 57, 188, 216, 218, 221-223, 225, 231, 233, 372, 387, 397

**Amortization,** 23, 90, 104, 107-108, 121, 135, 209, 391, 394, 396

**Audit,** ix, 49, 114, 119, 154, 275-280, 282, 285, 293, 298, 306-307, 318-319, 325, 331, 334, 348, 357, 359, 365, 380-381

**Automobile expenses,** 54

## B

**Bankruptcy,** xii, 291, 301, 398

**Basis,** 21-22, 41, 45, 55, 82, 96, 98, 112, 133-136, 144-146, 149-150, 152-155, 169-171, 175, 177, 181, 194, 207, 213, 240, 266, 304, 336, 358, 360, 364, 379, 395

## C

**Casualty loss,** 206

**Capital Gains and Losses,** 50, 134, 138, 140, 142, 150-151, 154-155, 313, 392, 395

**Charitable Contributions,** 28, 39, 51, 158, 187-191, 193-194, 196, 202-203, 217-218, 236, 330, 362, 369, 396-397

**Child tax credit,** 4, 41, 43, 51, 393

**Child and dependent care credit,** 4

**Computer,** 32, 40, 57, 76, 94, 101-102, 104, 107, 112, 114-115, 119, 126, 132, 136, 194, 208-209, 211, 270, 276, 293, 306, 309-310, 319, 348-350, 357, 359, 365, 379

**Consultants,** 55, 57, 121, 125-127, 249, 304

**Corporation,** 20, 55, 57-66, 68, 70, 74-84, 91, 98, 120, 125-127, 172, 183, 209, 227, 229-230, 250, 286, 319-320, 351, 362-364, 367, 372, 383, 385, 387, 392-393, 396

    **C Corporation,** 55, 57-59, 62-66, 74-75, 77, 79, 82-83, 125-126, 183, 320

    **S Corporation,** 20, 74-79, 82, 84, 91, 126, 172, 183, 319-320, 392-393, 396

**Correspondence audit,** 276-277, 280, 293, 319, 331

**Court,** 43, 212, 280-285, 294, 342

    **US Tax Court,** 284

    **Court of Federal Claims,** 284

    **United States District Court,** 284

**Coverdell Education Savings Account,** 259, 273

# D

**Dependents,** 2, 8, 10, 13, 32, 50, 95, 158, 160, 166, 183, 185, 225, 265, 300, 375, 398

**Depreciation,** 20-23, 90, 100-102, 104-110, 121, 123, 125, 130, 135, 146-148, 165, 192, 208-209, 320-321, 336-337, 345, 391, 394, 396

**Dividend income,** 15-16, 67, 127, 276, 391-393

**Divorce,** 5, 11, 18, 37, 42, 144, 161, 212-213, 313, 325, 339

# E

**Education credit,** 267

**Educator expenses,** 28, 32-33, 50, 209, 216

**Employee,** 26-27, 42, 44-45, 65, 87, 92-97, 108, 112-113, 115-118, 128-130, 203, 208-209, 219, 226, 228-229, 240, 242-243, 245, 247, 249-251, 272, 299, 305, 310, 314-315, 345-346, 354, 359, 363-364, 367, 369-370, 375, 393-397

**Employee stock purchase plan,** 243, 245

**Employee fringe benefits,** 87, 115

**Employer provided educational assistance,** 210

**Employer sponsored retirement plans,** 242, 249, 253

**Estate taxes,** 27, 113, 135, 170, 227, 234, 271, 316-318

**Expensing,** 54, 87, 100-101, 103-107, 109-110

# F

**FICA,** 44-46, 51, 77-78, 95-98, 315

**Franchises,** 119-120

**Field audit,** 279-280, 293, 331

**Fringe benefits,** 87, 115, 130

## G

**Gambling,** xi, 14, 23-25, 50, 208, 214-217, 219, 392, 396

**Gift taxes,** 18, 26, 238, 261, 264, 268-270, 273, 398

## H

**Head of household filing status,** 3-5, 9, 300, 338

**Health Savings Account,** 33, 116-118

**Holding period,** 137-138, 142, 154-155

**Home based business,** 119

**Home sale exclusion,** 147, 313

**Home improvements,** 178-179, 186, 358

**Home equity loan,** 173, 178, 180-181, 184-185, 226

**Home office expense deduction,** 171, 174, 359, 365

**Hope Credit,** 32, 43-44, 266-268, 273

## I

**Incentive Stock Option (ISO),** 224, 229-232

**Independent contractor,** 87, 92-94, 122, 129, 346, 348, 354, 359-360, 363-364, 369, 381, 395

**Innocent spouse relief,** 7, 323-325, 392

**Installment payment plans,** 49, 288

**Interest income,** 15-16, 128, 183, 298, 391, 396

**Investments,** 15, 18, 27, 30, 36, 44, 81, 117, 127-128, 151-152, 178, 213, 216, 237, 240-241, 245, 259-260, 265, 273, 318, 343, 382, 388, 397

**Investment clubs,** 127-128

**IRA,** 28-30, 33, 36, 50, 166, 240, 247-248, 250-254, 256-258, 262, 272, 331, 341, 343, 347, 349, 356, 365, 375, 378, 398

   **Roth,** 29, 252-254, 256-258, 272, 331, 341, 375

   **Traditional,** 29, 45, 116-117, 130, 182, 250, 252-253, 256-258, 272, 341, 343, 375

   **Early Withdrawals,** 254-256

   **Regular Distributions,** 254-255

   **Hardship distributions,** 254-255

   **Loans,** 15, 30, 48, 52, 105, 172-173, 175, 177-178, 180-181, 183-185, 226, 254, 256, 258-259, 272, 324, 339, 342, 346, 351, 354, 363-364, 367, 370, 381-382

   **Rollover,** 254, 257, 375, 378

**IRS Notices,** 275, 294

**Itemized deductions,** ix, 9, 16-17, 19, 23-24, 27-28, 33, 36, 38-39, 51, 86, 113, 126, 128, 157-158, 160, 166-168, 170-174, 185, 187-188, 203, 207-208, 210-214, 216-220, 222, 224-229, 233-236, 259, 299, 304, 310, 312, 318-319, 322, 329-330, 345, 357, 373, 387, 394-396

## J

**Job hunting expenses,** 209-211, 219, 310, 345, 352

## K

**Keogh plan,** 240, 251-252, 272, 347, 349, 356, 365, 375, 378

**Key person policy,** 87, 118

## L

**Leased assets,** 87, 110

**Levy,** 280, 288-289, 291-292, 295, 374

**Lifetime learning credit,** 32, 43-44, 266, 268, 338

**Limited partnership,** 68, 70

**Limited liability company,** 19, 55, 68, 79, 81-82, 126, 183, 250, 286, 320, 335, 351, 364, 372, 383

**Legal fees,** 21, 88, 134, 212, 310, 379

## M

**Married filing jointly status,** 6

**Married filing separately status,** 7

**Matching,** 78, 95, 138, 152, 154, 244, 249-251, 326, 343

**Meals and entertainment,** 87, 114-115, 130, 208, 345, 349

**Medical Expenses,** 9-10, 13, 18, 28, 36, 39, 50-51, 117, 158-166, 185, 217-218, 224, 226, 228, 235-236, 255, 270, 300, 312, 330, 339, 342, 376

**Mileage expense,** 193

**Miscellaneous itemized deductions,** 16, 19, 24, 27, 33, 86, 126, 128, 203, 207-208, 210-211, 216, 218-219, 224, 228-229, 236, 259, 310, 345

**Money purchase pension plan,** 243, 247, 251

**Mortgage interest,** 21, 23, 113, 171-174, 176-178, 180-182, 184-185, 226-227, 233, 236, 276-277, 299, 316-318, 321, 337, 357, 375, 395-396

**Moving expenses,** 28, 34-35, 50, 352, 357, 391-392, 396

## N

**Nanny Taxes,** 44-46, 51, 315-316, 341

**Netting,** 132, 138-142, 152, 155

**Notice of Audit adjustment (30 Day Letter),** 280, 293

**Notice of Federal Tax Lien,** 289, 291

**Notice of Levy,** 291, 374

## O

**Offer in Compromise,** 285-286, 294, 398

**Office audit,** 277-280, 293, 331

**Organizational expenses,** 88-90

## P

**Partnership,** 19, 54-55, 67-74, 77, 80-84, 98, 120, 125-128, 153, 172, 183, 250, 286, 320, 335, 351, 364, 372, 383, 387, 392-394, 396

**Payroll taxes,** 63, 87, 95, 97-99, 128-129, 319, 364, 367, 381

**Personal exemptions,** 5, 9, 11-13, 32, 38-39, 42, 50, 224-227, 236, 300, 329, 339

**Personal interest,** 172, 180, 184

**Personal property tax,** 171

**Personal use property,** 144, 148-150

**Phase-outs,** 13, 28, 51, 216-217, 373

**Points,** 23, 135, 174-181, 185-186, 318, 342, 344, 357

**Prize income,** 14

**Professional corporation,** 126

**Profit sharing plan,** 243, 246-247

**Property donations,** 188, 194, 197

**Protest letter,** 281-282, 293

## Q

**Qualifying widower,** 2, 13, 39, 223

## R

**Roth IRA,** 29, 252-254, 256-258, 331, 341, 375

**Real property tax,** 170

**Rental real estate,** 14, 19-20, 22-23, 50, 76, 81, 98, 119, 123-125, 148, 155, 182, 321-322, 329, 335-337, 383

**Repairs,** 10, 21-23, 104, 109, 111-112, 135, 165, 178, 194, 336-337, 348, 357-359, 365, 378-379

**Retirement plans,** 29-30, 36, 238, 240-243, 245, 247-252, 254-256, 272, 349, 370, 379, 392, 398

## S

**S corporation,** 20, 74-79, 82, 84, 91, 126, 172, 183, 319-320, 392-393, 396

**Sales price,** 133-134, 144-146, 149-150, 152, 154, 170, 177, 311, 395

**Self employment tax,** 28, 36-37, 44, 50, 73, 98, 166, 392-394

**SEP IRA,** 36, 247, 250-251, 257, 272, 347, 349, 356, 365, 375, 378

**Simple IRA,** 36, 247-248, 251, 257, 272, 347, 349, 356, 365, 375, 378

**Single filing status,** 3, 6

**Sole proprietorship,** 19, 55-58, 61, 65-66, 68, 70, 75, 81, 83, 98, 113, 118-119, 183, 212-213, 250, 279, 286, 303, 306, 359, 364, 383

**Solo 401(k),** 247-249, 251-252, 257, 272, 349, 365, 378

**Standard deduction,** 2, 6, 16, 28, 38-39, 51, 86, 157, 173, 175, 177, 224, 338

**Start-up expenses,** 87-88, 90, 120, 129

**State and local income tax deduction,** 167-168

**Statutory Deficiency Notice (90 Day Letter),** 280

**Student loan interest deduction,** 28-31, 50, 183, 259

**Support test,** 10, 362

# T

**Tax planning and preparation expenses,** 208, 211, 219

**Tax rates,** 38, 40, 64-65, 83, 131, 246

**Tax refunds,** 14, 16, 50, 291, 293, 358

**Timing,** 151-152, 234

**Traditional IRA,** 29, 250, 252-253, 256-258, 341, 343, 375

**Tuition and fees deduction,** 28, 32, 50, 259, 267

# U

**Uniform Gifts to Minor Account (UGMA),** 259, 264-266, 273, 370

**Unreimbursed employee expenses,** 27, 203, 226, 228, 310, 345, 375

**US Savings Bond,** 15, 259, 263-264, 273

# V

**Volunteer Expenses,** 188, 191, 194, 219

# W

**Wages,** 14, 42, 45, 47, 50, 64, 79, 95-97, 99, 115, 123, 139, 149, 245, 272, 276, 280, 283, 285-286, 288, 290-292, 295, 315, 346, 355, 360, 374

978-0-595-34895-4
0-595-34895-5

Printed in the United States
33953LVS00003B/61-99